To my friends in
Johnstown. Best wishes.
Matt Kane

HEAVENS UNEARTHED
IN NURSERY RHYMES
AND FAIRY TALES

HEAVENS UNEARTHED
IN NURSERY RHYMES
AND FAIRY TALES

MATT KANE

Illustrated by
JOE SERVELLO

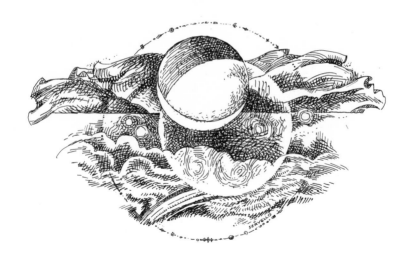

Golden Egg
Books

Golden Egg Books
P.O. Box 150
Altoona, PA 16603
Toll Free 1-877-999-8765
http://www.goldeneggbooks.com

398.362
K165h
CCL
3/99
24.00

Library of Congress Catalog Card Number: 98-96658

Publisher's Cataloging in Publication
(Provided by Quality Books, Inc.)

Kane, Matt (Matthew James), 1946-
      Heavens unearthed in nursery rhymes and fairy tales /
By Matt Kane ; illustrated by Joe Servello. — 1st ed.
      p. cm.
      Includes bibliographical references and index.
      ISBN: 0-9667076-1-3

      1. Stars—Folklore. 2. Moon—Folklore. 3. Fairy Tales
—History and Criticism. 4. Nursery rhymes—History and
Criticism. I. Servello, Joe II. Title.

GR625.K36 1999   398'.362
                          QBI98-1275

Acknowledgments

It has been gratifying to receive so much help in this project from old friends and new acquaintances alike.

One major area of study that *Heavens Unearthed* explores is that of astronomy and myth. I want to thank two of the most recognized authors in that field for their help. E. C. Krupp, Director of the Griffith Observatory, provided me with valuable articles and gave insightful criticism of my first draft that helped me to avoid a number of pitfalls. Anthony F. Aveni, the Russell B. Colgate Professor of Astronomy and Anthropology at Colgate University, acted as a mentor to me in this investigation, advising on further research and on the organization and presentation of the book.

The other major area of study in *Heavens Unearthed* is the field of folklore and fairy tales. Maria Tatar, Professor of Germanic Languages and Literatures at Harvard University, has written extensively on the tales of the Brothers Grimm. Her kind words and encouragement have been of great benefit.

Other writers who offered their suggestions include Dinty Moore of the Pennsylvania State University and my long-time friends John S. Morreall and James R. Hall. Thomas Cooney spent many hours helping me review the astronomy facts in the book, and Amy Sprouse assisted with translations from the French.

Other readers include John and Olga Orr, Glenn and Sonia Keiper, Keith Gordon, and Joyce Czuprynski. It should be noted that being acknowledged as a reader of this book does not imply the reader's endorsement of it. Any errors to be found are solely my responsibility.

Joe Servello, who illustrated this book, shared his enthusiasm and his knowledge of the book trade. Aline D. Wolf, author and owner of Parent Child Press, gave of her time to teach me about publishing. Cover designer Tracy Baldwin did a tremendous job of turning my ideas into images, and my editor, Deborah A. Stuart of P. M. Gordon

Associates, enabled me to make this a book I am proud to have authored.

I want to thank all the libraries that provided books for my research, especially the Carnegie Library of Pittsburgh, the Pennsylvania State University Libraries, and the Schlow Memorial Library of State College, Pennsylvania. But most of all I wish to express my appreciation to the staff (both past and present), the friends, and the board members of the Altoona (Pennsylvania) Area Public Library. Their support and generosity have been vital to my success.

Finally, I am most grateful to my wife, Mary Lou, our son, Steve, and our daughter, Melanie, for listening and believing. To everyone who has helped in this undertaking, many thanks.

HEAVENS UNEARTHED
IN NURSERY RHYMES
AND FAIRY TALES

Contents

Chapter 1

Introduction

The Full Moon

"It must be the full moon!" teachers and parents exclaim when children are particularly rambunctious, and most of us have used the phrase when we see adults acting like "lunatics." From the Latin word for moon, lunacy refers to the effect the moon has on our minds and emotions.

But why is the full moon considered so potent? Those who know the oceans' tides are aware that the new and the full moons are the times when the tides are at both their highest and their lowest and that the half moons are the times when the tides are more moderate. It is understandable, then, that people assume that the new and the full moons have the greatest effect on humans and other creatures. It is also understandable that people assume that the moon is strongest and has the most effect when it is the brightest, that the full moon, therefore, is more powerful than the new moon.

Furthermore, the full moon provides light for predatory animals that are not by nature nocturnal, such as wolves. Their eerie howl on moonlit nights instills fear in their prey. Even today in rural Italy some believe that anyone who sleeps outdoors under the full moon on a Friday either will turn into a werewolf or will be attacked by one.[1]

Ancient Myths

Our beliefs about the moon can be traced back to ancient times. Many span the globe, and many can be traced even to the last Ice

Age. By examining our most popular fairy tales and nursery rhymes, we can see that they are based on ancient myths about the sun and the moon and about solar and lunar eclipses.

I begin by explaining what led me to these discoveries, including how the number seven is related to the moon and why it is so significant, not only in "Snow White," but in our oldest stories. I show that Snow White's biting of the poisoned apple is a depiction of a lunar eclipse. I go on to describe ancient bear ceremonies and stories from around the world to show why the bear is a symbol of the moon and why Ice Age bear myths are predecessors of our fairy tales and nursery rhymes.

In this book we meet various men and women in the moon, including Rumpelstiltskin, who tries to eclipse the sun, and Santa Claus, whose sliding down the chimney is the Man in the Moon sliding down the shadow of the eclipse. We discover what Achilles' heel, Captain Ahab's missing leg, and Captain Hook's missing hand all have in common with the moon. We learn about children in the moon, including John in "Diddle, Diddle, Dumpling," Jack in "Jack Be Nimble," and Polly in "Little Polly Flinders." We meet various sons of the moon, including Jack, whose magic beans hold the secret of the winter and summer solstices. We see how Little Red Riding Hood is a daughter of the moon who is swallowed by the wolf just as the moon is swallowed by the shadow of the eclipse, and we see how Cinderella is another daughter of the moon whose slippers are the crescent moons. Finally, we uncover the Ice Age themes found in "Cinderella" and learn about the hidden meaning of her foot.

Ancient Myth or Coincidence?

As we look at stories from around the world, it is important that we not jump to conclusions. Just because two myths from different places and times are very similar does not mean that they came from one source or that one is derived from the other. For example, that the Inca House of the Moon in pre-conquest Cuzco was decorated all in silver and that the Ephesian shrines dedicated to the Greek moon goddess Artemis were made of silver does not require that these traditions had a common origin.[2] One could say that it was merely coincidence; but a more likely explanation is that for both, silver was chosen to suggest the cool, pale light of the moon. The association of

·RABBIT IN FULL MOON·

Figure 1

silver with the moon is an "elementary idea" or what Carl Jung called an "archetypal image" of the collective unconscious.[3]

But not all myths are so easily explained. For example, the rabbit is pictured in the moon or associated with the moon in the ancient native folklore of Canada, the United States, Mexico, China, India, Greece, and Germany, as well as in many countries of Africa. (See Figure 1.) An exception is Australia, which did not have aboriginal rabbit lore because rabbits or hares were not introduced to the continent until the time of European colonization. The Easter Rabbit of Western Christian custom was originally a companion of the moon goddess Eostre, for whom Easter was named.[4] (For more about the rabbit, see Chapter 8, "Jack Be Nimble.")

This myth is probably not an elementary idea, because it is little known today. (The only modern connection I can find between the rabbit and the moon is that Bugs Bunny is a member of the "Looney" Tunes family.) One could say, as for the association of silver and the moon, that the rabbit/moon myth coincidentally appeared throughout the world. But perhaps a better explanation is that it evolved in separate places under similar circumstances. Earlier societies were much more conscious of the activities of both the heavens and of animals. They would have noted that the thirty-day gestation period for rabbits is almost exactly the same as the twenty-nine-and-one-half-day lunar cycle. Because they both have such a short "reproduction" period, both the rabbit and the moon became symbols of fecundity. Additionally, the rabbit is a nocturnal animal and therefore a subject of the moon, who rules the night sky. In ancient tradition, the night and the moon were associated with the underworld, just as the day and the sun were associated with the upper world. Since the rabbit burrows and lives underground, both the rabbit and the moon are denizens of the underworld. It is possible that separate societies in separate places saw these similarities and made the same association.

The simplest explanation is that the myth spread over the world through a process of historical diffusion. The infiltration of the myth into the Americas can be explained by the migration of Asiatic peoples across a land bridge that today is the Bering Strait. It has been suggested that over generations the Asiatic newcomers brought the rabbit myth with them.[5] I like this theory because it is straightforward and because it allows more than ten thousand years for the myth to disperse widely in both the Old World and the New.

The End of the Last Ice Age

The end of the last Ice Age was a turning point in the human story. The last Ice Age, which reached its peak in 20,000 B.C., created huge ice sheets around both poles, greatly lowering temperatures and reducing the water in the oceans and in the atmosphere. Sea levels were as much as 330 feet lower than they are today, uncovering lowlands previously underwater. Land bridges connected Alaska to Siberia and Australia and Indonesia to Southeast Asia, the British Isles to Europe, Ceylon to India, and so on. Living conditions were difficult for plants and animals as well as humans. Because of the lack of moisture, deserts were larger than they are today, and much of the land was covered with ice. Humans, who lived in hunting-and-gathering societies, skillfully adapted to a large variety of harsh environments; but the human population, compared with now, was very sparse.

Then, between 13,000 B.C. and 8000 B.C., the ice sheets melted, and temperatures and ocean levels rose. Land bridges gradually were immersed again, and by the end of the period the climates and coastlines of the world were similar to what they are today. In the Americas, peoples who had already established settlements in the Yukon and on the land bridge between Siberia and Alaska had been unable to travel south until about 13,000 B.C., when two ice sheets receded enough that a western corridor opened the way to a new land. By the end of this period humans had reached across the Americas, and the land bridge had disappeared. Throughout the world, warmer climates caused an expansion of forests and grasslands. Wildlife abounded and humans began a population expansion that has never since been seriously interrupted. During this period dogs were first domesticated, mammoths became extinct, pottery was invented, and the first agricultural communities were established in the Fertile Crescent of the Middle East.[6]

Ice Age Controversy

Just as the end of the Ice Age was a turning point for human progress, it was also a turning point for the development of human myth. Ice Age societies produced representational and symbolic art. They developed complex rituals, such as the bear ceremonies of northern peoples, and complex structures of religious belief, such as the belief that shamans could fly to the upper and lower worlds and guide souls in those worlds. And these societies made up stories and myths to inspire, to teach moral lessons, and to explain the surrounding world. As the ice sheets melted, societal and economic changes caused these art forms to evolve.

As people migrated, stories and myths, held before the late Ice Age by a relatively small population in limited portions of the world, began spreading to an expanding population in a much greater area. But at the same time, because of the receding shorelines, the continents of North and South America and Australia gradually became cut off again from the rest of the world. The Americas were especially isolated because the Atlantic and Pacific Oceans are so vast. Therefore, whenever indigenous peoples in widely scattered parts of the world, including the Americas, tell the same story or myth, there is a good possibility that the story or myth derived from the late Ice Age or before. The more widely held the tradition, the stronger the possibility.

When folklorists claim, however, that certain stories derive from the late Ice Age, controversy follows. Jack Zipes, in *Breaking the Magic Spell,* states that most folktale themes can be traced back to the behaviors and beliefs of primitive societies. He notes, for example, that the German word *konig* ("king") is frequently used in folk and fairy tales. Etymologically it is related to the Latin word *gens*, meaning "clan," and originally referred to the oldest man or head of the clan. Similarly, *konigin* ("queen") referred to the matriarch of the clan.[7] Zipes cites August Nitschke as saying that there was a transition in behavioral attitude in the late Ice Age in which women assumed a greater role than animals in the social order, and that many tales reflect that transition.[8] For example, "Cinderella" originated near the end of the Ice Age and was produced by a hunting-and-grazing society that accorded women a place of honor.[9]

This connection between "Cinderella" and the place of women in Paleolithic society is "pure claptrap," says folklorist Neil Philip. "No such demonstration is possible."[10] He agrees, however, that some versions of the tale of Cinderella may be two thousand or more years old.

The Solar Theory
Another area of controversy in the study of folklore is the "solar theory." In the late nineteenth century, the renowned Oxford linguist

Max Muller promoted the "solar theory" for interpreting myth and folklore. Muller and his followers saw myth as accounts of the light of the sun doing battle with the darkness of night and the sun each year going down into the darkness of the underworld in winter and returning victorious in the spring. Each character in a story took on the role of a different natural phenomenon, such as the clouds, the dawn, or thunder and lightning. Muller's contemporary, the brilliant journalist and folklorist Andrew Lang, ridiculed the theory for its simplemindedness, pointing out that every myth and story is open to endless explanations. Lang's discrediting of the theory was so complete that most folklorists today eschew naturalistic theories of the origin of myth.[11]

In fact, twentieth-century folklore studies are concerned with the structure and function of myth, rather than its origin.[12] The astronomer E. C. Krupp, for example, who has contributed immensely to the study of the lore of the heavens, sees his role as "spotlighting the social uses of celestial analogy."[13] This approach has been very valuable in developing a large body of research on the myths and folklore of specific peoples that is not clouded by assumptions and vague generalizations. At the same time, I believe that we should look at myths cross-culturally to try to identify those oldest myths from which many of our traditions and stories are derived.

One mistake of solar theorists was that they did not carry their theory far enough. In their emphasis on the paternal solar deity, they de-emphasized the maternal lunar goddess; and furthermore, they underestimated the sophisticated knowledge that ancient peoples had of the sun and the moon. Just as archaeoastronomers today are discovering moon and sun sight lines in ancient temples around the world that attest to this sophisticated knowledge, now is the time for folklorists and mythologists to discover the intricate symbolism of the sun and moon in ancient tales. This new approach may be called a lunar theory because the moon was preeminent in the stories and myths of ancient peoples.

Why the Moon?

Why was the moon so significant in ancient myth? Compared with the simple and methodical path of the sun, the moon's path is complex and wide-ranging. During every lunar cycle the moon moves from a narrow arc low in the sky to a wide arc high in the sky and then back down again. At the low point there are approximately ten hours between moonrise and moonset, whereas at the high point there are approximately fourteen hours. So each month the moon appears to spiral around the earth, moving upward part of the month and then back downward again like the thread on a spindle.

Furthermore, the moon is a shape-shifter, never remaining the same. As the full moon, it struts across the night sky; as the new moon, it steals invisibly across the daytime sky. In addition the moon has other, more subtle changes. Sometimes it is closer to earth and looks larger; sometimes it is farther away. Sometimes its highest and lowest arcs are farther apart and sometimes they are closer together. With all this instability, it is easy to understand how it was linked to mental instability.

The moon's cycles make the sun's daily spiral, ever higher to the summer solstice and ever lower to the winter solstice, seem rather plodding in comparison. We relate to complexity because of the complexity of our lives. The moon's path is a labyrinthine puzzle to be solved. Similarly, our stories often tell of problems that must be overcome, because it is in wrestling with problems that we find our fulfillment.

But complexity is not the only feature that attracts us to the moon. The moon shines when we need it most—in the midst of darkness. And the full moon shines brightest when the sun shines the least. The full moon has a path that complements the sun's path, so when the sun's path is highest in the sky at the summer solstice, the full moon's path is at its lowest and vice versa. The new moon, in contrast, follows close to the sun's path through the year. This means that in the Northern Hemisphere in December, when the sun is weakest and the days are shortest, the full moon rises early in the evening, passes almost directly overhead during the night, and stays out the longest in the morning. It is our guide in the darkest hours.

Finally, the moon is more accessible than the sun. It is closer to us than the sun, and we can look at it without being blinded. It is an intermediary, mirroring the sun's light and making the night beautiful. The sun may be the source of our existence, but the moon mirrors our everyday struggle to survive. Together they complement and balance each other. Ancient peoples revered the sun and the moon. They followed their journeys and knew their meanderings.

Lost Wisdom

For most of us, knowledge of the heavens in this age of technology has been relegated to astronomers. Today, if we read a novel that describes a crescent moon overhead at midnight, few of us would recognize that that is impossible because the crescent moon is never in the sky at midnight. To people of the distant past back before the invention of writing, this mistake would have been obvious because they lived close to the sun, the moon, and the earth. Some of them were even able to predict solstices and eclipses.

Since the Industrial Revolution, however, folk wisdom has gradually disappeared. This disappearance has become nearly complete in our century. The scientific mind of the modern era has no room for learning customs such as planting corn during the waxing of the moon to ensure that it prospers or for believing that successful fishing may depend on an awareness of the phases of the moon.

Intent

In past centuries people living close to the earth knew more about the heavens, but does that mean that the folk narrators intentionally included the sun and the moon and the eclipses in their tales? It is impossible to say. In Western Europe the sun and the moon are usually objects in fairy tales and folktales (in "The Moon," by the Brothers Grimm, the moon is a lamp), whereas in most of the rest of the world the sun and the moon become characters in stories.[14] But no matter where one is in the world, the narrator is not the creator of a folktale. The narrator participates in the re-creation process and draws upon tradition rather than innovation.[15] Tales do change from time to time and from society to society. Narrators do vary structures and motifs, but they draw from the storehouse of the past for the source of their variation.

Therefore, our search is not for the intent of the narrators of fairy tales but rather for the origins of the motifs from which fairy tales are constructed. These origins are in stories and myths that are ancient, often going back to the late Ice Age. In these early myths we can find the sun and the moon and solar and lunar eclipses.

I look at nursery rhymes from the point of view of sun and moon lore. Since there is no way for us to know the intent of their anonymous authors, I examine the rhymes for their references to ancient themes and traditions. Nursery rhymes draw heavily from the store-house of myth.

Just Sun and Moon Lore?

Can fairy tales be reduced to tales about the heavens? Perhaps they can be, but they should not be. Fairy tales have moral, social, artistic, spiritual, and psychological meaning that still affects us today. I touch on some of these areas in this book, but my focus is to uncover the celestial significance of the tales.

We will find that the moon expands our understanding of nursery rhymes and fairy tales and of ourselves. Mircea Eliade, who has led the way in cross-cultural study of the sun and the moon, calls the rhythms of the moon "'the lowest common denominator' of an endless number of phenomena and symbols." "The rhythms of the moon," he says, "weave together harmonies, symmetries, analogies and participations which make up an endless 'fabric', a 'net' of invisible threads, which 'binds' together at once mankind, rain, vegetation, fertility, health, animals, death, regeneration, after-life, and more."[16]

This investigation of nursery rhymes and fairy tales will provide an understanding of the language of the sun, the moon, eclipses, and solstices found in lore around the world and in the customs of everyday life. We will find a deep myth that reaches back many millennia.

Chapter 2

The Discovery

The Birth of an Idea

Nothing in my training or experience prepared me for the discovery that occurred at 11:00 P.M. on Thursday, September 26, 1996.

As an undergraduate in philosophy and English and as a graduate student in library science and comparative literature, I had an on-going interest in folklore and folk customs as well as in moon lore and the moon in literature. As a librarian since the early 1970s, I have considered it a duty as well as a pleasure to read widely. But my search for hidden meaning in folklore and myth did not begin in earnest until the late 1980s when I was in my early forties.

Like many others my age, I was reflecting on some of the deeper questions of life and read Joseph Campbell's *The Power of Myth* when it came out in 1988. This led me to other books about mythology, such as Barbara Walker's *The Woman's Encyclopedia of Myths and Secrets* and Margaret Stutley and James Stutley's *Harper's Dictionary of Hinduism.* While studying world mythology, I began to wonder whether there was a symbolic relationship between the order of the seven Hindu chakras and the order of our days of the week.

Our days of the week come from the Greeks and Romans, who named them after the seven visible planets, which for the ancients included the sun and the moon. The Hindu tradition bases the days of the week on the same seven planets placed in the same order as in our days of the week. In medieval alchemical tradition, the seven planets each influenced a specific metal. Alchemists also connected these metals and planets with spiritual qualities. The chakra system of Hindu yoga teaches that there are seven wheels (chakras) or centers of energy within the body that correspond to the seven levels of spiritual attainment. In order to determine whether there were any significant relationships to be found, I juxtaposed the seven days of the week and their corresponding planets and metals to the seven body locations of the chakras. In the following list, I have used the metals as presented in Chaucer's *Canterbury Tales* (*Canon's Yeoman's Tale*, 825–29). In analyzing the list, I have followed Joseph Campbell's explanation of the chakras.[1] Following the natural progression from the lowest to the highest level of accomplishment, the assessment of the list begins at the bottom and works upward.

Weekdays	Planets	Metals	Chakras
Sunday	Sun	Gold	Crown
Monday	Moon	Silver	Forehead
Tuesday	Mars	Iron	Throat
Wednesday	Mercury	Quicksilver	Heart
Thursday	Jupiter	Tin	Solar plexus
Friday	Venus	Copper	Sexual organs
Saturday	Saturn	Lead	Base of spine

Here Saturn is related to the first chakra at the base of the spine, which controls the energy of survival. Saturn was one of the Titans, who were gods of enormous size and strength. Many mythologies have a tradition of an old race of giants that were overthrown. This fits the experience of children to whom all adults appear as giants. Saturn is the Lord of Death and Father Time, who closes out the old year at the winter solstice. The Romans celebrated the Saturnalia at the end of the year in honor of Saturn, the father of the gods who was overthrown by his son Jupiter. The Roman god Saturn is linked to the Greek god Cronus, whose name means "time" and who attempted to eat all his children to prevent them from usurping his power.

The Romans depicted Saturn as a ruler over a golden age of prosperity. He is heavy, sated by the pleasures of this world, and he rules the slowest of the ancient planets. Saturday is the Jewish sabbath, the seventh day, when God rested, an appropriate day for Saturn, the sluggish god. His metal is lead, which is the heaviest; and his color is black—the color of death. Lead comes from black ore. Black also represents the black soil, a symbol of fecundity and new life. Our modern Santa Claus draws upon the tradition of the December festival of Saturnalia, which was a time of gift giving; and he has evolved into a kind old Father Time who rides in a sleigh distributing gifts. In contrast to Saturn, an eater of his offspring, old Santa Claus is loved by children. Old age is sometimes referred to as a second childhood, a time when the higher faculties fail. Old Father Time ushers in the New Year in the form of a child. Childhood is an experiential age—a time controlled by what Sigmund Freud called the "id," the undifferentiated source of human instincts or drives. If unchecked, these drives lead to the sated, sluggish old Saturn. Instincts or drives are based on the need to survive and are associated with the lowest level of the chakras, the base of the spine. It is the stage of division, diversity, and multiplicity.

Friday is the German goddess Fria's day, which to the Romans was Venus's day. (Compare the French word for Friday—*vendredi*.) Venus's color is green—the color of fertility—and her metal is copper, which comes from green ore. Venus matches the second chakra, which corresponds with the human sexual organs and controls sexual and romantic energies. The second chakra is the age of adolescence and is dominated by subjective feelings. It is when the ego, which according to Freud develops during childhood, comes into bloom.

Venus is the goddess of life and love. Her reign as the morning star before she disappears from the morning sky and her reign as the evening star before she disappears from the evening sky each last nine lunar cycles—the length of time of a woman's pregnancy. This association with life and fertility implies love and beauty. As the brightest heavenly body after the sun and the moon, Venus is the beautiful wishing star, the first star in the evening sky and the last in the morning light. (Etymologically, *Venus* is related to *wish*, as well as *venerate, venereal, win, winsome, wistful*, and *wont*.)[2]

The third step of our seven-storied mountain—the third chakra—corresponds to Thursday. Our word *Thursday* comes from Thor, the Norse god of thunder, a position held by Jove or Jupiter in the Roman pantheon. The French for Thursday—*jeudi*—means "Jove's day." Jove represents the world of power. Traditionally, his color was gray and his metal was tin. According to psychologist Abraham Maslow, after survival (the first chakra) and sex (the second chakra), the next greatest human need is for power (the third chakra).[3] In Freudian terms, it is the level of the superego—the conscience and ideals. This is the level of duty and objectivity. It is the transition from adolescence to adulthood. The third chakra is positioned at the solar plexus.

The fourth chakra corresponds to Wednesday, named for Woden, the high god of the Germans, who died on the world tree, Yggsdrasil, in order to gain the secret of the runes. Woden was equated with the Roman god Mercury. The French for Wednesday is *mercredi*—"Mercury's day." Mercury was the messenger of the gods, who could travel in the heavens, on earth, and in the underworld. His metal is mercury and his color is blue—the color of the sky. We derive from him words such as *commerce* and *mercurial*. Mercury is also the god of thieves, and he can steal heaven as well as bargain for it. As the fourth level, Mercury is in the middle between the upper and lower worlds. The fourth chakra is located in the heart, which is in the middle of the body. Our hearts can see us through even when our ideas fail. The fourth level is the level of unity. For Jung it is the self. Joseph Campbell calls it the chakra of Christ and Buddha. It is the halfway point of life—balanced between the spiritual and the physical worlds.

The fifth chakra, which corresponds to Tuesday, is the level of fear and death. Tuesday is named for the German god Tiw—to the Romans, Mars, the god of war. The French *mardi* means "Mars's day." Mars is the red planet, which is appropriate for the bloody god of battle. Iron is the metal of Mars—the metal of weaponry. Iron ore is red as well. The Hindu emblem for the fifth chakra is a picture of a monstrous god with a terrible grimace. This stage goes beyond the physical world to the metaphysical first step—the experience of Nothingness. It is the age when some experience a mid-life crisis. It is when we come to grips with our mortality. In Freudian terms, it is the level of the subconscious; and in Christian mystical terms, it is the Dark Night of the Soul or the *Via Negativa*.

The fifth chakra is located in the throat. The throat is a constricted or narrow passage. The Latin word for narrow is *angustus*, which comes from the Indo-European root *angh* or *ang*. Related words include *anger*, *anxiety*, *anguish*, *angina*, *hang*, and *strangle*. The Persian god of destruction was Angra Mainya, which means "destructive thought."

The sixth chakra corresponds to Monday or the "Moon's day." The French word for Monday is *lundi*, which has the same meaning.

CADUCEUS

Design from the
Libation Cup of King
Gudea of Lagash, Sumer.
2,000 B.C.

Figure 2. Adapted from The Inner Reaches of Outer Space *by Joseph Campbell, HarperCollins, 1986.*

The moon (Becoming) is the intermediary between the blinding sun (Being) and the black earth (Nothingness). We are unable to look into the pure light of Being, but we can enlighten our darkness with the reflective light of Becoming. The color and metal of the moon is silver—the color of mirrors. The moon acts as a mirror that allows us to look at the absolute. Because the moon's shape is ever changing, the moon is the symbol of change and transformation. In the sixteenth century Edmund Spenser in the *Fairie Queene* told how Lady Mutability usurped the throne of the moon and ruled over everything within the circle of the moon, including our ever-changing world.[4]

The sixth chakra is the level of the forehead and is related to the expression of the absolute rather than the absolute itself. It is the level of creativity and awakening—the stage between the subconscious and consciousness. It stands between Nothingness and Being. The moon is the level of the eyes and of vision. It is a time for leadership and for sharing what our lives have given us.

The seventh chakra is equivalent to the first day of the week—Sunday. Known as *dimanche* or the "Lord's day" in French, it is the Christian sabbath. As the sun, it is the blinding light of pure Being. Both the metal and color of the sun is gold, the most precious metal to the ancients. It is consciousness and enlightenment. It is the source of creativity. It is placed at the crown of the head and is symbolized by the Hindu thousand-petal lotus blossom—the sign of enlightenment. It is the level beyond expression, both ineffable and inscrutable. This is the final stage of our lives.

Our Seven Heavens

I became interested in a question posed by Joseph Campbell about why the number seven was so predominant in our myths. He pointed out the seven intersections in the coiled serpents of the caduceus, symbol of wisdom among the Greeks and other ancient peoples. The caduceus was carried by the god Mercury and is still used today as a symbol of the medical profession. (See Figure 2.) Campbell compares the seven levels of the caduceus to the seven levels of Dante's *The Divine Comedy* and to the seven levels of a corn plant in a Navaho sand painting for a Blessing Chant. For him, Carl Jung's theory of "the archetypes of the unconscious" helps to explain these coincidences.[5]

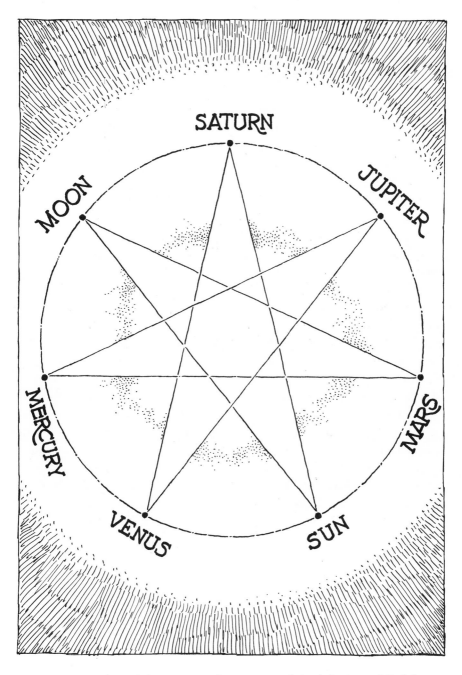

Figure 3. Adapted from Jesus Christ, Sun of God *by David Fideler,*
Quest Books, 1993.

Not fully satisfied with this explanation, I began to search for the historical roots of the significance of the number seven. First I learned that both the East and the West used the weekday order of the planets in religion and astrology.

The Seven Days of the Week

The Egyptians assigned ten days to a week, but the Hebrews divided the days into groups of seven, and the Greeks assigned each of the seven days a planet. This most likely took place in Alexandria, Egypt, in the second century B.C. At that time, the order of the seven visible planets had been established according to the length of their orbital periods: Saturn, 29.46 years; Jupiter, 11.86 years; Mars, 686.98 days; the sun, 365.26 days; Venus, 224.70 days; Mercury, 87.97 days; and the moon, 29.53 days. An explanation for how the order of the planets in the names of the days of the week was derived was not recorded until the third century A.D., when the Roman historian Dio Cassius provided two answers, one based on the music of the spheres and the other on astrology.[6]

Dio Cassius had heard that the daily order of the planets was derived from the traditional order, based on the orbital periods, separated into "tetrachords" or groups of four with a perfect musical interval of a fourth between the first and fourth notes.[7] This can best be visualized by placing the planets in their traditional order around the outside of a circle. (See Figure 3.) Counting from each planet as point one, go around the circle to point four both clockwise and counterclockwise to determine the planet that follows and precedes it. Connecting the planets in this weekday order makes a heptagram or seven-pointed star.[8] This solution is in keeping with the Pythagorean School with its emphasis on music, geometry, and the mysticism of numbers.

The second explanation of Dio Cassius took into account the close relationship between the days of the week and astrology. In the second century B.C., the day was divided into twenty-four hours and the planets were ordered according to their orbital periods. Also during this century the astrological theory of "chronocratories" was developed. It held that each hour of the day was ruled by a different planet or chronocrator ("ruler of time"). The planets were aligned with the hours of the day in the traditional order of the planets, beginning with Saturn. The planet ruling the first hour of the day was known as

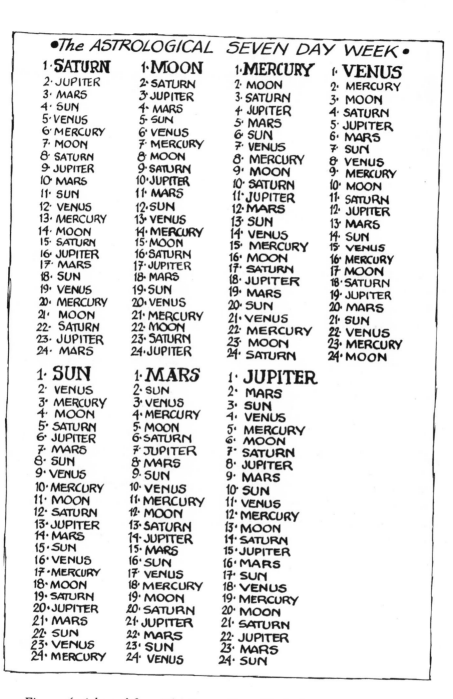

•The ASTROLOGICAL SEVEN DAY WEEK•

1·SATURN	1·MOON	1·MERCURY	1· VENUS
2· JUPITER	2· SATURN	2· MOON	2· MERCURY
3· MARS	3· JUPITER	3· SATURN	3· MOON
4· SUN	4· MARS	4· JUPITER	4· SATURN
5· VENUS	5· SUN	5· MARS	5· JUPITER
6· MERCURY	6· VENUS	6· SUN	6· MARS
7· MOON	7· MERCURY	7· VENUS	7· SUN
8· SATURN	8· MOON	8· MERCURY	8· VENUS
9· JUPITER	9· SATURN	9· MOON	9· MERCURY
10· MARS	10· JUPITER	10· SATURN	10· MOON
11· SUN	11· MARS	11· JUPITER	11· SATURN
12· VENUS	12· SUN	12· MARS	12· JUPITER
13· MERCURY	13· VENUS	13· SUN	13· MARS
14· MOON	14· MERCURY	14· VENUS	14· SUN
15· SATURN	15· MOON	15· MERCURY	15· VENUS
16· JUPITER	16· SATURN	16· MOON	16· MERCURY
17· MARS	17· JUPITER	17· SATURN	17· MOON
18· SUN	18· MARS	18· JUPITER	18· SATURN
19· VENUS	19· SUN	19· MARS	19· JUPITER
20· MERCURY	20· VENUS	20· SUN	20· MARS
21· MOON	21· MERCURY	21· VENUS	21· SUN
22· SATURN	22· MOON	22· MERCURY	22· VENUS
23· JUPITER	23· SATURN	23· MOON	23· MERCURY
24· MARS	24· JUPITER	24· SATURN	24· MOON

1· SUN	1· MARS	1· JUPITER
2· VENUS	2· SUN	2· MARS
3· MERCURY	3· VENUS	3· SUN
4· MOON	4· MERCURY	4· VENUS
5· SATURN	5· MOON	5· MERCURY
6· JUPITER	6· SATURN	6· MOON
7· MARS	7· JUPITER	7· SATURN
8· SUN	8· MARS	8· JUPITER
9· VENUS	9· SUN	9· MARS
10· MERCURY	10· VENUS	10· SUN
11· MOON	11· MERCURY	11· VENUS
12· SATURN	12· MOON	12· MERCURY
13· JUPITER	13· SATURN	13· MOON
14· MARS	14· JUPITER	14· SATURN
15· SUN	15· MARS	15· JUPITER
16· VENUS	16· SUN	16· MARS
17· MERCURY	17· VENUS	17· SUN
18· MOON	18· MERCURY	18· VENUS
19· SATURN	19· MOON	19· MERCURY
20· JUPITER	20· SATURN	20· MOON
21· MARS	21· JUPITER	21· SATURN
22· SUN	22· MARS	22· JUPITER
23· VENUS	23· SUN	23· MARS
24· MERCURY	24· VENUS	24· SUN

Figure 4. Adapted from The Seven Day Circle *by Eviatar Zerubavel,*
Macmillan, 1985.

the "regent" for the entire day. A horoscope ("a look at the hour") charted the stars and planets that influenced a person at the hour of birth. Therefore both the planet that ruled the hour and the planet that ruled the day were important. Figure 4 shows the astrological seven-day week with its chronocratories, beginning with Saturday. As you can see, the regents, which are in large letters, are in the same order as the modern days of the week.[9]

By 19 B.C. Romans identified the days of the week using the same planetary order that we use today except that Saturday was the first day of the week. With the expansion of the Roman Empire the practice spread quickly and widely. Eventually Christians changed the first day of the week from Saturday to Sunday and made it their sabbath, as was the practice among the followers of Mithra, the god of the sun. Meanwhile Saturn's day became the Jewish sabbath. (For example, *samedi* in French means "Saturday" and originally meant "sabbath.") Probably because of Mithraism's Persian roots, the present-day order of the days of the week with Sunday as the first day had already appeared in India by the first century A.D. Through India's influence, the practice spread to Nepal, Tibet, Ceylon, Burma, Thailand, and Indochina.[10]

The Planets and the Spiritual Journey
Mithraism was a very popular religion in the early centuries of the Roman Empire, particularly among the military. Evolving from the Zorastrian religion in Persia, Mithra became the god of the sun. Mithraism had much in common with Christianity, including an emphasis on humility and brotherly love. Mithraic rites included baptism and communion. Their god was born on December 25 and was adored by shepherds. Sunday was their holy day, and they believed in the soul's immortality, the last judgment, and the resurrection.[11] Many early churches were built on top of temples to Mithra, as can be seen in Rome today.

In the West in the third century A.D., Mythraic initiation ceremonies included a ladder with rungs. Each rung was assigned a different metal and a different planet. The metals were somewhat different than those later assigned to the planets by alchemists. Each rung was a "heaven" to be ascended: Saturn was lead, Venus tin, Jupiter bronze, Mercury iron, Mars "the alloy of money," the moon silver, and the sun gold. There was an eighth rung assigned to "the sphere of the fixed stars," which led to Empyrean, the highest heaven.[12] One of the reasons that the weekday order of the planets is found so often in Mithraic art is that Mithra was worshipped as a chronocrator.[13]

Like the followers of Mithra, Christians also connected the planets with spiritual growth. In the third century, Saint Ambrose stated that there were seven gifts of the Holy Spirit, each of which was connected to a spirit and a heaven. The first and highest heaven was wisdom, the second understanding, the third counsel, the fourth fortitude, the fifth knowledge, the sixth piety, and the seventh the fear of the Lord.[14] These gifts were lost in the descent to earth and had to be regained in the ascent back to heaven.

In the fifth century the Neoplatonist pagan philosopher Macrobius connected the seven deadly sins to the seven planets. He contended that as human souls left their fiery heavenly home in Empyrean and traveled past the fixed stars down through each planet's sphere, the souls drew with them the sloth of Saturn, the lust of Venus, the anger of Mars, and so forth. He also said that the soul received benefits from each planet as it descended. He used the order of the planets favored by the famous second-century Greek astronomer and astrologer Ptolemy, which was based on the lengths of the planets' orbital periods. According to Macrobius, in Saturn's sphere the soul receives "reasoning and intelligence," in Jupiter's "the power of acting," in Mars's "the fiery ardor of spirit," in the sun's "a nature for feeling and opinion," in Venus's the "motion of desire," in Mercury's "speaking out and interpreting," and in the moon's "corporeal begetting and growing."[15]

Almost eight hundred years later, this view of the world had changed very little as Dante described his spiral climb of the mountain of Purgatory and his ascent through the planetary spheres. In *The Purgatorio* he begins with those who have committed the most deadly sins and travels upward past the proud, the envious, the wrathful, the slothful, the avaricious, the gluttonous, and the lustful. In *The Paradiso,* to reach the fixed stars and then Empyrean, he first ascends the seven heavens: the moon, Mercury, Venus, the sun, Mars, Jupiter, and Saturn.

Even in the sixteenth century, Shakespeare in *As You Like It* still lists the seven ages of man as taught by Ptolemy fourteen hundred years earlier, beginning with infancy ruled by the moon and ending with senility ruled by Saturn.[16]

The planetary order of the days of the week can be found, too, in Eastern astrology and religion. Hindu astrology still uses this order of the planets today. And as in the West, the East also connected the planets with spiritual attainment. In the sixth century A.D. the great Indian astrologer and astronomer Varahamihira, considered to be the founder of Indian astrology, summarized the astronomical and astrological theories of his day. The following passage shows similarities with Macrobius and demonstrates Varahamihira's knowledge of Greek astrology: "The Sun is the Self of Time, the Moon is his Mind, Mars his Courage, Mercury his Speech, Jupiter his Knowledge and Happiness, Venus his Desire, and Saturn his Sorrow."[17]

An early reference to the seven chakras states, "All beings that exist in the seven worlds are to be found in the body."[18] This is from the *Purana*, medieval metrical stories, none of which dates earlier than third-century India.[19] We can see that the Western connection of spiritual attainment with the seven heavens and seven planets and the Eastern connection of spiritual attainment with the seven worlds and seven centers of the human body both appeared after the order of the seven days of the week had been spread throughout the Roman Empire and India. Hindu astrology, which promotes spiritual development, would have helped to promote the similarity of the weekday order of the seven planets and the order of the seven worlds and the seven chakras.

The Pervasiveness of Seven

The number seven has many other uses besides the ordering of the planets and the days of the week. Once I began to collect examples of how seven is used, I found that it is generally the most significant number throughout the world in literature, mythology, religion, and folk custom. My examples include: 7 angels before the throne of God, 7 auspicious signs of Buddha, 7 days of creation, 7 gifts of the Holy Spirit, 7 heavens, 7 names of God, 7 sacraments, 7 sacred trees of Ireland, 7 Irish saints that never died, 7 steps to heaven, 7 virtues, 7 ages of the Church, 7 ages of man, 7 animal sacrifices of the Siberian hero, 7 branches of the Menorah, 7 bishops of the early Church, 7 clouds of glory that followed the Israelites, 7 days of great festivals, 7 doves of the Pleiades, 7-fold alchemical process, 7 genies, 7 levels of a ziggurat, 7 liberal arts, 7 metals, 7 musical tones, 7 stars in the Big and the Little Dipper, 7 Buddhist offerings, 7-pillared temple in *Proverbs*, 7-story mountain, 7 temples of Inanna, 7 years of enchantment, 7 brides for 7 brothers, 7 priests marched around Jericho for 7 days, 7 Hindu Rishi (wise men), 7 Greek sages, 7th son, 7 assistants of Siberian Over-God, 7 Egyptian wise ones, 7 Hathors, 7 against Thebes, 7-days wonder, 7 forehead marks of Berber women, 7 hills of Rome, 7 fat and 7 lean years, 7-league boots, 7 locks of Samson's hair, 7 Native American directional points, 7 seas, 7x7 years in a jubilee, 7 wonders of the world, 7 deadly sins, 7-headed dragon or ogre or serpent, 7 hells, 7 sleepers of Islam, 7 steps of hell, 7-year itch, 7 years bad luck, 7 oriental veils, and the 7-year statute of limitations.

Geoffrey Ashe in *Dawn Behind the Dawn* looks beyond the seven planets and beyond universal archetypes to discover that the seven stars within the constellation of the Great Bear were influential throughout Asia, Europe, and North America. He points out that ancestors of Native Americans probably brought with them from Siberia the tradition of bear worship and that they too saw a bear in the stars that make up the Big Dipper.[20] The idea of finding concrete influences giving rise to our myths fascinated me, preparing me for the next series of discoveries.

In the Mountains of West Virginia

In August 1995 my wife, Mary Lou, and I vacationed in the Canaan Valley in West Virginia. The area is unpopulated and unpolluted as well as mountainous. During the summer it is wonderful for hiking. At night, during the new moon, the skies are ablaze with starlight; then it is easy to see why ancient peoples were so influenced by the sky. The Milky Way is like a road to heaven.

On that trip I had the rare opportunity to read a book straight through. The book was *Celebrate the Solstice*, by Richard Heinburg. I read with interest Heinburg's account of Anna Sofaer's discovery that, at the summer solstice, a thin dagger of light cuts through a spiral petroglyph that looks like a snake at the top of Fajade Butte in Chaco Canyon, New Mexico. Like the caduceus, this Anasazi spiraling snake has seven coils. In addition, there are two daggers of light that appear there at the winter solstice and delimit the outer edges of the coiled snake. At the equinoxes, one dagger of light falls on the coiled snake and a second dagger falls on a second, smaller coiled snake depicted nearby.[21]

I learned also that the Hopi, descendents of the Anasazi, used a horizon calendar to determine the time for planting and harvesting. The three points on the mountainous horizon that would not change from year to year when seen from the same location are the rising of the sun at the winter solstice, at the summer solstice, and at the equinoxes. (The sun rises at the same point for both the spring and fall equinoxes.) Other important dates, such as the time for planting beans and corn, could be determined by noting where the sun rises on those days and remembering the landmark for it.[22]

Based on this leisure-time reading, I was able to make two discoveries in the weeks and months to come. The first discovery was that the sun, as it arches overhead, appears to be circling the earth, spiraling every day a little bit farther north or south. That is why Native Americans used a spiral, depicting the sun, to designate the solstices. In the same way, the intertwined snakes of the caduceus portray the sun's path, spiraling upward to reach the summer solstice and turning around and spiraling back down again.

The second discovery was why the number seven is associated with the serpent. I arrived at this discovery by imagining the Hopi noting the location of the sunrise at the day of the full moon each month. I realized that one of the reasons that the number seven is so significant is that if the full moon occurs on or near the winter solstice, there will be a total of seven full moons before the summer solstice. Similarly, if the new moon occurs on or near the winter solstice, there will be a total of seven new moons before the summer solstice. The solstice, which means "sun standing still," appears to last for several days before the sun reverses its direction. There are always either seven full moons or seven new moons between the beginning of one solstice period and the end of the next. (For more on the length of the solstice period, see Chapter 11, "Jack and the Beanstalk.")

Jacob's Ladder

The paths of the full moons are seven descending rungs on a ladder between the winter and summer solstices. (See Figure 5.) The rungs are descending because the path of the full moon, unlike the path of the new moon, complements the path of the sun. The full moon is high in the winter sky when the sun is low, and it is low in the summer sky when the sun is high. The ladder can be used to determine when the next solstice will be by counting the moons down toward

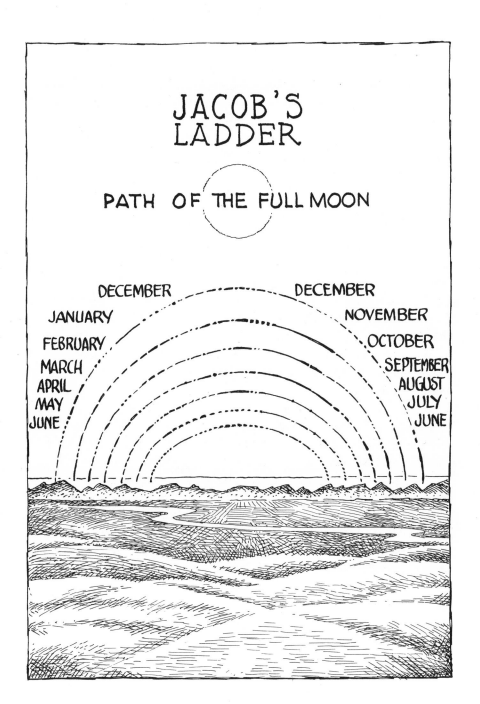

Figure 5

the summer solstice and counting them up toward the next winter solstice.

This ladder can also be used to calculate lunar eclipses. Counting six rungs along the ladder after a lunar eclipse can reveal when the next lunar eclipse will occur. William H. Calvin explains in *How the Shaman Stole the Moon* how ancient peoples used this technique to predict when a lunar eclipse would occur. About 56 percent of all lunar eclipses occur at the sixth full moon following an observed lunar eclipse.[23] It seems to me that by using the ladder as a simple calculator, it would be easy to see when the greatest likelihood of a lunar eclipse would be. In his book, Calvin then goes on to show how the ancient sky watcher could have used observations of light, shadow, and landmarks to locate the precise relationship of the sun and the moon in order to very accurately predict lunar eclipses and in some cases solar eclipses as well.

Babylonians said that seven devils were holding the moon prisoner when there was a lunar eclipse.[24] This is appropriate because there are seven full moons in the period from one lunar eclipse to the point of the greatest likelihood of another. (In ancient counting systems there was no zero, because it had not yet been invented. Therefore the starting point for counting was often called "one." For example, Christians believe that Christ rose on the third day after the Crucifixion, while by modern count there are only two days between Good Friday and Easter Sunday.)

Counting up and down the moon's paths is reminiscent of Jacob's vision: "And he dreamed that there was a ladder set up on the earth, the top of it reaching to heaven; and the angels of God were ascending and descending on it" (Gen. 28:12).[25] The angels would be the spirits governing the sun and the moon as well as the other five visible planets, which vary each month of the year because of their wanderings. The five planets arc across the southern sky (in the Northern Hemisphere) on paths close to the paths of the sun and the moon. Sometimes none, sometimes one or a few, and sometimes all five are visible in the sky at once.

Serpents and Dragons

These discoveries opened the floodgates of my imagination. I was finding serpents and dragons and the number seven everywhere. In the chakra teaching, there are "two subtle nerves or channels" of vital energy that wind around the central spinal column and around the chakras, much like the two snakes of the caduceus. The red channel carries solar energy and is "'masculine' fiery, poisonous, and deadly," while the white or yellowish channel carries lunar energy and is "'feminine' cooling and as refreshing as dew." They spiral around a central channel that is black.[26] The two spiraling channels imitate the sun's spiral growing upward toward summer and the full moon's spiral growing downward toward winter.

There is no question that these symbols are very ancient. Serpents can be found in early cave paintings, and snakes and spirals signifying the rhythms of the moon have been found in the Siberian cultures of the Ice Age.[27] In Mexico, the rain god Tlolac is associated with the moon and is represented by two twisted snakes.[28] The Aztecs pictured the twisted snakes being worshipped at an altar.[29] Twisted serpents are often used as symbols of wisdom in Hindu mythology, and in Ireland, the "Right Hand of God" is pictured on top of two twisted snakes on a tenth-century stone cross.[30]

The Maya placed the glyph for the lunar eclipse above the open jaws of a hungry serpent.[31] In Chinese, Hindu, Finnish, and Islamic myth the dragon, a relative of the serpent, eats the moon, causing a lunar eclipse.[32] Armenians, too, accused the dragon of causing eclipses, while the Balts blamed dragons, serpents, and witches.[33] In modern astrology, the times when eclipses can occur are referred to as the head and tail of a dragon. The Cherokee tell of four snakes that attempted to kill the sun, first Spreading Adder and Copperhead, and then Rattlesnake and Water Monster. They killed the sun's daughter by mistake, and seven men with seven sticks had to be sent to capture her spirit in a box in order to bring her back to life.[34]

Another connection of the number seven and the serpent is a seven-part serpent of light that can be seen at the equinoxes at the Castillo at Chichan Itza in the Yucatan. E. C. Krupp, in his exciting book *Beyond the Blue Horizon*, provides a photograph of the seven triangles of light that move down the side of the stepped pyramid to a crafted serpent's head that is also lit up near sunset in the fall and the spring. The tenth-century structure built by a group of Putun Maya was dedicated to the god Kukulcan (Quetzalcoatl), whose name means "feathered serpent" and who brought civilization to humans.[35] The serpent is worshipped at the halfway point in its trip between the solstices, midway among the seven new or full moons. (For more about the feathered serpent, the number seven, and the prediction of solstices and equinoxes, see Chapter 11, "Jack and the Beanstalk.")

Snakes are lunar animals because they shed their skins periodically, just as the moon sheds its garment each month and puts on another. Snakes are the source of magic, knowledge, and secrets and can predict the future. It was widely believed that by eating a snake, one could speak the language of animals, particularly of birds.[36]

The Seven Days of the Moon's Ascent

After our vacation, the year went quickly. In September 1996, Mary Lou took a teaching position in tidewater Virginia while I continued working in Pennsylvania. Visiting Virginia on weekends taught me two things. First, I began to understand the relationship between the tides and the moon—something I had not experienced before. I saw how the tides were highest and lowest at spring tide during the new and full moons and how the tides were the least noticeable during neap tide at the first and third quarters of the moon. ("Spring" comes from the German *springen,* which means "to leap up" and does not refer to the season of spring in this context.)

Second, during the drive I learned that the moon is essentially on a seven-day cycle. If on a Friday night there was a new moon as I drove south, the next Friday I would see the half (first quarter) moon, and the following Friday I would see the full moon. This pattern would have to be adjusted by one or two days each lunar cycle, but it was easy to see how people would associate the number seven with the moon.

Each month the moon spends most of its time in the day sky half of the month and most of its time in the night sky the other half. If one observes the moon each night at midnight beginning at the waxing half-moon, for seven days the moon would be a little higher above the western horizon each day, culminating in the full moon at the top of the sky on the seventh day. For the next seven days it would decline in the sky.

Similarly, if it were possible to observe the moon every day at noon beginning with the waning half-moon, each day it would be higher above the horizon, until on the seventh day it would reach its apex as the new moon. For the next seven days it would decline. Figure 6 depicts the phases of the moon each day. If Sunday were the moon at the top of the sky, then Saturday would be the moon at the

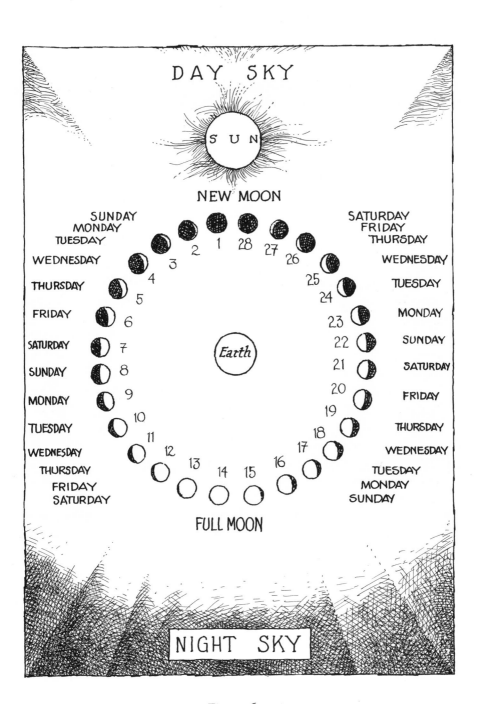

Figure 6

horizon, again stressing the importance of the number seven. This twenty-eight-day cycle is only an approximation of the twenty-nine-and-one-half-day lunar cycle, but it is the traditional number of the phases of the moon, and astrologers used to refer to twenty-eight lunar mansions.[37]

Moon Mountain

The moon ascending for seven days into the daytime sky and then descending for seven days back to the horizon is a seven-story mountain, just like the seven-stepped pyramids of Babylonia known as ziggurats. Ziggurat originally meant "pinnacle" and was a cosmic mountain. The ziggurat at Borsippa had a level for each of the seven planets.[38] There are rare times when all seven of the ancient planets will be in the sky on the same evening or morning. They are like seven stepping stones arching up the seven-story mountain, all hovering above or below the path of the moon.

Besides being Jacob's ladder, the seven arcs of the full moon can also be seen as seven mountains one behind the other. (See Figure 5.) Mountains are widely used in myth and are often linked to the moon. The Snoqualmie say that Mount Si in the state of Washington is the moon, Snoqualm, who fell to earth when a rope broke while he was climbing down from the sky after Beaver, who had stolen the sun.[39]

In Hindu myth, one of the great peaks of the Himalayas, Mount Mandara, stands on Vishnu, the god of creation, in his tortoise incarnation. Demons twisted Mandara like a pestle by pulling the great serpent Vasuki, which was coiled around it, and churned the ocean to produce the essential objects for the survival of the gods and humans, including the sun, the moon, and soma, the elixir of immortality, which comes from the moon.[40] The Ganges, which fell from the moon, springs from the foot of Mount Mandara.[41]

I believe that there is an etymological connection between *month* and *mountain*. They both have the identical Indo-European root—*mens*. In Sanskrit the word *mata* means both "mother" and "moon." The two words derive from the shorter root *ma* which means "to measure" and are related to the Sanskrit *manas*—"mind"; *masa*—"month"; *Manu*—the first "man"; and *mantra*—a formula of words and sounds. So too in English, all of these groups of words are related to the moon, including words about mountains:

1. Moon, month, menstrual, Monday
2. Human, woman, man, manikin
3. Mind, mental, remember, comment, vehement, mean, mad, mania, maniac, manic, amnesia, amnesty, automatic, necromancy, mandarin, mantis, martyr
4. Monitor, admonition, premonition, monstrance, monster, monument, remonstrate, demonstrate, muster, summon
5. Measure, mete, meter, metric, commensurate, geometry, mathematics
6. Mother, mamma, mom, maternal, mammal, matriculate, metropolitan, matrimony, matrix, matter, material
7. Mountain, promontory, mount, amount, amenable, demeanor, eminent, imminent, mane, marmot, menace, mental (pertaining to the chin), monte, paramount, and prominent.[42]

A good example of the measuring moon mother is the lunar Egyptian goddess Ma'at, who measures out justice at the end of life just as the moon measures out time. With her male counterpart, Toth, she weighs her feather against a person's heart to see if it is light enough to enter heaven. She is usually shown wearing her ostrich feather. She and Toth determine whether a person is ready to "go to the top of the mountain."

The Discovery
The discovery that pulled together all of the ideas that had been evolving over the previous decade occurred on Thursday, September 26, 1996. Regarding the number seven, I found it interesting that many Bible stories and fairy tales could be divided into seven episodes. I had been working on the concept that the story of Snow White was a story about the moon and its travel from the winter solstice to the summer solstice in seven steps. It all worked very well, but why was Snow White described as being as red as blood, as white as snow, and as black as ebony? At 10:30 P.M. I talked to Mary Lou by telephone and suggested that she go outside and try to see the total lunar eclipse. I had been looking forward to seeing it myself, but there was too much cloud cover in Pennsylvania, and so I had to miss it.

Figure 7

At 11:00 P.M. Mary Lou called back, excited to tell me that the eclipse was beautiful. It was a rich dark red. She had never seen anything like it before. As she spoke, a seed began to grow in my mind. I had always thought, in my ignorance, that the lunar eclipse was the black shadow of the earth swallowing the white moon. However, depending on weather conditions on earth, the sun's light is refracted by the earth's atmosphere, causing the moon sometimes to turn dark red. That was it—the three colors of the lunar eclipse are red, white, and black, the colors of Snow White!

Again, one idea led to another, and I was finding examples of both lunar and solar eclipses throughout folklore and myth. It made sense that all ancient peoples feared eclipses not just because they were afraid that the sun or moon would never return. Rather, they saw it as a time when the upper world of the heavens interacted with the lower world, causing fear, but also hope. Figure 7 shows the path that the shadows of the eclipse follow. The shadows act as two-way passages for both good and evil spirits. The shadows lead to the inconstant moon, but they also allow an opening past the circle of the moon to the predictable world of the planets, the sun, the fixed stars, and beyond—a world of constancy and permanency unlike our chaotic one.

Make a Great Noise!

The making of a great din during both solar and lunar eclipses is one of the oldest and most widespread traditions in the world. In an ancient Sumerian ritual the people were told what to do as a lunar eclipse began: "A dirge for the fields thou shalt intone; a dirge for the streams that the water shall not devastate, thou shalt intone. . . . Until the eclipse is past, they shalt shout."[43] They are to cover their heads with their garments, and they are to cry aloud and sing to the moon so that catastrophe, murder, and rebellion would not approach them. Throughout the world the moon is seen to influence vegetation and rain.[44] Because the moon grows large each month, it is associated with growing things. Because it moves the tides, it is linked to water and therefore rain. Because it dies each month it is linked to death; and because it is ever changing, it is linked to chaos and instability.

In Turkey and Italy, people beat kettles and basins to drown out the charms of witches during lunar eclipses.[45] This ritual is based on the ancient Greek belief, as pictured on vases and described in the *Voyage of the Argo*, that the lunar eclipse is caused by witches calling down the moon from heaven to mix it with their herbs.[46] Here the purpose of the noise appears to be to break the spell cast on the moon. The ancient Romans beat pots and pans and threw torches into the sky.[47] In India, people beat with utensils on pots and pans to frighten the demon Rahu, who attempts to swallow the sun and the moon.[48] In China, the purpose of the clamor was to cause the dragon, which had the moon, to lose hold of it.[49]

The Welsh and Irish also made a racket, and Greenlanders got on their roofs to beat their kettles.[50] In the nineteenth century in what is now Uzbekistan, people used cymbals, tambourines, and drums during a lunar eclipse. The Buryats screamed and threw stones into the air to frighten Alkha away during an eclipse.[51]

In the New World, up until recent times Native Americans used their voices to make noise. The Toba of Paraguay and Argentina shouted to scatter the spirits of the dead, who took the form of jaguars trying to eat the moon; while the Galibi of French Guiana made noise and shot arrows into the air during an eclipse. In South America, the Tupinamba sang to their ancestors while the women wailed and fell to the ground with their children. In California, an old man of the Kawaiisu sang to the sun or moon to cure it of its illness, while the Serrano tried to prevent the spirits of the dead from eating the sun or moon by shouting, listening to singers and dancers, and avoiding food. The Luiseno of California sang songs to cure a sick moon, and at Mission San Luis Rey they clapped and shouted to frighten the animal attempting to eat the moon.[52]

Spirits of the Dead

As we have seen, the eclipse is a time when the sun or moon was believed to be ill and to be eaten by the spirits of the dead. The Talmud refers to one who "walks through the valley of the shadow of death" (Ps. 23:4) as one "who sleeps in the shadow of the moon," that is, one who sleeps during a solar eclipse.[53] I imagine that in ancient times it was pretty difficult to sleep during an eclipse, with all that hubbub. In China, two inebriated court astronomers who fell asleep during a solar eclipse were put to death.[54]

African pygmies believed the moon was their mother and the refuge of ghosts.[55] According to the Malayan Besisi, there is a man in the moon who hunts the souls of the dead with his bow and arrow.[56] The Saliva of South America thought that the moon was a paradise for souls with no mosquitoes, and the Guaycurus saw the moon as the home of their dead chiefs. So did the people of Polynesian Tokelau. The Greek Plutarch said that the souls of the dead resolve into the moon, and in medieval times hell was said to be in the moon.[57]

The moon was both a transporter of souls and a portal through which souls passed. Isis prayed that her brother Osiris's soul would go up to heaven on the moon's disc.[58] In the early Roman Empire, the followers of Mani believed that the moon was a boat that ferried souls from the sun to the "pillars of glory." The Inuit (Eskimo) believe that the soul travels from the moon to the sun.[59] The ancient Iranian view was the same. Hindus say that the moon's path is the path of reincarnation, whereas the sun's path is the path of freedom from illusion. Pythagoras taught that the Elysian Fields, where the souls of heroes dwelled, was in the moon. He also said that the moon reabsorbs souls and recreates them. This was a widely held belief about the moon. As he stated, "Only what is beyond the moon is beyond becoming."[60]

While being the home of the dead, the moon is a sign of hope as well. For Australian aborigines, Gidja, the moon, is a man who watches the "good gate at the portal of the new horizon." Just like the Egyptian measuring moon mother Ma'at, no one can pass through into life after death without Gidja's approval.[61] The moon is also a place of birth. There is a Native American tradition that babies cry when they are born because they have left the Moon Land and their Moon Mother.[62]

What Is Black and White and Red All Over?

What do the moon, the eclipse of the moon, and the colors white, red, and black have in common? The three colors of the moon are the black new moon, the white full moon, and the immense red moon, known as the harvest moon because it appears most often in the fall. Weather permitting, the beautiful lunar eclipse is always preceded by a large reddish moonrise.[63] That is the one time when the moon manifests all three colors—the moon of the lunar eclipse. A lunar eclipse can only happen at the full moon, when the moon is white. In the transition to a total lunar eclipse the portion of the moon that enters the earth's umbra sometimes appears to be near black, but then, in the totality of the lunar eclipse, the moon turns a bright orange or a deep red. There are also times when, because of heavy cloud cover on the earth, no light is transmitted and the moon is totally black and even invisible. Only one thing is certain about lunar eclipses—that no two are exactly alike.

The White, the Red, and the Black

Besides being literally white, red, and black, the moon and the three colors are also symbolically connected. In classical times, the three Fates or Moirai were believed to obtain their power from the moon and to be part of the moon.[64] The life threads that they spun, measured, and cut off were made of three colors—white, red, and black. This agrees with the Hindu Tantric tradition that there are three strands in the thread of fate, which are white, red, and black. The Mahabharata tells of three goddesses who weave the veil of days and nights in an underground city of serpents using threads of white and black together with the red thread of life.[65]

Some of the earliest religious symbols were painted on cave walls with red ochre. Red symbolizes birth, life, love, and death. Children come into this world covered with placental blood. Menstrual blood is a sign of a woman's fertility, hymenal blood is a sign of first love, and at death blood flows from the body as does the soul.

In Sumeria doorways were painted red to symbolize the "blood of life," and Egyptians smeared their doorways with real blood during religious ceremonies.[66] The Hebrews painted their doorposts with the blood of the lamb in the spring, and the Babylonians painted the temple of Nabu with sheep's blood in their spring New Year festival.[67] Even today the Chinese paint their gateways red for their New Year celebration. Eclipses symbolize the sun or moon going through a door. On Vancouver Island, the Nootka believed that eclipses were the sun or moon being swallowed by the "door of heaven."[68]

Hindu and Chinese art and architecture still often use gold, red, and black. Gold is often used as the color of sunlight or moonlight and in this case replaces the color white. In ancient Europe (including imperial Rome), unlike today, white was considered the color of death, associated with white bones; and black was the color of life, linked to the rich black earth. This ancient tradition is still seen today in China, where a bride might wear red for her wedding but would never wear white, which is reserved for funerals.[69] The Roman Catholic Church has changed in recent years to using white vestments for funeral masses instead of black.

The three colors have both religious and natural origins. The ancients used fire to burn offerings to the heavens. Red blood of the victims spilled onto the black earth, and red fire wafted the offering to the white or golden lights of heaven. Between the white or golden light of daytime and the black of night is the red of sunrise and sunset. Between the gold or white of the summer solstice and the black of the winter solstice are the red sap and buds of spring and the red leaves of fall. Between the black darkness of the womb and the white light of day is the red doorway of birth. A wound is the red doorway between the light of consciousness and the blackness of death.

The Sun, the Moon, and the Night

The moon's creatures are white, red, and black. We will find them in the old stories and nursery rhymes. In Native American ceremonies the bear, which is a symbol of the moon, is painted using white, red, and black.[70] Io, the Ionians' moon goddess, who took the form of a cow, was able to turn herself from white to red to black. In Celtic myth, the Hounds of Annwn or dogs of the underworld were white, red, and black.[71] Another creature of the moon is the Devil. Looking at Figure 7, it is easy to see why the full moon, the time when lunar eclipses occur, would be seen as being at the bottom of the underworld. Dante places the Devil at the very bottom of the underworld, with a head with three faces. The right face is white or yellow, the left face is black, and the middle face is red.[72]

There is a story about the three colors from Papua, New Guinea, entitled "The Man Who Paddled to the Moon's House." It tells how the Moon had a white house, The Night had a black house, and the Sun had a red house. Similarly, the Moon ate white bananas, taros, and yams, the Night ate black bananas, and so on.[73] Often the sun is portrayed as fiery and red, and the moon is shown as cool and white. In the Munsee-Mahican Delaware World Renewal Ceremony, white represented peace, women, and the moon.[74] In Europe the moon was known as the White Goddess or the White Lady.

At eclipses the red sun, white moon, and black shadow join together. In Europe, an eclipse foreboded ill.[75] In old European ballads, a white, a red, and a black cock crow to herald the departure of the dead.[76] In "Snow White" the colors foretell both birth and death.

Chapter 3

Snow White

and the Seven Dwarfs

The Making of a Woman

Take one part flesh and blood; add one part sun, moon, and stars; then stir the mixture briskly with the wind. Allow it to warm a while; and, voila, you have a human being. "Snow White and the Seven Dwarfs" is the story of the making of a woman, but who is Snow White? Yes, she is the heroine; but she is also much more. She is all of us—she is the human soul. Her story follows the path of initiation, the path of the moon.

The number seven reappears throughout "Snow White." There are seven dwarfs and seven mountains, Snow White is taken into the forest when she is seven, and seven times the looking glass upon the wall is queried and seven times it responds. Seven is the number of the moon. The moon ascends for seven days to the top of the sky. Seven moons measure the time between solstices and the time between eclipses.

Seven Moons Between Solstices

The story of Snow White begins near the winter solstice:

It was the middle of winter, and the snow-flakes were falling like feathers from the sky, and a queen sat at her window working, and her embroidery-frame was of ebony. [1]

"Midsummer" has traditionally described the time near the summer solstice. For example, Shakespeare's *Midsummer Night's Dream*

Snow White and the Seven Dwarfs

takes place on the night before Midsummer Day, which in England is June 24, the nativity of John the Baptist. Similarly, "the middle of winter" can stand for the winter solstice in December, also known as "midwinter." Just as midday is when the sun is highest in the sky and midnight is when it is farthest away, it makes sense that midsummer is when the sun is northernmost in the sky and midwinter is when it is southernmost.

We will follow the story of Snow White, as told by the Brothers Grimm, from the midwinter of longing to the midsummer of fulfillment. Just as there are seven moons between the solstices, there are seven parts to our story, each symbolically related to the new and full moon.

First Month—New Moon
Blood on the Snow

Raka, the Hindu goddess of the full moon, is the patron of childbirth and prosperity.[2] In the *Ramayana* she is asked to sew with a needle that cannot be broken.[3] That magic needle can be seen as the needle formed by the shadow of the eclipse. (See Figure 7, p. 32.) But before there can be the full moon and childbirth, there must first be the dark of the new moon:

And as she worked, gazing at times out on the snow, she pricked her finger, and there fell from it three drops of blood on the snow.

This is a depiction of a solar eclipse, which can happen only during the new moon. The three drops of blood are the three dark days of the new moon. The new moon lasts for two to three days but is traditionally counted as three. The point of the needle is the thin dark shadow of the solar eclipse.

The ebony frame is the monthly circle of the moon encompassing our world and separating us from the eternal, predictable world of the sun and stars. The thread is the thread spun by the paths of the sun, moon, and stars weaving together across the sky, weaving a tapestry, weaving life's story. According to ancient tradition, and still believed in astrology today, activities in the heavens above influence the everyday happenings of our world here below.

The queen pricks the skin of her finger. Skin is also a tapestry. Up close it has tiny lines woven together, telling the stories of our lives—stories that palm readers attempt to interpret. But the needle breaks the story—breaks the paths of the heavenly orbs. To the ancients, eclipses were unpredictable. They could be forecast by a few hours or a few days, but for the most part eclipses were a break in the rules of the heavens—a break in the skin of the sky and therefore in the story of our lives.

And when she saw how bright and red it looked, she said to herself,
"Oh, that I had a child as white as snow, as red as blood, and as
black as the wood of the embroidery frame!"

This is a moment of foreboding—a moment when the rules of heaven are set aside and when intimations of Love and Death—the unpredictable but inevitable lawbreakers of our world—remind us of their power. Snow White's mother saw her desires fulfilled in the future, which resides in the absolute world of the sun and stars, but her vision up the shaft of the needle of the eclipse would cost her dearly.

At the moment of an eclipse the queen can directly communicate with the heavens along the shaft of the shadowy needle. The sun can be looked at directly in the moments of totality, and the stars come out during the day. For a moment laws are cut through and wishes are fulfilled.

First Month—Full Moon
The White, the Red, and the Black

The girl was to be white, red, and black—the sacred colors of ancient times. In India, yellow (replacing white), red, and black are all colors protective against evil spirits.[4] In this story, the colors are only partially successful:

Not very long after she had a daughter, with a skin as white as
snow, lips as red as blood, and hair as black as ebony, and she was
named Snow-white. And when she was born the queen died.

The full moon and the lunar eclipse are reminiscent of conception, pregnancy, and birth. First, just as the three drops of blood on the snow imply the three days of the new moon, they also imply menstrual blood. Since the lunar cycle approximates the length of time of a woman's menstrual cycle, and since the dark of the moon symbolizes menstruation, it follows that the full moon is linked to the time of conception.

Second, the waxing of the moon mimes pregnancy, culminating with birth at the full moon. Third, the long dark shadow cast by the earth upon the moon recalls the birth canal. It portrays the passage of the child's soul from the sky to the earth as well as the physical passage of the child from the womb into the world. Also, the dark red of the eclipse imitates the appearance of the little red child covered with placental blood. Because fertility and conception are symbolically linked with the full moon and because pregnancy averages almost exactly nine lunar cycles, it follows that birth is also associated with the full moon.

Snow White's mother dies giving birth and her soul escapes up the same passageway to the upper world that Snow White had just descended. The mother goes to the moon, the residence of the spirits of the dead. The moon plays out the close relationship between birth and death, which was so much a part of the ancient worldview.

Similarly, death and birth are associated with the winter solstice, when the sun becomes weak and old and dies to make way for the birth of the new sun. Solar and lunar eclipses were not the only times during which ancient peoples made lots of noise. At the time of the winter solstice when the sun stands still, ancient peoples believed that good and evil spirits bringing life and death could enter the world. In order to chase away evil and to get the sun moving again, people made lots of noise to frighten these spirits, thus giving rise to noise-makers on New Year's Eve. Dressing as spirits and supernatural beings and mimicking combat are part of winter solstice rites in both the Eastern and the Western Hemispheres. Halloween may originally have been a New Year's Eve celebration, along with many of the winter carnival celebrations of the Old World. In China, the New Year's fireworks are set off, and door posters welcome Gods of Wealth and Babies and tell evil spirits to go away.[5] In the New World there are winter solstice dances, and offerings are made to the dead.[6]

The celebration of the birth of Jesus attests to the winter solstice as a time of birth, as do the births of savior gods such as Attis, Adonis, and Mithra. So, too, Snow White is born. For a little while there is peace, but then her troubles begin.

Second Month—New Moon
Looking Glass upon the Wall

Here we meet the character that makes the whole story possible—the looking glass upon the wall:

After a year had gone by the king took another wife, a beautiful woman, but proud and overbearing, and she could not bear to be

surpassed in beauty by anyone. She had a magic looking-glass, and she used to stand before it, and look in it, and say,
> *"Looking-glass upon the wall,*
> *Who is fairest of us all?"*
And the looking-glass would answer:
> *"You are fairest of them all."*
And she was contented, for she knew that the looking-glass spoke the truth.

In the Italian Snow White story, it is the moon rather than a mirror that declares the heroine, Giricoccola, the most beautiful of three sisters.[7] In our version, both the new queen and the looking glass are personifications of the new moon. The queen is usually portrayed as a dark beauty like the dark beauty of the new moon. She resembles Hecate, the Greek goddess of witches and the new moon.

The Mirror and the Moon

Aristophanes, in *The Clouds*, speaks of hiring a witch to draw down the moon at night and shut it up in a round helmet case, like a mirror. The moon is often compared to a mirror. In Siberia, an Altaic myth tells of a spirit who found two mirrors and hung them in the sky as the sun and moon so that they could give light to the world.[8]

Mirrors are also associated with the number seven, the number of the moon. The best-known association, of course, is the seven years bad luck for breaking a mirror. The ancient Japanese believed that each time a person looked into a mirror, a bit of that person's soul was captured by the mirror. Even after a person dies, her or his reflection and thus soul would remain in the mirror.[9] The breaking of a mirror, therefore, would release spirits, both good and bad. That is why mirrors are treated with such respect in Japan. Around the world the moon is seen as the home of the dead. No wonder in Europe it was once considered bad luck to see the new moon in a mirror.[10] Who would want to risk absorbing all those spirits residing in the moon?

Truth and Beauty

How is it that the looking glass always knows the truth and is such an expert at beauty? The ancient Japanese held that mirrors could see the human heart and reflected it in the images of people, making them either ugly or beautiful. The followers of Plato in the West and

Buddha in the East believe that the material world is a mirror that reflects reality darkly.[11] There is a time when the moon reveals truth darkly—during a solar eclipse. During totality the stars will come out during the day. And even when the stars are hard to see, the new moon of the solar eclipse is particularly an expert in beauty because it reveals the planet Venus. Venus is the daystar because it is so bright that the unaided eye can see it in the daytime sky if an observer knows where to look to find it. And, during a solar eclipse, even the untrained observer cannot miss the revelation of the goddess of beauty! So, at the solar eclipse the new moon becomes an expert in both truth and beauty.

The looking glass upon the wall becomes the catalyst of our story. Each time it speaks is another turning point:

Now Snow-white was growing prettier and prettier, and when she was seven years old she was as beautiful as day, far more so than the queen herself. So one day when the queen went to her mirror and said,

> *"Looking-glass upon the wall,*
> *Who is fairest of us all?"*

It answered,

> *"Queen, you are full fair, 'tis true,*
> *But Snow-white fairer is than you."*

This gave the queen a great shock, and she became yellow and green with envy, and from that hour her heart turned against Snow-white, and she hated her. And envy and pride like ill weeds grew in her heart higher every day, until she had no peace day or night.

This is the second time the mirror has been questioned and the second time it has answered. The first time could have occurred anytime earlier, even before Snow White was born. It represents the first monthly cycle in the story and the first solar eclipse. This latest question and response represent the second monthly cycle and the second solar eclipse.

Snow White is seven years old. In the Roman Catholic tradition seven is the age when the rational mind is developed and children are able to know right from wrong. Therefore, in the nineteenth century when this story was collected, it was the traditional age for the reception of the sacraments of Penance and Holy Communion. Snow

White has reached the age when she will be tested, because she is now a threat to the embodiment of evil, the wicked queen.

Second Month—Full Moon
Venus Meets the Lord of Death

At last she sent for a huntsman, and said,

"Take the child out into the woods, so that I may set eyes on her no more. You must put her to death, and bring me her heart for a token."

The huntsman consented, and led her away, but when he drew his cutlass to pierce Snow-white's innocent heart, she began to weep, and to say,

"Oh, dear huntsman, do not take my life; I will go away into the wild wood, and never come home again."

And as she was so lovely the huntsman had pity on her, and said,

"Away with you then, poor child;" for he thought the wild animals would be sure to devour her, and it was as if a stone had been rolled away from his heart when he spared to put her to death.

At seven, Snow White is already leaving behind the age of childhood, the age of Saturn, whose festival, the Saturnalia, occurred at the winter solstice. The huntsman, who, with his dogs, hunts and kills wild game, is the Lord of Death and Father Time. But Snow White is beloved by the huntsman, who, like Father Christmas, loves children. Snow White leaves the huntsman, which means leaving behind her childhood, and seeks her own identity. She is leaving the first month and the winter solstice and entering the next stage of her life.

The Boar's Heart

The cutting out of Snow White's heart symbolizes a total lunar eclipse. The red moon is her heart, and the earth's long shadow is the sword cutting out the moon. Fortunately, the huntsman finds a substitute:

Just at that moment a young wild boar came running by, so he caught and killed it, and taking out its heart, he brought it to the queen for a token. And it was salted and cooked, and the wicked woman ate it up, thinking that there was an end of Snow-white.

Because the boar is a scavenger and eats corpses, it has been associated with death. The boar killed many lunar gods of death and resurrection, including the Egyptian Osiris, lover of Isis; the Syrian Adonis, lover of Aphrodite; the Phrygian Attis, lover of Cybele; and the Irish Diarmuid, lover of Grainne.[12] The boar's huge size, terrible visage, dangerous tusks, fierce dark bristles, and irascible temper make it a Lord of Death that in each of these stories jealously attacks the lovers of its goddess.

Like the bear (which is etymologically related), the boar is associated with the moon. Joseph Campbell tells us that the evil Egyptian god Set in the form of a black boar is the new moon. His white tusks are the crescents of the waning and waxing moon. He used them to cut the lunar god Osiris into many pieces and to injure his son Horus. The Malekulans of the New Hebrides also saw the black boar as the new moon.[13] The feet of the boar are cloven like the moon, which is cloven into crescents at the total lunar eclipse and at the new moon. The crescents just before the moon disappears and just after it appears again together make the cloven footprint. The sun is also cloven in the same way during a total solar eclipse.

As well as being a Lord of Death, the boar or pig is also a sacrificial victim around the world. In ancient Egypt eating pig's meat was forbidden, and it still is among the Malekulans and among Jews around the world. Malekulans, however, did eat pig's meat during sacrificial communion.[14] Egyptians ate pork one time annually when they sacrificed pigs to the moon and to Osiris, whose death was commemorated on November 13.[15]

Similarly, in the United States there still are customs of eating the porker at New Year's celebrations. It is traditional to eat ham both on New Year's Day and on Easter Sunday. (The First of April used to be the first day of the year in Northern Europe, even up until a few centuries ago.) A German tradition that has been transported to America is the eating of sauerkraut and pork on New Year's Day to bring good luck throughout the year. Grocery stores in Pennsylvania are redolent with this vinegary meal during the holiday season. In old Peking, pork dumplings were eaten at the winter solstice.[16] There is an old Yule custom of serving a boar's head or a suckling pig with an apple in its mouth. (Later in our story we will see that the apple is the lunar eclipse.) At the New Year in Estonia, Denmark, and Sweden, cakes were made in the shape of a boar, using the grain from the first sheathes of the harvest.[17] This is reminiscent of Egypt, where those who could not afford to offer up a pig at the winter solstice made cakes to take the place of pork.[18]

In Scandinavia, "Valhalla's boar" was a substitute for human sacrificial victims to satisfy the appetites of the gods.[19] Throughout Oceania, including both Polynesia and Melanesia, the "death pig" was the substitute sacrifice for a human so that the soul could pass through the fiery gate into the afterworld.[20] So in "Snow White," the lunar boar is the sacrificial victim that allows Snow White to pass unharmed through the jaws of death and into the underworld of the deep woods.

Now, when the poor child found herself quite alone in the wild woods, she felt full of terror, even of the very leaves on the trees, and she did not know what to do for fright. Then she began to run over the sharp stones and through the thorn bushes, and the wild beasts after her, but they did her no harm.

Although the huntsman thought that the beasts would eat Snow White, she was not touched by them, despite her fears. Like the goddess of the full moon—Diana (Artemis) the Huntress—Snow White is a friend of beasts; and they recognize her power, even though she is not aware of it herself. The full moon dominates the night sky, which is the lower world—the dwelling place of beasts. Therefore, the full moon is familiar with the haunts of animals. Snow White has left the stage of childhood and of animal senses, but she is in control of her senses and of the animal world.

Snow Whites Meets Seven Little Men

The Brothers Grimm appear to enjoy embellishing the description of the encounter between their heroine and her seven new friends:

She ran as long as her feet would carry her; and when the evening drew near she came to a little house, and she went inside to rest. Everything there was very small, but as pretty and clean as possible. There stood the little table ready laid, and covered with a white cloth, and seven little plates, and seven knives and forks, and drinking-cups. By the wall stood seven little beds, side by side, covered with clean white quilts. Snow-white, being very hungry and thirsty, ate from each plate a little porridge and bread, and drank out of each little cup a drop of wine, so as not to finish up one portion alone. After that she felt so tired that she lay down on one of the beds, but it did not seem to suit her; one was too long, another too short, but at last the seventh was quite right; and so she lay down upon it, committed herself to heaven, and fell asleep.

When it was quite dark, the masters of the house came home. They were seven dwarfs, whose occupation it was to dig underground among the mountains. When they had lighted their seven candles, and it was quite light in the little house, they saw that someone must have been in, as everything was not in the same order in which they left it. The first said,

"Who has been sitting in my chair?"

The second said,

"Who has been eating from my little plate?"

The third said,

"Who has been taking my little loaf?"

The fourth said,

"Who has been tasting my porridge?"

The fifth said,

"Who has been using my little fork?"

The sixth said,

"Who has been cutting with my little knife?"

The seventh said,

"Who has been drinking from my little cup?"

Then the first one, looking round, saw a hollow in his bed, and cried, "Who has been lying on my bed?"

And the others came running, and cried,

"Some one has been on our beds too!"

But when the seventh looked at his bed, he saw little Snowwhite lying there asleep. Then he told the others, who came running up, crying out in their astonishment, and holding up their seven little candles to throw a light upon Snow-white.

"O goodness! O gracious!" cried they, "what beautiful child is this?" and were so full of joy to see her that they did not wake her, but let her sleep on. And the seventh dwarf slept with his comrades, an hour at a time with each, until the night had passed.

In myth, seven men are connected to the eclipses. Instructions for the Babylonian observances during a lunar eclipse say, "Seven workmen of the people of the country, the family, the dwelling, the river, their eyes, their hands, and their feet, shall be anointed."[21] As we noted previously, Babylonians thought that seven devils imprisoned the sun or the moon during an eclipse, and, in Cherokee legend, seven men were sent to capture the spirit of the sun's daughter after she was killed instead of her mother. The seven dwarfs also have a girl in their possession and must decide what to do with her.

When it was morning, and Snow-white awoke and saw the seven dwarfs, she was very frightened; but they seemed quite friendly, and asked her what her name was, and she told them; and then they asked how she came to be in their house. And she related to them how her step-mother had wished her to be put to death, and how the huntsman had spared her life, and how she had run the whole day long, until at last she had found their little house. Then the dwarfs said,

"If you keep our house for us, and cook, and wash, and make the beds, and sew and knit, and keep everything tidy and clean, you may stay with us, and you shall lack nothing."

"With all my heart," said Snow-white; and so she stayed, and kept the house in good order. In the morning the dwarfs went to the mountain to dig for gold; in the evening they came home, and their supper had to be ready for them.

Who are the seven little men, and in whose house do they live? In the Italian "Snow White," the moon rescues Giricoccola from the persecution of her sisters. She is taken to the moon's house to live. In the Grimms' story, the house in the woods is also the house of the moon in the underworld. And the seven dwarfs are the seven phases of the moon at midnight that climb from the half moon at the horizon to the full moon at the top of the sky, as well as the seven moons between solstices and the seven full moons used to predict eclipses.

The dwarfs go out to dig for gold. As we have seen, the dwarfs are miners who dig under the mountains. It is appropriate that they are small to fit in the low mine shafts. The shafts are the curved paths of the moon through the underworld, and the gold nuggets the dwarfs gather are the golden phases of the moon. According to Roman folk etymology, the temple of Juno Moneta, which was the Roman treasury, was related to the word *monere,* meaning "to warn." This would relate *money* to the words *monitor, mind,* and *moon.*[22] In actuality, the word *money* may be more closely related to the word *mint,* but, nonetheless, bright gold and silver coins are traditionally symbols of the full moon. The story "The Moonrakers" tells of foolish men who try to rake the moon's reflection out of a lake because they think it is a mound of gold. Just as the moon stores the gold of sunlight under the earth in the night sky, so our little lords of the underworld discover heavenly gold underground.

Third Month—New Moon
The Looking Glass Pierces the Woods

And the plot thickens:

All the day long the maiden was left alone, and the good little dwarfs warned her, saying,

"Beware of your step-mother, she will soon know you are here. Let no one into the house."

Now the queen, having eaten Snow-white's heart, as she supposed, felt quite sure that now she was the first and fairest, and so she came to her mirror, and said,

> *"Looking-glass upon the wall,*
> *Who is fairest of us all?"*

And the glass answered,

> *"Queen, thou art of beauty rare,*
> *But Snow-white living in the glen*
> *With the seven little men*
> *Is a thousand times more fair."*

Then she was very angry, for the glass always spoke the truth, and she knew that the huntsman must have deceived her, and that Snow-white must still be living.

For the third time the looking glass speaks, and this time its gaze not only pierces the daylight but also reaches into the deep woods— just as the shadow of the eclipses not only pierces daylight but reaches into the underworld as well.

Then the queen begins to plot:

And she thought and thought how she could manage to make an end of her, for as long as she was not the fairest in the land, envy left her no rest. At last she thought of a plan; she painted her face and dressed herself like an old pedlar woman, so that no one would have known her. In this disguise she went across the seven mountains, until she came upon the house of the seven little dwarfs.

The queen lives in the castle in the seat of power, which represents the upper world, whereas Snow White lives in the deep wood, which represents the lower world. In terms of the solar year, the queen, who lives in the upper world of the summer solstice, would travel over seven moons or mountains to reach the abode of darkness—the winter solstice. The seven mountains could also be the seven arcs of the moon for seven days as it ascends from the half moon at the horizon to the full moon at the top of the night sky.

Wrinkles in Time

Disguises are common in folklore and myth. Heroes and villains alike don guises to fool their opponents. Besides adding humor and entertainment to stories, the device is central to an understanding of the prehistoric worldview. To ancient peoples, the real world was the world of the sun, moon, stars, and planets and the spirits or gods that governed them. Our world below the moon was merely one of fleeting apparitions. In fact, our world was a reflection of the heavens just as the trees and mountains seen in a pool of water were but a reflection of the real trees and mountains. Accordingly, as our souls descended to earth, they donned earthly garments or disguises until death, when they were discarded. This can be seen in the Greek and Roman tradition of picturing the celestial Venus as nude while clothing the earthly Venus as a sign of her physical incarnation.[23]

How are these earthly garments woven? The moon, whose path spirals up and down monthly like a thread on a spindle, is the weaver of destinies and the creator of the fabric of life. In Hindu thought, the air weaves the world. Just as five winds weave the Cosmos, so five breaths (*pranas*) weave human lives into a whole.[24] Stars and planets also become involved. Today, when people speak of being an Aries, a Libra, or other zodiac sign, they are identifying themselves by the pattern of the heavens at the time they were born. Marsilio Ficino, the Renaissance philosopher, believed that different planets dominated different people, so that some people were more solar, some more lunar, some more saturnine, and so on.[25] We are like bodies of water reflecting the course of the heavenly orbs, and the vapors that can be seen vibrating in the air above the water on a warm summer's day are the threads being woven into our lives. The ripples on the water and on the sand are caused by the air, which in ancient times was thought to reach all the way to the heavens.

As we age, the paths of the celestial bodies continue to mark us in the lines of our skin. The lines interlace, creating a costume or disguise. The path of the sun also traces interlacing lines. Watching the sun every day, one would see the sun arc across the sky, each day rising a little bit farther north until the summer solstice. Then the path would reverse itself, each day progressing a little farther south. The paths would cross over each other in the sky, the northward-bound arcs intersecting the southward-bound. By the time the winter solstice is reached, there are 365 arcs cutting across one another, creating, in effect, a thick woven mat, like the thick matted hair of one who has a lifetime of growth or even the wrinkled skin of an old person. When the Old Year has literally "shuffled off this mortal coil" (*Hamlet*, 3.1.67), then the New Year can begin with the smooth skin of a newborn babe. Santa Claus and Father Time with their long beards are good examples of interlaced sun lines at the winter solstice. So are the Yule Boar with its spiny hide and the queen disguised as an old peddler woman with her long white hair and wrinkly skin. Like the sun's path, the moon, planets, and stars also create interlaced patterns that become different earthly destinies for each creature below.

Like the moon, the queen can quickly change her appearance. The moon goes from the youth of the waxing moon to the maturity of the full moon and then to the old age of the waning moon all in the short span of a month.[26] And the moon is the ultimate shape-shifter. In the African Mossi story *Princess of the Full Moon* from Burkina Faso, a monster from the new moon captures the Princess and prepares to sacrifice her. When others attempt to save her, the monster changes into a cloud, a lion, a giant, a mosquito, and a seven-headed snake.[27] Similarly, the Mansi Voguls of Eastern Europe celebrate a bear festival in which the dead bear, a lunar animal, comes back to life and first appears to be the size of a mouse, then an ermine, then a wolverine, and finally a full-grown bear again.[28] These creatures, like the moon each night, continue to change in shape and size.

Third Month—Full Moon

The New Lace

The queen, who never appears as her real self in the underworld of the deep woods, begins her trickery:

> *And she knocked at the door and cried,*
> *"Fine wares to sell! fine wares to sell!"*

TYPICAL BULGARIAN FOLK COSTUME OF A CENTURY AGO

Figure 8. Adapted from Women's Work *by Elizabeth Wayland Barber,*
W. W. Norton, 1994.

Snow-white peeped out of the window and cried,
"Good-day, good woman, what have you to sell?"
"Good wares, fine wares," answered she, "laces of all colours;"
and she held up a piece that was woven of variegated silk.

The lace the queen brings to Snow White is reminiscent of the three-colored thread of fate, made of white, red, and black strands—made from the colors of the lunar eclipse. The strands of fate can reach even to the cottage in the deep woods, just as the earth's shadow can reach into the underworld of the night sky to darken the full moon.

"I need not be afraid of letting in this good woman," thought
Snow-white, and she unbarred the door and bought the pretty lace.

"What a figure you are, child!" said the old woman, "come and
let me lace you properly for once."

Snow-white, suspecting nothing, stood up before her, and let her
lace her with the new lace; but the old woman laced so quick and
tight that it took Snow-white's breath away, and she fell down as
dead.

"Now you have done with being the fairest," said the old
woman as she hastened away.

The lace itself represented the knowledge of the pathways of the heavens, and whoever possessed that knowledge possessed the ability to predict both solstices and eclipses. Interlaced patterns on women's clothing like that shown in Figure 8 have been used for many thousands of years.[29] The six horizontal diamond shapes on the twentieth-century folk costume represent both the interlacing of the path of the sun as it travels north to the summer solstice and the path of the full moon as it travels southward to the summer solstice at the same time. If the pattern is turned vertically, it matches the Greek caduceus, the intertwined serpents symbolizing wisdom (Figure 2, p. 15).

The sun's path also creates a great net that covers the sky. If you imagine the spiraling trip of the sun around the earth, moving ever northward, it would look like a giant Slinky. If you step outside the Slinky and attempt to draw a picture of it, it would look like a giant net or latticework. This latticework is a trellis on which the vines of our lives grow up and up until we reach our summer solstice. Then they travel down again, growing ever thicker, until, at the winter solstice, the vine is choking out sunlight and must be cut off at its root so that a new vine can begin to grow. But Snow White is being asphyxiated before her time, thanks to the wicked science of the queen.

Fortunately, the queen fails to wrest control of our heroine's life:

Not long after that, towards evening, the seven dwarfs came home, and were terrified to see their dear Snow-white lying on the ground, without life or motion; they raised her up, and when they saw how tightly she was laced they cut the lace in two; then she began to draw breath, and little by little she returned to life.

The knife that cut the lace was the crescent after a lunar eclipse. The path of the sun and the moon had woven Snow White's fate, but fortuitously the eclipse was cut short of totality, and the dwarfs manage to cut short the plans of death. They warn her again:

When the dwarfs heard what had happened they said,

   "The old pedlar woman was no other than the wicked queen; you must beware of letting any one in when we are not here!"

The dwarfs were kinder than the moon was when a witch turned Giricoccola into a statue by sticking her with a pretty brooch. The moon first scolded her soundly before removing the brooch.[30]

Fourth Month—New Moon
A Fourth Time the Looking Glass Speaks

And when the wicked woman got home she went to her glass and said,

   "Looking-glass against the wall,
   Who is fairest of us all?"

And it answered as before,

   "Queen, thou art of beauty rare,
   But Snow-white living in the glen
   With the seven little men
   Is a thousand times more fair."

When she heard that she was so struck with surprise that all the blood left her heart, for she knew that Snow-white must still be living.

The mirror, as the new moon, has the ability to magically reach through time and space from the upper world of the castle down into the lower world of the deep woods, just as the shadows of the eclipses together form a straight line between the upper and lower worlds. (See Figure 7, p. 32.)

Fourth Month—Full Moon
The Poisoned Comb

> *But now," said she, "I will think of something that will be her ruin." And by witchcraft she made a poisoned comb. Then she dressed herself up to look like another different sort of old woman.*
>
> *So she went across the seven mountains and came to the house of the seven dwarfs, and knocked at the door and cried,*
>
> *"Good wares to sell! good wares to sell!"*
>
> *Snow-white looked out and said,*
>
> *"Go away, I must not let anybody in."*
>
> *"But you are not forbidden to look," said the old woman, taking out the poisoned comb and holding it up. It pleased the poor child so much that she was tempted to open the door; and when the bargain was made the old woman said,*
>
> *"Now, for once your hair shall be properly combed."*

Snow White tries to resist the temptation of the old woman, but like Eve in the garden she is dealing with cosmic forces.

The comb is a well-known goddess symbol. Even today European peasant women and children wear comb pendants around their necks to ward off illness and death after childbirth. Combs in the shape of the mother goddess have been found in Switzerland dating from 4000 B.C. up to the Celtic Iron Age.[31] Some combs have nine tines connoting the nine months of pregnancy, while other combs have seven tines recalling the number of the moon. The comb is an excellent instrument of measurement. Each tine of the seven-tine comb denotes a lunar cycle. The comb brings the hair under control and gives it order, just as the moon brings the planets and stars under control and gives them a way to be measured. The comb also breaks the course of the hair just as an eclipse breaks the course of the sun and moon on their journey.

And so again the queen prevails:

> *Poor Snow-white, thinking no harm, let the old woman do as she would, but no sooner was the comb put in her hair than the poison began to work, and the poor girl fell down senseless.*
>
> *"Now, you paragon of beauty," said the wicked woman, "this is the end of you," and went off. By good luck it was now near evening, and the seven little dwarfs came home. When they saw Snow-white lying on the ground as dead, they thought directly that it was*

the step-mother's doing, and looked about, found the poisoned comb, and no sooner had they drawn it out of her hair than Snow-white came to herself, and related all that had passed. Then they warned her once more to be on her guard, and never again to let any one in at the door.

Here we have another example of a lunar eclipse. Women's hair was once associated with the moon and with magic. Ropes made with it were strong enough to capture the sun. The comb represents the measurement of time and fate. The tines are the times when lunar eclipses can occur. During a lunar eclipse time stops and spirits leave the earth. By removing the comb the dwarfs thwarted time, fate, and death.

In the story of Giricoccola, the moon was very upset with the witch who used a comb to turn the girl into a statue. The moon warned her that if it happened again, she would get no more help.[32] In Europe in recent times, seeing a woman combing her hair by the light of the full moon was considered bad luck.[33] For Snow White and Giricoccola, it was bad luck even for the girls whose hair was being combed.

Fifth Month—New Moon
Still Again the Mirror Speaks

And the queen went home and stood before the looking-glass and said,

> *"Looking-glass against the wall,*
> *Who is fairest of us all?"*

And the looking-glass answered as before,

> *"Queen, thou art of beauty rare,*
> *But Snow-white living in the glen*
> *With the seven little men*
> *Is a thousand times more fair."*

When she heard the looking-glass speak thus she trembled and shook with anger.

"Snow-white shall die," cried she, "though it should cost me my own life!" And then she went to a secret lonely chamber, where no one was likely to come, and there she made a poisonous apple. It was beautiful to look upon, being white with red cheeks, so that any one who should see it must long for it, but whoever ate even a

little bit of it must die. When the apple was ready she painted her
face and clothed herself like a peasant woman, and went across the
seven mountains to where the seven dwarfs lived.

Fifth Month—Full Moon
The White Apple with Red Cheeks

What a perfect description of the lunar eclipse! As the eclipse approaches totality, the white of the full moon acquires a red blush on its cheek that turns dark red at its peak. Then, as the umbra recedes, again the whiteness of the moon appears with a red tinge. The three colors of an apple also recall the three colors of a lunar eclipse: the black seeds, the white flesh, and the red skin.

The Greeks believed that the moon was bewitched and that witches and sorcerers caused the lunar eclipse by drawing down the moon from heaven in order to put it in their herbal brews and give them an evil froth.[34] What better picture of an eclipse than the white and red moon being dipped into the black shadow of the witch's cauldron and then being pulled out again.

Once more the stepmother uses the lunar eclipse to try to end Snow White's life:

And when she knocked at the door Snow-white put her head out of
the window and said,

"I dare not let anybody in; the seven dwarfs told me not."

"All right," answered the woman; "I can easily get rid of my
apples elsewhere. There, I will give you one."

"No," answered Snow-white, "I dare not take anything."

"Are you afraid of poison?" said the woman, "look here, I will
cut the apple in two pieces; you shall have the red side, I will have
the white one."

For the apple was so cunningly made, that all of the poison was
in the rosy half of it. Snow-white longed for the beautiful apple,
and as she saw the peasant woman eating a piece of it she could no
longer refrain, but stretched out her hand and took the poisoned
half. But no sooner had she taken a morsel of it into her mouth
than she fell to the earth as dead.

Fruit is a key image in Western myth. Paris awarded the golden apple to Aphrodite (Venus) for her beauty, thus provoking the jealousy of Hera (Juno) and beginning what was to become the Trojan

War. Persephone (Proserpine) took a bite out of a pomegranate while she was in Hades, and so we have winter and death. Eve partook of the forbidden fruit in the garden and shared it with Adam, thus beginning the cycle of life and death. The moon is a natural symbol for fruit because it begins as the tiny new moon and grows into the bright round fruit of the full moon. A hymn to the Babylonian moon god Sin describes the moon as "a fruit growing from itself."[35] It is a natural step to compare the biting of the fruit to the lunar eclipse. The total lunar eclipse is even more appropriate for fruits such as pomegranates or apples because of their rich red color.

By cutting the apple in half, the queen is imitating the partial eclipse in which half of the moon is white and half is red. It is important that Snow White eats the red half, because it is the dark half—the half of death. The concave shadow of the earth against the white globe during a partial eclipse even looks like someone taking a bite out of a piece of fruit.

The queen finishes by reminding the girl of her mother's wish. Like her mother, Snow White would die during a lunar eclipse:
And the queen, casting on her a terrible glance, laughed aloud and cried,
  "As white as snow, as red as blood, as black as ebony! this time the dwarfs will not be able to bring you to life again."
In Giricoccola's story, it is the moon who in anger washes her hands of the girl. The witch turned her into a statue by giving her a beautiful gown to wear. The moon sells the statue to a chimney sweep for a few pennies.[36]

Sixth Month—New Moon
The Mirror Is Half-Right
  And when she went home and asked the looking-glass,
      "Looking-glass against the wall,
        Who is fairest of us all?"
  at last it answered,
        "You are the fairest now of all."
  Then her envious heart had peace, as much as an envious heart can have.

The looking glass, in its role as the new moon of the solar eclipse, was not totally accurate—perhaps this time the mirror achieved only a partial solar eclipse. It turns out that the mirror was fooled by the appearance of death:

The dwarfs, when they came home in the evening, found Snow-white lying on the ground, and there came no breath out of her mouth, and she was dead. They lifted her up, sought if anything poisonous was to be found, cut her laces, combed her hair, washed her with water and wine, but all was to no avail, the poor child was dead, and remained dead. Then they laid her on a bier, and sat all seven of them round it, and wept and lamented three whole days. And then they would have buried her, but that she looked still as if she were living, with her beautiful blooming cheeks.

During a total solar eclipse birds stop flying, there is a hush in the air, and the temperature lowers. So too, Snow White's breath stops and her body turns cold. In their solicitousness, the dwarfs wash her with water and wine. They are attempting to revive her with placental waters of birth, with the fertile juices of first love, and with the white and red of the lunar eclipse. The followers of Jesus are baptized with water in order to enter into divine life; and the followers of Mithra were baptized in the warm blood of a bull that was slaughtered over-head in order to receive eternal life. But Snow White instead receives the water and blood of death, as flowed from the wound in the side of Jesus on the cross. In the Roman Catholic mass, in remembrance of that event, water is mixed with wine in the chalice. However, all of the dwarfs' ministrations were apparently for naught. Their three days of lamentation are the three days of the darkness of the new moon. Yet, even in her death, her red cheeks were reminders of her true nature—the moon of the lunar eclipse.

So they said,

"We cannot hide her away in the black ground." And they had made a coffin of clear glass, so as to be looked into from all sides, and they laid her in it, and wrote in golden letters upon it her name, and that she was a king's daughter. Then they set the coffin out upon the mountain, and one of them always remained by it to watch. And the birds came too, and mourned for Snow-white, first an owl, then a raven, and lastly, a dove.

Picture the seven dwarfs carrying the coffin up the mountain, which is the path of the moon. Each man is a day of the week carrying the moon to its position at the top of the sky. The clear coffin is the day sky, where the new moon resides.

The three birds are all representations of the moon. The white dove with its wings outstretched looks like the white half moon. It is a messenger or spirit, which travels between the upper and lower worlds, halfway between the new moon and the full moon. The dove is Noah's messenger of hope; and a dove representing the Holy Spirit is often painted with the Blessed Virgin at the Annunciation, when Jesus is conceived. The Annunciation occurs on March 25, halfway between the winter and the summer solstice. The dove is also the companion of Aphrodite, goddess of life, youth, and beauty.[37] The raven is a carrion-eating bird whose black color likens it to the new moon. It is the companion of Odin, the Scandinavian high god of death and wisdom. The owl is the full moon and is the harbinger of death around the world. In parts of Europe, even today, it is believed that if an owl alights upon a roof, someone in the house will soon die.[38] The Comanches believe there is an owl holding a club in the moon, and many Native Americans believe the owl's call is a portent of death.[39] The owl is also a symbol of wisdom and was the emblem of Athena (Minerva), the goddess of wisdom. Its horned ears are reminiscent of the crescent moon; and the wink of its keen eye mimics the decreasing and increasing phases of the moon through the month.

So the three sacred birds encompass the moon's journey including the half moon (dove), the full moon (owl), and the new moon (raven); but they also embrace the life of Snow White as girl (dove), woman (owl), and crone (raven). They are also the three Fates spinning, measuring, and cutting the threads of life. Since the lunar eclipse is sometimes brown or copper in color, rather than red, the birds could also be seen to represent the colors of the three strands of the thread of life: white (dove), red-brown (owl), and black (raven).

Now, for a long while Snow-white lay in the coffin and never changed, but looked as if she were asleep, for she was still as white as snow, as red as blood, and her hair was as black as ebony. It happened, however, that one day a king's son rode through the wood and up to the dwarfs' house, which was near it. He saw on the mountain the coffin, and beautiful Snow-white within it, and he read what was written in golden letters upon it.

Like the saints whose bodies never decayed, Snow White never loses her beauty. The king's son was far away from his father's kingdom. The young man had wandered into the underworld of the deep woods. In most cultures in both the Old and the New Worlds, the sun and moon tend to be of opposite genders. Since Snow White is the stepdaughter of the new moon, it can be presumed that the prince's father is the sun, thus making the prince and Snow White the inheritors of the sun and the moon. So the new sun travels far from its home at the summer solstice to the underworld of the winter solstice. The young man begins as the weakest sun of the month of December, when the days are the shortest. He is the sun/son who is born anew with the New Year. As he returns to his rightful kingdom, which is the summer solstice, he will grow stronger until he is able someday to take his father's place in the summer sky. In the meantime, he has found the daughter of the moon. Although the full moon glows longest and highest in the underworld of the winter solstice, he longs to take Snow White with him to his upper world.

Then he said to the dwarfs,

"Let me have the coffin, and I will give you whatever you like to ask for it."

But the dwarfs told him that they could not part with it for all the gold in the world. But he said,

"I beseech you to give it to me, for I cannot live without looking upon Snow-white; if you consent I will bring you to great honour, and care for you as if you were my brethren."

In a sense, the seven dwarfs are like brothers to Snow White, since they are all related to the moon. Therefore, their becoming like brothers to the prince would be a kind of marriage between Snow White and the prince.

Sixth Month—Full Moon

The Bush

When he so spoke the good little dwarfs had pity upon him and gave him the coffin, and the king's son called his servants and bid them carry it away on their shoulders. Now it happened that as they were going along they stumbled over a bush, and with the shaking the bit of poisoned apple flew out of her throat. It was not long before she opened her eyes, threw up the cover of the coffin, and sat up, alive and well.

The descent of the mountain is the descent from the new moon of the day sky. The bush suggests the burning bush that appeared to Moses on the mountain and the thicket that entangled the ram on the mountain in the story of Abraham and Isaac. Just as the beard of Santa Claus represents the spiraling path of the sun, moon, and stars through the year, so too does the bush. The bush is the wisdom that comes with the knowledge of the solstices and the eclipses. In medieval liturgical writing, the burning bush was used to describe the Blessed Virgin Mary, who is also associated with the moon.[40] Additionally, the Man in the Moon is sometimes seen as carrying a thorn bush.[41] The Man in the Moon can be seen in the full moon—the time of the lunar eclipse.

The bit of poisoned apple flying out of her throat is the lunar eclipse—the bite of the dark shadow of the earth, which appears and then disappears, leaving the moon in all her brilliance again. Snow White is like the bear, which grows large and goes underground like the moon growing full in the night sky. Like the bear and the moon, she too leaves the underworld and awakens to the day.

Seventh Month—New Moon and Full Moon
The Execution and the Wedding

"Oh dear! where am I?" cried she. The king's son answered, full of joy, "You are near me," and, relating all that had happened, he said,

"I would rather have you than anything in the world; come with me to my father's castle and you shall be my bride."

And Snow-white was kind, and went with him, and their wedding was held with pomp and great splendour.

But Snow-white's wicked step-mother was also bidden to the feast, and when she had dressed herself in beautiful clothes she went to her looking-glass and said,

> *"Looking-glass upon the wall,*
> *Who is fairest of us all?"*

The looking-glass answered,

> *"O Queen, although you are of beauty rare,*
> *The young bride is a thousand times more fair."*

*Then she railed and cursed, and was beside herself with disap-
pointment and anger. First she thought she would not go to the
wedding; but then she felt she should have no peace until she went
and saw the bride. And when she saw her she knew her for Snow-
white, and could not stir from the place for anger and terror. For
they had ready red-hot iron shoes, in which she had to dance until
she fell dead.*

The story's ending telescopes the punishment of the wicked queen
and the wedding—the new moon and the full moon. It is almost as
though two different endings were merged into one. Coincidentally,
this condensation fits the story of the heavens, for it is possible to
have seven new moons or seven full moons between the winter and
summer solstices, but it is not possible to have both seven new moons
and seven full moons between them.

Let's look at the wicked queen's torment and execution. As always,
the dark queen and her mirror portray both the new moon and the
solar eclipse; but the red-hot iron shoes also represent the crescents of
the sun before and after totality. The blacksmith symbolizes the shaman throughout the Old World.[42] In Russian folktales he is the assistant to witches.[43] His red-hot crescents are made into horseshoes,
which were placed over doorways and were considered lucky because
they are pieces of the red-hot sun stolen and brought to earth. In ancient Ireland, Luno, which means Moon Man, was the lame smithy
in the sky. Christian folklore says that Cain was the Man in the
Moon and that his name means "Smith."[44] German tales also see a
smith in the moon with his hammer and anvil.[45] It is appropriate that
the blacksmith is the moon, because it is the moon that steals the
sun's red-hot crescents at the solar eclipse so that they can be placed
on the wicked queen's feet.

Death and weddings have been linked in the past. In Indonesia,
where the head hunt was a sacred act, a young man had to first kill
before he could marry and become a father.[46] The queen's death,
which seems to be a merry event, is juxtaposed to the merriment of
the wedding.

Happily Ever After

Besides being the summer solstice, which symbolizes enlightenment
and fulfillment, June was a good time to marry for practical reasons,

because it would mean that a child might be born nine months later, in the spring, when both mother and child would have the greatest chance of survival. Both the new moon and the full moon have been said to be auspicious for weddings. The Greeks traditionally held weddings at the full moon, while on the Orkney Islands couples married at the waxing of the moon.[47] Estonians, Finns, and the Yakut celebrated weddings at the new moon.[48] In *A Midsummer-Night's Dream* the couples in the story are married at the first light of the new moon after the summer solstice (1.1.1–11). Plutarch justified marriage at the new moon, saying that it is the time when the sun and moon are joined together.[49] The first waxing of the moon can be justified because it was the customary time for farmers to begin planting. But an argument can also be made for marriage at the full moon. Between the winter and summer solstices a woman has seven periods of fertility, which correspond to the seven full moons. The seventh full moon is the summer solstice, which is June—the month of weddings.

The lunar eclipse also symbolizes a wedding. The shaft formed by the darkness of the solar and lunar eclipse and the cup formed by the concave path of the moon on its monthly sojourn through the night sky depict the conjugal act. (See Figure 7, p. 32.) The red moon of the lunar eclipse is the blood of the hymen traditionally broken on the wedding night. From Siberia to Sicily a crude custom that existed even into the twentieth century was the public display of the bloodied bedclothes after the wedding night to prove that both parties had properly kept the nuptial contract.

Have Snow White and the prince reached the apex of their lives? In ancient tradition they have. The king must die so that a new king may live, and the death of the king begins at the conception of offspring. In a sense this applies to all parents in that they must die to themselves for the benefit of the young. In "Snow White" it is the queen who must die, first Snow White's mother at the beginning and then her stepmother at the end. Now Snow White has ascended to the summer solstice, and from there she will descend again to winter.

Journey through the Seven Planets

Although we are left wondering what happens to Snow White and her prince, as a story about initiation and about the journey of the soul, this story is complete. We have followed Snow White through the seven new and full moons, but what about her journey through the seven days of the week and the seven planets? The seven utterances of the looking glass fit with beliefs about the seven planets. Medieval and Renaissance Cabalists believed that the will of the seven planetary spirits could be read using seven mirrors, each made out of a metal corresponding to a day of the week and its planet.[50]

Beginning at the bottom with Saturday and Saturn, here is an analysis of her journey:

Weekday	Planet	Episode
Sunday	Sun	Marriage
Monday	Moon	Awakening
Tuesday	Mars	Apple
Wednesday	Mercury	Comb
Thursday	Jupiter	Lace
Friday	Venus	Beauty
Saturday	Saturn	Childhood

The bottom story of the moon's seven-story mountain, the day when the moon is at the horizon and is closest to earth, is Saturday—dedicated to Saturn, the Titan, who represents all adults as they appear to children. Hence, it is the time of childhood. The huntsman takes Saturn's place as the Lord of Time and Death. Snow White is forced to leave the first stage of life and ascend to the next phase of the moon, the second story of the mountain, which corresponds to Friday—dedicated to Venus, the goddess of beauty. The wicked queen cannot endure the blossoming of Snow White into the age of beauty and attempts to eat her heart—thus destroying her ability to feel. But the heart of a boar was substituted for Snow White's heart. Swedish priests, who wore boar masks, were treated as incarnations and husbands of Freya, the German goddess of beauty. In this case the boar gives its life for its goddess of beauty.

After arriving at the seven dwarfs' house, Snow White tastes of each plate and cup and tests each bed, foreshadowing her ascent of the seven steps to her fulfillment. Just as the moon ascends the sky in seven days, so her soul must progress through seven stages to completion. Carolyn Myss compares the seven dwarfs to the seven chakras. She relates the cleanliness of the dwarfs to Kundalini Yoga adepts who cleanse and purify their chakras.[51]

At this stage in her development, Snow White leaves adolescence to take on the work and duties related to Thursday—dedicated to Jupiter, king of the gods. When the wicked queen tricks her, Snow White is rudely introduced to the realities of the objective world, the realm of Jupiter, the ruler of the physical world. The lace around Snow White's waist was positioned at the solar plexus, the same position as the third chakra.

The comb an excellent symbol for the fourth level of transformation. The very bargaining in the story is watched over by Mercury, the god of commerce. The European tradition of wearing combs as pendants placed the combs in front, at the level of the heart or the fourth chakra, or in back, again at the place of the heart.[52] In stories such as "Rapunzel," hair becomes a rope that allows us to reach the sun and the upper world, just as Mercury travels between the worlds.

The fifth chakra is located in the throat, and it turns out that the bite of apple was lodged in Snow White's throat. At the fifth chakra we confront Nothingness and the subconscious, just as Snow White confronts Tuesday—dedicated to Mars, the god of war. Red is the color of the apple and of Mars. Finally she awakens and opens her eyes, completing her journey through the sixth level, the level of the eyes and forehead. She has entered the sixth chakra, which corresponds to Monday or "moon day." It is the level of creativity and expression, the level when the young couple express their love for each other. Snow White has fully become the moon and rises to the seventh level, Sunday—dedicated to the sun. The sun and moon join in marriage symbolizing integration and completion.

How Old Is Snow White?

The origin of the days of the week and the Hindu chakras date back only about two thousand years, whereas there is a deep myth about the solstices and the eclipses within this story that has roots that are much older. Although the seven days and seven chakras appear to fit comfortably within the story, that may be explained as being the result of "elementary ideas" or "archetypal images." For example, it is natural to think of the human faculties as progressing from the lower faculties to the higher faculties. It is also natural to relate lower faculties to lower parts of the body and higher faculties to higher parts of the body, as was done in the East. Furthermore, it is natural to rank virtues and vices from top to bottom, as was done in the West.

Therefore, the similarity of the progress of Snow White and the progress of the days of the week and the chakras may be due to their development parallel to each other, effected by similar influences. Insights and inspiration can be gained by comparing them with each other, but it would be incorrect to presume that one directly influenced the other.

Investigation of other versions of "Snow White" will lead us to other stories about the eating of forbidden fruit from prehistory, and we will find similar stories that go back even to the late Ice Age. Snow White, who seems so young to us, may turn out to be more than ten thousand years old.

Forbidden Fruit

In prehistory people waited at the full moon for the chance that a lunar eclipse would occur—a chance that a red apple would appear on the tree that is the black shadow of the earth stretching up into the night sky. Despite their fears, they hoped for the chance that the apple would be bitten into and that an uneaten seed, fallen to earth and forgotten, would spring to life and renew the world.

Chapter 4

Snow White,

Persephone, and Eve

Snow White

Prehistoric Roots

There are many stories of youths who have the colors of Snow White. In the Brothers Grimm story "The Juniper Tree," a woman cuts her finger and sees her blood on the snow. She wishes for a child as red as blood and as white as snow. A boy is born and the mother dies. His new stepmother kills him as he is reaching for an apple, and she serves him up as a stew for his father to eat. The boy returns to life at the end of the story.[1]

In the tragic story of Deirdre, she sees a raven drink the blood of a slaughtered calf on fresh snow. She wishes for a husband with hair as black as the raven's, cheeks as red as the blood, and a body as white as the snow. She receives her wish, but her marriage ends in tragedy and in the ruin of Ireland.[2] In medieval romance, the object of Peredur's love has jet-black hair and skin of red and white. When he sees a crow and blood in the snow, he falls in a trance thinking of his love and cannot awake.[3] Although these stories remind us of "Snow White" because of the repetition of the colors red, white, and black, we can learn more about ancient myths that are linked to the eclipses and the solstices by examining the many versions of "Snow White." The characters in the story and their motivations have changed dramatically over the millennia, but the underlying themes and key elements of the story have remained the same.

Evolution of the Grimms' "Snow White"

Collected by the Brothers Grimm in Cassel, the story of "Snow White" evolved with each of the seventeen editions of the Grimms' tales from 1812 to 1856. In an 1810 manuscript the jealous queen is Snow White's natural mother rather than her stepmother, and it is the mother herself who takes the girl to the forest and abandons her there. It is the girl's father who finds her in a coffin and has his physician tie her body by ropes to the four corners of the room to cure her. By 1812 it is still the natural mother who exiles her daughter, but now there is a huntsman who is to bring back her liver and lungs. And a prince now retrieves the coffin, but his servants revive her when they strike her on the back in anger. By the final text the natural mother has been separated from the evil queen, but it is evident that this literary editing was done by the brothers in order to satisfy the bourgeois sensibilities of their readers.[4]

There is a literary history for "Snow White" going back to Giambattista Basile's *Pentamerone* (Day 2, Tale 8), published in 1634. In it Lisa, like Snow White, is seven years old. She appears to have died when a comb becomes stuck in her head. Her uncle hides her away in a crystal coffin in a room of the castle, and there she stays and grows as if she were alive, her casket growing with her. Then her uncle's wife discovers her and thinks she is her husband's mistress merely fallen asleep. In a fit of jealous rage, she drags Lisa by her hair and in so doing dislodges the comb from her head and revives her.[5]

The Oral Tradition

There is a large oral tradition of stories related to "Snow White" in Europe, Africa, Asia, and the Americas. Steven Swann Jones researched over one hundred of them, finding a common theme of a heroine who is expelled from home, threatened for her life, apparently killed, and rescued and reawakened. He briefly summarizes twenty-four of these in his dissertation.[6] Kay E. Vandergrift abstracts passages from thirty-six text versions of the tale on her web pages.[7]

The heroine has various names in these many tellings. In each of the following she is the title character. In the Grimms' version she is called either Snow White or Snow Drop. In the Celtic "Gold-Tree and Silver-Tree" she is Gold-Tree. In the Armenian version she is Nourie Hadig (Little Piece of Pomegranate). In the Greek version she

Snow White, Persephone, and Eve

is Myrsina (Myrtle). In the Italian version she is Giricoccola, and in the North African tale she is Rimonah (Pomegranate).[8]

In the Norwegian "The Knights in the Bear Hut" she is Schneekind or Snow Child. In the Icelandic version her mother's name is Vala, and she is called Vilfridr Fairer-than-Vala. In the Swiss "The Little Earth-Cow" she is Greta. In the Mallorcan tale "Na Magraneta" (The Little Pomegranate) a childless queen eats a pomegranate and wishes for a child she could call Little Pomegranate, and her wish comes true. In the Spanish version she is Blanca Flor (White Flower). In the Rumanian version she is "Florita [Flower-Child] in the Deep Forest." In the Aegean "Marietta and the Sorceress, Her Stepmother," she is Marietta. In the Mexican "The Princess Who Became a Priest" the girl is called Blanca (White).[9]

Little Pomegranate

It is curious that in Armenia, North Africa, and Mallorca Snow White is Little Pomegranate. The pomegranate is a thick-skinned edible fruit about the size of an orange with many seeds in a reddish pulp. It has an agreeable acid flavor. (The word *pomegranate* is from Latin and means "fruit with many seeds.") In the Armenian tale the child has white skin and rosy cheeks like the little piece of pomegranate that gives her her name. All of these tales are describing the moon at near total lunar eclipse. The white of the moon is still visible at the crescent edge while the moon turns gradually more red as it nears totality.

These tales are all reminiscent of the Greek myth of Persephone, who takes a bite of a pomegranate, as well as the Biblical tale of Eve, who eats the forbidden fruit. Persephone, the daughter of Demeter, the earth mother, is abducted into the underworld by Hades and made his queen. Demeter grieves for her daughter and Hades finally gives her up. But because Persephone ate from the pomegranate, she must spend part of the year with him. It is interesting that in Greece Snow White is called Myrsina or Myrtle. Throughout Europe young girls and brides wear myrtle.[10] In ancient Greece it was used to communicate with the dead.[11] Hades, god of the underworld, wore myrtle.[12] It also happens that the pomegranate is a member of the myrtle family.[13]

Mirror on the Wall

The mirror on the wall varies significantly in the many versions of "Snow White." In "Gold-Tree and Silver-Tree" the messenger is a trout in a well. In "Giricoccola" it is the moon, and in "Nourie Hadig" it is the new moon. In "Myrsina" it is the "sun on the sun porch." In "Rimonah" the queen has a favorite porcelain bowl in which a face appears when she fills it with water.[14]

In the French "The Enchanted Stockings" the queen hears from an old beggar woman. In the Italian "The Crystal Casket" the queen hears from an eagle. In the Hungarian "The World's Beautiful Woman" a witch from the bottom of the hill prophesies that the girl will be more beautiful than her mother. In the Greek "The Three Sisters" a goddess prophesies the beauty of one sister, and the other two later learn from the sun that she is still alive. In the Swahili "The Most Beautiful Woman" a sultan's wife speaks to the sun and the moon. In "Marietta" the stepmother asks the sun. In "The Princess Who Became a Priest" the queen has an old woman as an informant. In the Puerto Rican "The Envious Mother" the informant is a beggar woman. In all of the other versions either a mirror or a passerby informs the queen.[15]

The Informants

In short, the queen's informants include a trout in a well, a face in a bowl of water, the sun, the moon (especially the new moon), an old woman or witch, an eagle, a mirror, and passersby. In "Snow White," the informant, the talking mirror, is the sun and new moon during a solar eclipse. This is appropriate because it is during a solar eclipse that Snow White (as the moon) is forcibly removed from the upper world and begins her decent below. The well is an excellent image of the shadow of the moon during an eclipse, and in most primitive cultures a bowl of water is a way to capture or see the sun before and after a total eclipse without looking directly at it. (This is not a safe way to observe an eclipse.)[16] It is very widely held that the person or persons in the moon carry a gourd or bucket of water.[17] The old woman is a metaphor for the new moon, and the eagle is a metaphor for the sun. (Worldwide, the eagle symbolizes the sun because of its soaring flight, its keen eyesight in daylight, and its spiraling path.) The sun and moon are also informants in the myth of Persephone.

Adoption

In the various "Snow White" stories, there are many different characters that give the heroine a home in the wilderness. In "The Knights in the Bear Hut" there are three knights who are bears by day. In "Vilfridr Fairer-than-Vala" there are two dwarfs. In "The Enchanted Stockings" there are three brothers, two of whom hunt and one who cooks. In "The Little Earth-Cow" there is a cow. In "Na Magraneta" thirteen giants provide a castle. In the Basque "The Jealous Mother and the Persecuted Girl" twelve thieves inhabit a castle. In the Tuscan "The Innkeeper of Paris" there are twenty-four bandits who are absent from their palace for fourteen days. In "The Crystal Casket" there is a crystal palace occupied by court ladies. In "Florita" there is a hunchback. In "The Three Sisters" the heroine is thrown down an abyss, where a Nereid (sea nymph) takes the girl in. In "Marietta" there are forty giant brothers. In "The Most Beautiful Woman" there is a group of Jinns. In "The Unnatural Mother" there are some cannibals. In the Louisianan "King Peacock" there is an ogre at the bottom of a well. In the Mexican "The Beautiful Stone" there are twenty brothers.[18]

Descent into the Underworld

These various characters are underworld figures who are often unsavory. The fourteen days that the twenty-four bandits are absent are the fourteen days that the moon stays in the daytime sky, away from its underworld home, and the number twenty-four refers to the twenty-four hours in a day. Twelve and thirteen refer to months or moons in a year, three implies the three days of the new or full moon, and forty is the forty days of Lent. Like the moon, Snow White is adopted by the denizens of the underworld.

In some of the stories the descent into the underworld is very specific. The heroine falls into an abyss in "The Three Sisters." In the French Canadian "The Mirror That Talks" she falls down a hole, and in "King Peacock" her nurse gives her three seeds. She drops one as she falls down a well, and the well dries up. All of this fits with the story of Persephone being taken through an opening in the ground into the underworld. The seeds are like the pomegranate seeds that Persephone ate.[19] The "Three Knights in the Bear Hut" is reminiscent of the story of the bear who abducted a woman and made her his wife in the underworld, except that in this version there are three bears rather than one.

Instruments of Death

There were also a variety of devices that the queen uses to cause the death of Snow White. In the "Knights in the Bear Hut" she uses shoes, a shirt, and finally a golden needle, which she sticks in her daughter's neck. In "Vilfridr Fairer-than-Vala" she uses a gold ring, gold shoes, and a gold belt, all of which bind her severely. In "Gold-Tree and Silver-Tree" Gold-Tree sticks her finger through a keyhole and her mother, Silver-Tree, stabs it with a poisonous needle. In "The Enchanted Stockings" a pair of stockings is used. In "Na Magraneta" a witch arrives after seven days and puts an iron ring on the heroine's finger. In "The Jealous Mother and the Persecuted Girl" white bread puts her to sleep for three months. In "The Innkeeper of Paris" a beggar woman combs the girl's hair and puts a dagger in it. In "The Crystal Casket" a poisoned piece of sweetmeat and then a dress put the girl asleep. In "The Three Sisters" the oldest sister puts a needle in the youngest sister's head. The Nereid finds it and removes it. The oldest sister then throws a poisoned grape through the roof. In "Marietta" the stepmother first uses a ring; then she throws a poisoned raisin into her room. In "The Most Beautiful Woman" she uses two poisoned combs and poisoned slippers. In "The Mirror That Talks" the witch uses a ring, a necklace, and a poisoned apple. In "King Peacock" the girl eats a seed.[20]

The Seeds of the Pomegranate

All of the instruments of death are images of eclipses. The ring, belt, and necklace are pictures of an annular or total solar eclipse. (See Chapter 5, "Rumpelstiltskin.") The shoes, stockings, and slippers are the crescents both before and after a lunar eclipse or a solar eclipse; and the shirt and dress are the darkness of the totality of a lunar eclipse. The needle, dagger, and combs are shafts of darkness that prick the moon at the lunar or solar eclipse. Finally, the bread, sweetmeat, grape, raisin, apple, and seeds are all foods that are bitten into just as the shadow of the earth bites into the moon during the eclipse. The fruits and seeds are similar to the pomegranate and its seeds that Persephone eats.

Persephone

Demeter and Persephone

What is fascinating about the Greek myth of Demeter (known as Ceres to the Romans) and Persephone (Proserpine) is that in mythology they are mother and daughter, and etymologically they belong to the same family as well. Demeter's name contains the Greek word for mother, and she was the earth goddess or earth mother in the Greek pantheon. We call her Mother Nature today. As Ceres, her name, like the word *cereal*, comes from the Indo-European root *ker* or *kere*, which means "to grow." Other words in the same family include *accrue, create, increase, crescent, procreate, recruit, Cora, Corrinna*, and most important, *Kore*. Kore is another Greek name for Persephone. It simply means "a young [growing] girl." Statues of a young girl (called a *kore*) with an enigmatic smile were placed on the tombs of the dead to signify rebirth. It is also noteworthy that Demeter is related to the word *moon* (See Chapter 2, "The Discovery."), while Ceres and Kore are related to *crescent*—Kore to the waxing crescent, when the grain is young, and Ceres to the waning crescent, when the sickle moon harvests the grain.

Other more distant relatives include words derived from the Indo-European root, *ger* or *gere*, meaning "to become ripe" or "to grow old." They include *corn, grain, kernel, pomegranate*, and *kirn* (the harvest festival), as well as *gram, granite, grenade, granule, engrain, grange, gravy, churn, grand, grandmother*, and *geriatric*. Another group of words, descended from the Indo-European root *ghro* or *ghros*, which means "to grow" or "young shoot" or "sprout," includes *grass, grow, green*, and *graze*. Persephone is the green grass and growing corn, which is celebrated in the spring, while Demeter is the cereals, grains, and kernels in the granary after the kirn. Her festival is the harvest celebration at the fall equinox.

The Rape of Persephone

Demeter is the daughter of Cronus (Saturn) and Rhea and the sister of Zeus (Jupiter), Poseidon (Neptune), and Hades (Pluto). She is swallowed by her father and later disgorged. Through union with Zeus, Demeter has a daughter, Persephone or Kore. One day Hades, who rules the underworld, catches sight of Persephone and falls in love with her.

He consults with his brother Zeus, who agrees to the match. But they know that Demeter will never agree to having her daughter taken into the bowels of the earth, so Zeus advises Hades to carry her away. Zeus also helps by encouraging Ge, the Earth, to produce a myriad of lovely flowers, including a hundred-blossomed narcissus, near where Persephone lives. While Persephone is gathering these flowers she is entranced by their beauty and becomes separated from her companions. Hades suddenly appears dressed all in black, in a chariot pulled by four black stallions. He snatches her up, and as he races away the earth opens up and allows him entrance back into his realm.[21] Some say that a swineherd named Eubuleus happened to be close by, and his pigs were swallowed up in the cavern down which Hades and Persephone vanished.[22]

Mother Nature Grieves

Unable to find her daughter, Demeter puts on black mourning clothes, and, not stopping to eat or bathe, she carries two torches lit at Mount Etna and searches the earth for her child. On the tenth day she meets Hecate, who has heard the girl's cries. Hecate leads Demeter to Helios, the sun, to ask if he has seen the abductor. Helios tells them that it was Hades but counsels the mother that he is an appropriate suitor. (In some versions it is the fountain Arethusa that tells Demeter of her daughter's whereabouts. Arethusa, in her travels underground, has passed the throne of Persephone.)

Upset that Zeus has promised her child to Hades without advising her, Demeter shuns Mount Olympus. She wanders the desolate earth and becomes a nurse to the child of the human Celeus. In her grief, she sometimes lashes out in anger. For instance, she turns a boy into a lizard for ridiculing how thirstily she drinks from a cup; and in some versions of the story of Celeus, she throws the man's son into the fire when she is discovered trying to turn the boy into an immortal. Because of their kindness to her when she was disguised as an old woman, the goddess teaches Celeus's family the rites of the Eleusinian mysteries. But nothing grows, nothing is harvested, and the gods are deprived of their sacrifices. They implore Demeter to let the earth be fruitful again, but she is punishing the earth for cooperating with Hades in her daughter's abduction. She will not relent or leave her temple at Eleusis until she is allowed to see Persephone.

The Return of Spring

At last, Hermes (Mercury) is sent to Hades to retrieve Persephone. The dark ruler agrees. However, those who have eaten in the underworld cannot return to the living without penalty. The girl has eaten a pomegranate seed. (Some say she ate seven seeds.) Ascalaphus spied her as she did it and told Hades. Persephone punishes Ascalaphus by turning him into an owl. The mother rejoices at her daughter's return but is saddened to learn that she must spend a third (some say a half) of each year underground. Relenting, Demeter allows the grain to grow again as long as her daughter is above the earth.

The Barley Mother

Demeter teaches a child of Celeus the arts of agriculture, which he spreads across the world. Mother and daughter return to Mount Olympus and are known as the two goddesses. The Eleusinian Mysteries celebrated at the fall equinox became the most influential of all Greek mysteries, and the Thesmophoria was an annual festival in late October for Athenian women.[23] At the Eleusinian Mysteries, a coffer was borne in a procession from Athens to Eleusis. It contained items sacred to Demeter, including a comb, a mirror, a snake figurine, and some wheat and barley.[24] The initiates consumed the drink *kykeon*, which consisted of meal and water mixed with fresh pennyroyal mint leaves.[25] During the nine-day festival, pigs, cows, bulls, fruit, and honey cakes were offered up to her. All vegetation save beans was sacred to her. (Eleusinians were not allowed to eat beans because of their association with the souls of the dead.)[26]

Their mysteries, which included communion with bread and wine, gave both Greeks and Romans hope for life after death as well as hope for this world. The rite included a priest and a priestess who retreated to an inner sanctum and returned with a sheath of corn that the priest displayed before the participants. Peasants believed that Demeter resided in the first or last sheaf of the harvest, which was called the Demeter, the Barley Mother, or the Old Woman, and which was often dressed in woman's clothing and laid in a manger to help the cattle prosper.[27]

Pigs and Snakes

Pigs were sacred to Demeter and were sacrificed at both the Eleusinia and the Thesmophoria. At the three-day festival of the Thesmophoria, pigs, cakes of dough, and pine branches were tossed into sacred caverns or vaults, which were the homes of serpents. The serpents devoured most of the sacrifice, but what remained was retrieved the following year for veneration. Women called "drawers" had the unenviable task of frightening the snakes away by clapping their hands and then collecting the decayed leftovers. The remnants of pig flesh and cakes were sown in the fields to ensure a good harvest.[28] The descent of the pigs reenacted Persephone's descent.

In western Ceram Island near New Guinea, a myth tells of the sun god (rather than the god of the underworld) who decides to marry a divine maiden. However, her parents put a dead pig in the marriage bed instead of the girl, and, in retribution, the sun god makes the girl sink into the ground. The girl calls out for her parents to slaughter a pig and make a feast. In three days she is seen in the sky as the moon, and her story is remembered in a feast for the dead.[29]

Persephone ruled the moon, according to Plutarch.[30] How can the divine maiden and Persephone have sunk into the ground and also be in the sky in the moon? Figure 7 (p. 32) suggests how. The dark shadow of the eclipses is the path to the underworld as well as to the sun. But if the underworld is in the sky above, does that mean that the upper world is underground? In a sense, yes. It can be thought of as a turning wheel. Sometimes the upper world ends on top and the lower world on the bottom, and sometimes the reverse is true.

The snake is an emblem of Persephone as well as of the moon. Persephone, Artemis, and Hecate all were moon goddesses and all were shown with snakes in their hands.[31] The snake is related to the moon because of the serpentine path of the moon through the month and through the year.

The Meaning of the Pomegranate

We have seen that the biting of the pomegranate is an image of the partial lunar eclipse. The pomegranate tree, being evergreen, symbolizes immortality. The pomegranate, because of its many seeds, is also a sign of fertility and a symbol of the womb wherever it is found in the world. The fruit was a universal womb symbol.[32] Solomon decorated the pillar of the temple with pomegranates and in the Song of Solomon, the loved one says to her lord, "I would give you spiced wine to drink, the juice of my pomegranates" (Song of Sol. 8:2).[33] In India, women drank pomegranate juice to prevent infertility, and the

Vietnamese say that "the pomegranate opens and allows a hundred children to emerge."[34] According to Robert Graves, the pomegranate's biblical name was *rimmon* from *rim* meaning "to bear a child."[35] The house of Rimmon, in which the Phoenicians worshipped, was sacred to the moon.[36]

Demeter and the Mirror on the Wall

Demeter's informants were Hecate and Helios. Hecate was a dark witchlike goddess associated with the moon, particularly the new moon. Helios, of course, was the sun. This is a direct link to the versions of "Snow White" in which the sun or new moon or both the sun and moon take the place of the mirror on the wall as the informants to the evil queen. And what occurs when the sun and new moon are both in the sky at the same time and in the same place? A solar eclipse. The underground fountain and the well that holds the informing trout reach underground, just as the shadow of the eclipse pierces through the underworld to the moon.

Hades and the Shadow of the Moon

What did Hecate and Helios observe? Hecate heard a commotion, but Helios actually saw the swift, shadowy Hades sweep across the landscape and grab up Persephone and carry her off underground. This is a perfect description of the event just before and after a solar eclipse. Before the eclipse, the shadow of the moon appears on the horizon, racing toward the observer at approximately one thousand miles an hour. The shadow engulfs the observer during totality and then races away toward the opposite horizon.

How does Persephone fit into this picture? She is the moon. Just as she wanders away from her companions, so the moon is invisible to others as the new moon in the daytime sky. In the days following the solar eclipse, the thin crescent moon becomes visible in the evening sky, growing larger and descending farther into the night sky each day. By the tenth day, when Demeter discovers where her daughter had been taken, the moon is nearing its fullness in the middle of the night for all to see. And what was the opening in the earth that allowed Hades and Persephone into the underworld? That was the shadow of the lunar eclipse, which opens a route through the earth to the full moon deep in the underworld.

Persephone and Snow White

The Similarities

Even though Demeter bears little resemblance to the wicked queen, a close examination reveals many similarities between Persephone in myth and ritual and the Snow White tale.

- **A daughter is beautiful and naïve**—In both stories the girl is very beautiful and too trusting. Snow White opens her door to strangers, and Persephone wanders off collecting flowers.

- **A young girl leaves home by force**—Snow White is exiled and Persephone is abducted, but both are removed against their will.

- **A mother is upset and cruel**—Both mothers are portrayed in dark clothes. In versions of "Snow White" the stepmother (or mother) is jealous of her daughter and is driven to such acts of cruelty as having her daughter's innards cut out and cooked. Demeter, on the other hand, is driven by bereavement for her missing daughter to act out in anger against those who provoke her.

- **An underworld figure forces a young girl to leave home**—In "Snow White," the huntsman is a man of the forest, and therefore of the dark underworld. Hades, the Lord of the Underworld, plays the part with Persephone.

- **A boar or pigs are killed**—A boar's heart is substituted for Snow White's, and pigs are engulfed along with Hades and Persephone.

- **There is a dark, reflective informant**—Whether it is Hecate, the new moon, an old woman, a face in a bowl of water, or a mirror, all of the stories have an informant who is able to travel or see what others cannot.

- **The mother possesses a mirror**—In "Snow White" it is the looking glass, in the Eleusinian Mysteries it is in Demeter's coffer.

- **The mother is told the whereabouts of the daughter**—In every version she learns through an informant.

- **The mother is angry at being betrayed**—The wicked queen is angry at the huntsman's deceit, and Demeter is enraged over the complicity of Zeus and the earth.

- **The heroine dwells in an underworld domain**—The dark forest is hidden from the light, just like the underworld of Persephone.
- **Her companions are underworldly**—The seven dwarfs spend their time digging underground, and in stories similar to "Snow White" the characters are mostly unsavory. Persephone's companions are the dead.
- **She is queen of the underworld**—Snow White's companions realize her great worth to them and treat her like royalty. Hades makes Persephone his queen.
- **There is an old woman**—In "Snow White" the wicked queen turns herself into an old woman selling wares; Hecate is usually portrayed as old.
- **The girl is entranced by pretty things**—Snow White is enthralled by pretty trinkets, while Persephone is enchanted by flowers.
- **There is a comb**—It is the poisoned gift to Snow White, and it is among the possessions of Demeter at Eleusis.
- **The girl eats forbidden fruit**—One eats a poisoned apple, the other a pomegranate.
- **It prevents her from returning to the upper world**—Snow White loses consciousness, while Persephone loses her right to return to the living.
- **There is a sacred drink mixed with water**—The body of Snow White is washed with water and wine. Eleusinian initiates drank the sacred *kykeon* in remembrance of Persephone.
- **There is a procession**—There is the funeral procession carrying Snow White's coffin to the top of the mountain, and in the Eleusinian Mysteries there is the procession with the coffer containing the possessions of Demeter.
- **The girl appears to have died but is only sleeping**—Snow White is in a deathlike sleep but awakens, and Persephone eats only a bit of the fruit and so is allowed above ground.
- **There is an owl**—An owl perches on Snow White's casket, and Persephone's betrayer is turned into an owl.
- **There is the number seven**—In one story there are seven dwarfs and seven mountains, and in the other there are seven seeds. Because of seven seeds, Persephone must remain in the

underworld for six months. This reflects the concept that
there are seven full or new moons in six months.

- **An intercessor brings the girl back to the upper world**—The
  prince, by moving the casket, dislodges the poison apple, and
  Hermes negotiates the return of Persephone.
- **The girl becomes a princess/goddess in the upper world**—
  Snow White becomes a princess. Persephone lives on Mount
  Olympus when she is not reigning in the nether regions.

The only emblem of Persephone that seems to be missing in the
Snow White story is the snake. But this fits with the one episode un-
accounted for in "Snow White"—the varicolored lace. As we noted
previously, if the interlace designs found on traditional women's folk
costumes were turned sideways, they would represent the intertwined
snakes of the caduceus.

The twenty-four common aspects listed above plus the fact that
Snow White is often known as "Little Pomegranate" make a strong
case for direct kinship between the two stories, even though the purpose of the story of Persephone and the motivation of the characters
has completely changed in "Snow White." These disparities are much
easier to overcome if we see both of these tales as depictions of solar
and lunar eclipses and the transition of the moon through the month
and through the year.

Persephone and the Bear

Persephone's marriage to an underworld god recalls a traditional
myth, dating from at least the late Ice Age, of a girl marrying a bear.
The bear eventually allows the woman's brother or other family
member to kill it, providing its instructions for the bear-hunt ritual
are carried out. Versions of the story are told over large parts of
northern North America and in Siberia. It is the most popular story
among the Athapascans, Tagish, Tutchone, and Tlingit. The
Koyukon still believe that if a woman is not careful, she will marry a
bear. Other Native Americans, including the Navaho and Apache
have similar stories, and the Lakota tell of a bear that came to steal a
virgin.[37] Throughout the Arctic Circle, including Europe, the story is
an integral part of ancient bear ceremonies.[38] Remnants of the story
can be seen in fairy tales such as the Irish "Brown Bear of Norway,"

the Norwegian "East of the Sun, West of the Moon," and the German "Bearskin."[39]

The Lesser Eleusinian Mysteries ceremony went on for three days at the beginning of February to celebrate the return of Persephone to the upper world and to provide a time of instruction for initiates.[40] February 2, or Candlemas in Christian tradition, is the day when Persephone returns from the underworld.[41] It is also the day when bears were supposed to emerge from their winter sleep. In Poland, Austria, and Hungary it is still known as "Bear's Day," when bears come out to look for their shadows. Until recently, in Arles-sur-Tech at the foot of the French Pyrenees, townsfolk held a sacred marriage rite on the Sunday after Candlemas. A mock cave was built in the town square, and a young man wore a bearskin and acted the part of a bear. He frightened the women in the crowd until he found his bride, "Rosetta." He then carried her back to his cave where they sat at a huge table eating cakes and wine. In Crete at Candlemas, in the cave of Acrotiri, the Virgin Mary is venerated as *Panagia* (Mary) *Arkoudiotissa* ("she of the bear"). Each of these spring ceremonies recalls the tale of the woman who married a bear and links Persephone to the bear as well as to Hades.[42]

The Bear and the Moon

Persephone ruled the moon, and the bear is a symbol of the moon in both the Old World and the New. In the World Renewal Ceremony of the Munsee-Mahican Delaware, the bear was the moon. The bear ceremony began at the new moon and a crescent moon represented the bear.[43] In sites in Bulgaria, Romania, Hungary, and Yugoslavia around 5000 B.C., figures of the bear as a mother goddess often picture her with crescents symbolizing the moon.[44] Just as the moon appears and disappears from the sky, so the bear appears and disappears with the seasons.[45] Just as the moon waxes and wanes, so the bear grows fat before hibernation and is thin afterward. Just as the full moon rules over the lower world of the night sky, so the bear is ruler of the lower world of the animals. Also, the bear's shaggy coat is dark like the new moon.

The bear is also the dark shadow of the eclipses. A Modoc tale from Oregon tells of grizzly bears eating the moon.[46] The Slavey of British Columbia tell how the bears kept the sun in a bag, and the Kutchin of the Canadian Arctic tell how a bear kept the moon in a bag.[47] In the Old World, in Istanbul, people adhered to the Arab belief that a bear caused the eclipse.[48] Besides causing eclipses and abducting young women, in some cultures the bear helps to forecast the weather.

The Bear and the Groundhog

In the United States we have the popular myth of Punxsutawney Phil, the prognosticating groundhog. He is so afraid of his shadow that he pops right back into his hole the moment he sees it. In Pennsylvania Phil appears every February 2, Candlemas Day. Traditionally, if the groundhog sees its shadow and returns to its hole, then there will be six more weeks of winter; while if it does not see its shadow and remains above ground, then spring will begin soon. In Germany a badger plays the same role, and in parts of Europe and the United States a bear was similarly used for weather prediction.[49]

These ancient rites are portrayals of a solar eclipse. The groundhog or bear is the dark of the new moon, whose shadow rushes across the landscape as he kidnaps a young girl. The groundhog hole or bear cave is the column of blackness made by the shadow of the earth traveling to the moon during the lunar eclipse. Each evening the girl shows herself in the sky as the light of the waxing moon growing larger as it descends into the realm of darkness.

And how does Phil's fear of his shadow fit into all this? He is afraid of the sun, that is, the brother or other family member of the moon. If the shadow of the new moon is visible on the ground, then a total solar eclipse is near, and the groundhog, as the dark of the moon, will have to do battle with the sun. Therefore he scurries back into his hole to avoid killing his wife's relative and to avoid being killed. However, when there is not a solar eclipse, the new moon has no shadow and is not in fear of being injured by the sun. In our current tradition, it could be interpreted that on a cloudy day Phil does not hurry to his hole because a solar eclipse would not be visible under such conditions. Therefore Phil is free from fear and stays above ground portending the blessings of an early spring.

Six More Weeks of Winter

The belief that there will be six more weeks of winter if the groundhog sees his shadow also has ancient roots. Aristotle, in agreement with Greek tradition, said that bears hibernated for six weeks. (In actuality they sleep much longer than that.) There is a biblical reference to the six-week hibernation of bears. The prophet Elisha was mocked by a group of children and called "bald head." He cursed them, and two she-bears rushed out of the woods and killed forty-two of them (2 Kings 2:23–24). (There are forty-two days in six weeks.)[50]

The numbers forty and forty-two are both numbers of darkness and initiation. Lent originally was for forty days, commemorating the forty days of rain in Genesis, the Israelites' forty years in the desert, and Christ's forty days in the desert. Just as Eleusinian initiates were trained at the Lesser Mysteries in February, so Christian catechists were trained during Lent in preparation for baptism at Easter. In addition, Christ was born in the forty-second generation after Abraham. In the Egyptian *Book of the Dead,* there were forty-two judges who questioned the dead regarding forty-two possible sins.[51]

Candlemas, or the Presentation, takes place one-third of a year after the end of the Greater Eleusinian Mysteries and forty days after Christmas. This is in keeping with the Persephone myth regarding one-third of a year for winter and with the myth of the bear hibernating for six weeks when winter begins. It is interesting to note that when Missouri officially declared February 2 as Groundhog Day, there was a debate in many states about whether February 14 should be the correct date. Many old-timers insisted on the later, less popular date.[52] It so happens that February 14 is forty-two days before March 27, when early Christians celebrated Easter and forty days before March 25, when they remembered Christ's death at the spring equinox.[53] Furthermore, Persephone's reappearance at the spring equinox is in keeping with the alternate story of her causing winter to last six months.

Like an old mother bear, Demeter is fiercely protective of her child. Until recently in Europe she was the Old Woman of last year's grain. Among the Cherokee, the Old Woman protects the corn for the coming year.[54] Similarly, the bear, who was not named directly in northern cultures, was sometimes called "Grandmother" or "Stepmother."[55] In Neolithic Europe the bear was a kind, nursing mother, but in Native American lore she is sometimes a violent and obscene mother.[56] In "Snow White," Demeter becomes split into two persons—mother and stepmother—splitting the good and evil that resides within her. Just as Demeter is the old harvest and the waning moon, so Persephone is the new grain and the waxing moon. Snow

White takes on these attributes as well. Just as Persephone rules over the dead and just as the Woman Who Married a Bear takes on bear-like qualities, so Snow White takes on aspects of the bear. Her hair is dark, like the bear's, and she also goes into hibernation. The bear has been part of initiation rites in Siberia since Paleolithic times and is also part of initiation ceremonies of the Pomo of Northern California.[57] So, too, Snow White's tale is one of initiation. Furthermore, as we have seen, in at least one Snow White story, her companions in the forest are bears; and, although the boar is the usual victim killed in place of Snow White, in at least one rendition a little bear is killed.[58]

The story of Demeter and Persephone drew upon beliefs about the bear, about the spirits of the fields, and about the moon as the source of growth and vegetation—beliefs that go back to the Ice Age. Their story both came from and had a strong influence on folk beliefs, and the worship of Demeter was still observed in Greece even in the nineteenth century.[59] Little wonder that their story was the wellspring for a popular fairy tale.

Eve

Naming the Animals

Another young woman who ate forbidden fruit was Eve. Like the reappearance of Persephone, the story of Adam and Eve traditionally takes place in the spring.[60] Before there were plants or animals, God took dust, formed it, and, breathing into it, made man. As the moon begins as a tiny sliver and grows to fullness, so too God begins with a handful of dust to make the human race. The word 'adam was not originally a proper name, but rather the word for "human being." In the story there is word-play with 'adamah, which means "ground, soil."[61] On Ash Wednesday in the Roman Catholic rite, ashes are placed on believers' foreheads with the words, "Remember, man, you are dust and to dust you will return."[62] This reminder of the ephemeral nature of life fits with the ancient belief in the sacredness of ashes, which we will examine in "Little Polly Flinders." First the Lord created the garden in Eden. Then, just as the Lord breathed life into Adam, so Adam used his breath to name the animals the Lord created. This was no ordinary garden, and these were not ordinary names that Adam gave, but names that expressed the very essence of the first animals: "and whatever the man called every living creature, that was its name" (Gen. 2:19). As we will see in "Rumpelstiltskin," in primitive society to know a person's name was to control that person's destiny. Therefore, it was often taboo to reveal one's secret name. Among some peoples who regard the bear with reverence, it is believed the bear can hear everything that humans say, so a special hunter's language is used to protect hunters from being understood.[63] It was a very widely held belief that snakes knew all secrets and that by eating a snake, one could become conversant in the language of animals, especially the language of birds.[64] Both snakes and birds are messengers of the moon.

The Thirteenth Rib
Genesis says, "And the rib that the Lord God had taken from the man he made into a woman and brought her to the man" (Gen. 2:22). Both men and women have exactly twelve ribs. Does this imply that Adam originally had thirteen ribs? The Venus of Laussel, which was sculpted in France between 16,000 and 23,000 B.C., portrays a full-figured nude goddess holding a buffalo horn with thirteen notches in it.[65] The horn likely represents the crescent moon. The thirteen notches would coincide with the thirteen new or full moons between the beginning of the winter solstice period in one year to the end of the next winter solstice period in the year. It could also represent the thirteen visible phases of the moon between the new and the full moon. The Paleolithic figure is both the mother goddess and the moon. It would be appropriate for Eve, the first mother, to be made from the thirteenth rib, signifying the moon. There are tales worldwide of humans being brought to life from a bone or bones.[66] It is fitting that Eve should be made from a single, crescent-shaped bone.

The Temptation
The followers of Demeter were not allowed to eat the pomegranate for fear of being pulled down into the flesh.[67] In some versions of the Persephone story the maiden is portrayed as succumbing to the temptations of sin. In the Homeric hymn to Demeter she makes excuses to her mother saying, "He secretly put into my mouth sweet food, a pomegranate seed, and forced me to taste against my will."[68] This sounds very much like Eve when she tells God, "The serpent tricked me, and I ate" (Gen. 3:13).[69] There is a tradition that the for-

bidden fruit of Eden was a pomegranate and that each pomegranate contains a seed from the garden.[70]

The Apple and the Pomegranate

There is also the tradition of the apple as the forbidden fruit. From this we derive the term "Adam's apple," referring to the projection in the neck that was supposedly created when Adam choked on the bite of the fruit. The words for apple and fruit were often interchangeable in Romance languages. *Pomum* is Latin means any kind of fruit, while *pomme* in French means "apple." The Latin for pomegranate is *malum granatum,* which means "apple with many seeds." By the way, *malum* with a long *a* is an apple, while, interestingly, *malum* with a short *a* is evil. It is easy to see why the apple became the forbidden fruit, since Latin was the universal language of the Roman church and since pomegranates were unfamiliar in northern climes.

The Trees in the Garden

The Lord had placed two trees in the middle of the garden, the tree of life, and the tree of the knowledge of good and evil. He strictly forbade the touching or eating of the fruit of the tree of the knowledge of good and evil, on punishment of death. The motif of the forbidden tree, where the fruit of all trees but one may be eaten, is extremely widespread and can be found in European, Semitic, Siberian, Latin-American, and Indonesian folktales.[71]

A Hindu tale tells of a toad named U Hynroh who climbed a tree to the sky in order to swallow the sun. The toad is a symbol for the moon.[72] In New Zealand, the Maori tell of a girl named Rona who went to a well to fetch water. On her return she tripped on the root of a tree. She grabbed the tree to save herself and cursed the moon for not lighting her way. The moon heard her and, in retribution, took her and the tree up to the sky, where they can still be seen in the moon today.[73] There is also a tale from India of the sun and moon stealing the tree of life, and another tale from the Finnish *Kalevala* tells of the sun and moon being placed at the top of the World Tree.[74]

Gardens in the Middle East were surrounded by walls, which represented the circle of the moon surrounding the earth each month. (See Figure 7, p. 32.) The tree of life is the shadow of the solar eclipse, which grows at the center of the garden. The tree of the knowledge of good and evil is the shadow of the lunar eclipse that also grows in the center of the garden. The one tree reaches toward the sun and eternal life, while the other reaches toward the underworld and death.

The Trickster Serpent

In Hindu and Greek mythology the serpent is portrayed as being wise. However, in the Garden of Eden, the serpent is more cunning than wise. As we have seen, the spiraling serpent is the path of the spiraling moon. The serpent is the yearly path of the full moon spiraling in ever-larger circles toward the winter solstice and the monthly path of the moon spiraling toward the midnight of the full moon where Eve bites the apple.

There are many myths of the moon sending a message to humans through an animal messenger—a rabbit, dog, lizard, or other. The message is, "As I die and rise to life again, so you shall also die and rise to life again." However, through ignorance or deceit, the animal changes the message to say that once dead, a human will not live again. This story can be found widely in Africa, as well as in Fiji, in Australia, among the Ainu of Japan, and elsewhere.[75] In New Zealand, the hero Maui wished humans to live forever, but the moon objected and said that they should "die and become like the soil."[76] Although the serpent in Eden may have been subtler, he accomplished the same end as the moon and the other lunar animals, by bringing death to humans.

The Naked Truth

Before the transgression, Genesis says, "Therefore a man leaves his father and his mother and clings to his wife, and they become one flesh. And the man and his wife were both naked and were not ashamed" (Gen. 2:24–25). Later, after they had eaten of the fruit, "Then the eyes of both were opened, and they knew that they were naked; and they sewed fig leaves together and made loincloths for themselves" (Gen. 3:7). Their clothing symbolizes the corporeal garments that all things wear. The spiraling serpent wove a new world and created garments of flesh. Just as the moon grows heavy as it goes down into the underworld, so Adam and Eve have fallen under the weight of their new garments. Even the Lord "made garments of skins for the man and for his wife, and clothed them" (Gen. 3:20–21). Animal skins, which are a sign of the animal aspect that humans have assumed, are warm and particularly helpful for the cold nights of the winter solstice, which they will endure in exile.

The Triple Curse
First the Lord curses the serpent:

> "Because you have done this,
> 　cursed are you among animals
> 　and among all wild creatures;
> upon your belly you shall go,
> 　and dust you shall eat
> 　all the days of your life."[77]

The snake eats dust and is covered with dust. Just as the moon is so often portrayed in stories as covered with mud or soot or pitch, so the snake is the dusty one. Unlike Eve, whose name means "Life" and who stands for the full moon, the snake stands for death and the dark new moon.

The Lord continues to speak to the serpent:

> "And I will put enmity between you and
> 　the woman
> 　and between your offspring and hers;
> they shall strike at your head
> 　and you shall strike at their heels."[78]

This statement is the beginning of a search, which will continue until the end of this book. The heel and the foot have been sacred symbols since the last Ice Age. We will discover why both the hand and the foot are significant and what they have to do with the moon. We shall examine Achilles' heel and the missing leg of Captain Ahab, the missing hand of Captain Hook, the missing eyes of pirates, the missing shoe in "Diddle, Diddle, Dumpling," and the limps of many characters in story and myth. Finally, we will find the Ice Age secret that makes the connection between the shoeless foot of Cinderella and the heels of Eve's offspring.

Throughout the world a goddess and her serpent are connected with the forming of the human race.[79] There are also depictions of a goddess bruising a serpent's head with her heel.[80] Many Roman Catholic statues of the Blessed Virgin show her foot upon the head of a snake. The bite of a snake brings death, and the winding snake is the path of the moon as it winds toward the sun in order to kill it at the eclipse. It is also the winding path of the moon to the solstice, when the sun dies. As we shall see, the foot contains a secret that will tame the snake.

The Lord also cursed Eve by increasing her pain in childbirth. Eve is the first mother. Many peoples believe that the moon or a lunar animal is the ancestor of their tribe. The Inca believe the moon was the root from which their emperors sprang.[81] The Snoqualmie believe that they descend from Snoqualm, the Moon.[82] The Tewa of North America believe that the moon was the first mother and that she gave up one eye so that she would not shine so brightly at night and her children could sleep. Our word *mother* is related to the word *moon*. How suitable that the first word from a child's mouth should be "Ma," meaning both mother and moon.

The Lord cursed Adam to endless toil. Just as the moon never ceases on its endless journey, so humans must work for their food until they return to the soil. The Tlingit of North America relate the story of the Angry Moon, which continues to roll up a gigantic mountain so steep that the moon keeps rolling back down.[83] Like the Greek Sisyphus, who endlessly rolls a rock up a mountain only to have it roll down again, so humans must labor without relief.

"Then the Lord God said, 'See, the man has become like one of us, knowing good and evil; and now, he might reach out his hand and take also of the tree of life, and eat, and live forever'" (Gen. 3:22).[84] This echoes a theme found in Babylonian mythology. God is fearful that, like the moon, humans will eclipse the sun and steal immortality. Like Snow White, Adam and Eve are cast out. Snow White, Persephone, and Eve have left the world of innocence and entered the world of good and evil.

An Ice Age Story

In the American Southwest, one of the favorite stories among the Tewa is "The Man Who Married the Moon."[85] Nah-chu-ru-chu, whose name means "the Bluish Light of Dawn," was a weaver and a leader of the Tewa, as well as the most eligible bachelor in those early days. After being badgered by the two Yellow Corn Maidens, he announces a contest to see whom he will marry. In four days he will hang a dipper of pearl on his door. Whoever can grind her corn meal so fine that it sticks to the dipper will be his bride. All of the girls work at grinding, but the Yellow Corn Maidens are confident that they will win. On the fourth day, the Moon, who is a girl in the village, returns home from visiting her father and learns of the contest. She is very beautiful, though she is blind in one eye, and she too wishes to marry Nah-chu-ru-chu.

She hurries to grind a little meal, and after all the women, including the Yellow Corn Maidens, have failed, she takes her turn. Every drop of her meal sticks to the shiny dipper! The handsome bachelor keeps his promise, despite the anger of the Yellow Corn Maidens, and marries the Moon. They are very happy, but he warns her to beware of the Yellow Corn Maidens. One day they invite her to go gathering roots with them. Her husband agrees to let her go as long as she promises not to do anything that they propose. On the way to the plains, the women have to go through a forest. In the center of the forest is a well. The Yellow Corn Maidens urge the Moon to take a drink, but she refuses. They then tell her to see how pretty she looks reflected in the water. The Moon has always been fond of looking at herself in the water, so she leans over the well. As she does so, the maidens push her in and drown her. They cover the well with earth and return home happily.

The Yellow Corn Maidens tell the Moon's husband that the Moon returned home ahead of them. He goes into mourning, and there is no rain, and the crops fail. The people send Eagle, Badger, Osprey, Coyote, and Turkey Buzzard to search for her, all to no avail. However, Turkey Buzzard, who flies so high that he burns the feathers off his head, sees a mound in the middle of the forest covered with beautiful flowers.

Nah-chu-ru-chu asks Turkey Buzzard to bring him a white flower from the middle of the mound, which he does. The Moon's husband places the flower between two of the Moon's dresses and begins to chant. The flower begins to grow. He sings more and the flower grows more. After he sings five times, he lifts away the cloth and there is his wife, alive again. The people celebrate, and Nah-chu-ru-chu makes a hoop and gives it to the Moon. When the Yellow Corn

Maidens visit, the Moon plays with her hoop. The maidens insist on playing as well, and when they grab onto the rolling hoop, they turn into two snakes. The Moon tames the snakes so they will harm humans no more.

The Yellow Corn Maidens reveal the evil side of the corn spirits. The short stories "The Lottery" by Shirley Jackson and "The Children of the Corn" by Stephen King are modern tellings of the corn spirits' demand for sacrificial victims.

The story "The Man Who Married the Moon" contains echoes of Snow White, Persephone, and Eve. Along with other Native American stories of maidens visiting the underworld, it shows that Snow White has roots that go back at least to the late Ice Age. There may, of course, have been some European influence on the story. It is interesting that the white flower in the story is also the name of the heroine in one of the Spanish versions of Snow White. But this is very much a story in the Tewan tradition. This story brings together parts of all the stories we have looked at and links them directly to the moon. All of these stories are vehicles, which allow us to travel back over vast expanses of space and time and to see life for a moment through the eyes of our predecessors.

Chapter 5

Rumpelstiltskin

Spinning a Yarn

"Rumpelstiltskin" is known, under different names, throughout Europe, including parts of Russia but is not found elsewhere except in its European form.[1] This is because "Rumpelstiltskin" is a commentary on the enslaving effects of the invention of the spinning wheel on women in Europe. The heroine of the story is a victim of circumstance and a victim of the men in her life.

But first, let's enjoy the tale and see what amazing details it has to say about the sun and the moon.

> *There was once a miller who was poor, but he had one beautiful daughter. It happened one day that he came to speak with the king, and, to give himself consequence, he told him that he had a daughter who could spin gold out of straw. The king said to the miller,*
>
> *"That is an art that pleases me well; if thy daughter is as clever as you say, bring her to my castle to-morrow, that I may put her to the proof."*
>
> *When the girl was brought to him, he led her into a room that was quite full of straw, and gave her a wheel and spindle, and said,*
>
> *"Now set to work, and if by the early morning thou hast not spun this straw to gold thou shalt die." And he shut the door himself, and left her there alone.*[2]

The miller, with his ever-turning millstone, is an allegory for Time. In *Hamlet's Mill: An Essay on Myth and the Frame of Time*, Georgio de Santillana and Hertha von Dechend compare the mill to the circle of the stars that moves through the eons, creating new ages by their movement.[3] The sun and the moon are also like a mill in that they circle through the year and through the month, measuring out time. The miller is Father Time, who risks the life of his daughter because of his boastfulness. He puts the poor girl into the hands of an avaricious and cruel king because he is unable to be either modest or honest. Both the miller and the king are interested in the girl's being productive at the wheel, because this was a form of income and a dowry, even without the talent of turning straw to gold.

Just as the miller represents Time, so too does the act of spinning. The word *spin* comes from the Indo-European root *spe(i)*, meaning "draw," "stretch," "spread," "swell," "be successful." Related words include *span, space, speed, prosper,* and *spontaneous.* Another related word that better fits our heroine's situation is *despair.* The Old High German word for spindle is *wirtel,* which comes from the Indo-European root *wert,* which means "to turn." *Weird,* meaning "fate," comes from the same root, as does *vortex, vertigo, anniversary, worm, worry, wrong, wrinkle, wring, wrench,* and *worth.* The Weird Sisters are the Fates, who spin the thread of life and measure out its span.

The heroine's father is such a braggadocio that he cannot just say that his daughter can spin huge quantities of flax into thread, as in other versions of the tale. Instead he boasts even more, insisting she can spin straw into gold.

Golden Spindles

For thousands of years in Europe, the technique for spinning thread from fibers involved the use of a distaff and spindle. A distaff was a long staff or board that held the loose fibers of wool, flax, and so on. The old word *dis-* meant "fuzz" or "fiber." Today *distaff* implies a woman's domain or the female side of the family. The spindle was a stick about a foot long inserted into a small disk or rock called a whorl, which helped the spindle spin like a top. The loose fiber was evenly fed from the distaff to the spindle, which hung down as it spun, both drawing and twisting the thread at the same time. When the thread almost reached the ground, it was wrapped around the spindle and the process continued.[4]

Golden spindles dating back to 2500 B.C. have been found at Alaca Hoyuk in central Turkey. They were also mentioned as gifts to

Rumpelstiltskin

Helen of Troy in *The Odyssey*. Highborn ladies of early Greece both spun and wove with the most expensive of materials.[5] They certainly would not have used straw, but they very well might have made threads that appeared to be golden. Elizabeth Wayland Barber points out that flax retted in running or standing water turns golden, while flax retted in night's dew turns silver. (Retting, which means "rotting," is the soaking of plants to rot the plant material from the fibers.)[6]

The spinning wheel was introduced into Europe in the late Middle Ages.[7] It allowed women to spin four times faster than the ancient method of using a distaff and spindle, and the production of thread became part of the economics of the household and the society, often debilitating the women who were forced to work long hours at it. Maria Tatar in *The Hard Facts of the Grimms' Fairy Tales* discusses all of the Grimms' tales about spinning and points out that although fairy tales may tacitly support the prevailing social order, humorous folk tales attack the sacredness of that order and undermine the work ethic. The fairy tales emphasize the redeeming value of spinning and sewing, but the folktales emphasize their deforming and enslaving aspects. She concludes that few tales "assimilated the craft of spinning in so thoroughgoing a fashion as 'Rumpelstiltskin.'"[8]

The Spinning Spider

What is it that spins gold in the night sky? It is the moon. Each night as it wends its way across the sky, it winds another turn of gold thread around the earth's spindle. Persephone was a spinning goddess associated with the moon.[9] The Mayan goddess of the moon was the patroness of weaving, and her attribute was a spider.[10] The word *spider* means spinner and derives from the word *spin*.

In many cultures around the world the female spider is the creator of the world. The Pueblo say that Spider Women wove the world using two threads, and her two daughters created the sun and the moon.[11] In Ghana Anansi the Spider created the sun, moon, and stars. In the Gilbert Islands of Micronesia, Nareau, the Lord Spider, is the creator god. In many instances, the spider takes on qualities specifically associated with the moon. The Incas believed spiders could predict the future, the Muisca of Columbia believed the spider carried souls across rivers into the underworld on its boat of spider webs, and the Aztecs believed the spider was god of the underworld.[12]

The Snoqualmie tell how Spider made a rope of cedar bark and stretched it to the sky so that Blue Jay and Fox could steal the sun and fire from Moon.[13]

The Kiowa of Oklahoma tell of Spider Grandmother. When the world was young there was no light, and all the animals complained that they could not see. Rabbit, Fox, Eagle, and Woodpecker all tried to find light, but to no avail. Spider Grandmother volunteered; and, despite being ridiculed, she set off to the Land of the Sun People, spinning her web behind her so she would not get lost. She formed a bowl out of clay along the way, and when she reached her destination, she stole a piece of their fire without being detected and put it in her bowl. As she returned home, the fire became larger and hotter, and she finally had to toss it high up into the sky, where it became the sun. However, she remembered to save a little in her bowl so that her people could have fire.[14] The clay bowl is the dark of the moon that eclipsed the sun and contained a piece of it to bring to the lower world. The fire growing larger and hotter is like the sun after an eclipse, when it becomes brighter and the temperature rises again. The piece of fire that Spider Grandmother saved for cooking and for lighting the night is like the moon that illuminates the underworld of the night sky. In Papua, New Guinea, people describe the moon as a fire in a pot.[15]

The story of Rumpelstiltskin is the story of another spinner who steals the sun.

The First New Moon

Baily's Beads

A little man comes to the rescue—for a price:

> *And so the poor miller's daughter was left there sitting, and could not think what to do for her life: she had no notion how to set to work to spin gold from straw, and her distress grew so great that she began to weep. Then all at once the door opened, and in came a little man, who said,*
>
> *"Good evening, miller's daughter; why are you crying?"*
>
> *"Oh!" answered the girl, "I have got to spin gold out of straw, and I don't understand the business."*
>
> *Then the little man said,*
>
> *"What will you give me if I spin it for you?"*

"My necklace," said the girl.

The girl is in the depths of despair. She is at the winter solstice in her life. There was a customary prohibition against using a spinning wheel on certain nights near the winter solstice, and, similarly, our heroine is not spinning.[16] Not only is she at the dark of winter, when the spiraling motion of the sun stops before starting up again, but also she is at the dark of the new moon. And the little man is the dark of the moon, which is about to steal a bit of the sun.

There is an interesting solar phenomenon that looks like a necklace. It is known as Baily's Beads, named after the British astronomer Francis Baily (1774–1844), who first described them. During a total eclipse of the sun, just before and just after totality, the thin crescent of the unobscured portion of the sun suddenly appears broken up. It becomes a band of bright points of different sizes separated by dark spaces. In other words, it looks like a "string of bright beads." Irregularities such as mountains and valleys at the edge of the moon's disk cause this phenomenon.[17]

Why should we connect the girl's necklace with Baily's Beads? There are clues that we are dealing with a solar eclipse. First of all, the heroine is weeping. It was customary throughout the world to grieve and wail when there was an eclipse of either the sun or the moon. The mourning was to continue until the eclipse had disappeared. Second, the little man is an underworld figure and is an agent of darkness. Pictures of Rumpelstiltskin usually show him as a bearded, gnarled, mean old man. These features fit with the Man in the Moon, particularly the dark new moon. And third, as we shall see, the little man takes the necklace. This fits with the new moon, which reaches the sun at the height of the sky and takes it out of the sky, taking its necklace of beads with it. Once the eclipse is over, the necklace disappears.

Seeing the necklace as Baily's Beads may seem like a big jump. But there is a substantial mythology to back up the claim. The stealing of a necklace is a common theme. Stealing the goddess Freya's necklace is a task in Icelandic lore, and an attempt to steal a fairy necklace is unsuccessful in Irish myth. In a Hindu tale, a hawk carries off the necklace of a queen and drops it by a lucky girl, who receives a reward. Another common theme is the retrieval of a necklace from the underworld. Again from India, a rescued princess leaves her necklace behind in the underworld and the hero returns for it and remains trapped there. Another Hindu tale relates the challenge of retrieving a necklace of rubies from the sea.[18] In Hindu astrology the sun is a ruby.[19] Also, the sun's chromosphere, which is visible just as totality begins after the first Baily's Beads, is usually "a deep ruby red."[20]

From Spain comes the exemplum of a crow that steals a necklace and drops it into a snake's nest. A man then retrieves the necklace and kills the snake, which had eaten the fledglings of the crow. The black crow is the dark of the moon that steals the necklace of the sun and drops it into the underworld of the snake's pit in order to exact retribution for the loss of its young. In a Hindu tale, the tree of heaven springs from the necklace of a goddess. She then hangs the necklace from one of its branches.[21] The tree is the shadow of the solar eclipse, and the necklace in its branches is Baily's Beads.

A famous necklace in Greek myth was to bring disaster upon the royal house of Thebes. Cadmus, the founder of Thebes, married Harmonia, the daughter of Aphrodite, the goddess of love. The goddess gave her daughter a necklace forged by Hephaestus, the smith of the gods, as a wedding present. The necklace was passed on from generation to generation, and tragedy pursued whoever possessed it, inspiring the plays *Oedipus the King, Antigone,* and *Seven against Thebes.* After the fall of Thebes, the necklace was taken to Delphi, where it was shown to pilgrims for hundreds of years.[22] It was subsequently stolen by Phayallus for his mistress, who died when her son went mad and burned her house and all her treasures.[23] As we have seen, a blacksmith is believed to reside in the moon. The new moon eclipses the sun and creates the necklace, whose powers are so strong that they are a curse to whoever possesses it.

One final tale from India is about an earring instead of a necklace, but I believe it makes the case for Baily's Beads. The Thoria, an Orissan tribe in the Kerba Koraput District, tells the tale "Sonwari and the Golden Earring."[24] In the days before there was a sun, the beautiful girl Sonwari receives a pair of earrings from her parents as a wedding present. They are in a wooden box, and each earring contains "spangled, wobbling pieces." One day while she is filling her pail at the well, which is in a circle of fire since there is no sun, a kite swoops down and grabs one of her earrings with its talons and rips it from her lobe. The kite, as it flies higher, becomes stuck in the star web of the great spider in the sky. The earring begins to grow and grow until it becomes the sun.

The "spangled, wobbling pieces" are the beads in Baily's Beads. The box is the new moon that causes the beads and the total solar eclipse. There are two earrings because Baily's Beads occur both before and after a total solar eclipse. The circle of fires is the circle of the phases of the moon in a month. The shaft of the well is the shadow of the lunar eclipse, and the kite is the shadow of the solar eclipse. The spider's web is the web that the moon weaves each month. The earring grows just as Baily's Beads grow into the globe of the sun.

Even though Baily's Beads were not named until 1836, primitive peoples most likely would have known about them. Although proper precautions should be taken against damage to the eyes, the beads can be seen with the naked eye or in a reflective surface. The secrets of the eclipses were of great importance to ancient peoples, and so it is very likely that a description of Baily's Beads would have been passed on from one generation to the next.

The Spinning Begins

The little man keeps his promise:

> The little man took the necklace, seated himself before the wheel, and whirr, whirr, whirr! three times round and the bobbin was full; then he took up another, and whirr, whirr, whirr! three times round, and that was full; and so he went on till the morning, when all the straw had been spun, and all the bobbins were full of gold.

This describes the action of the full moon during the night. The full moon lasts for three days according to tradition. Therefore, "three times round" means that the full moon goes three times around the earth before it is complete. Since the girl has many bobbins to fill, the little man has to make the bobbins go three times round many times. But by morning the full moon leaves the sky, and its work is completed, with the help of the underworld helper—the Man in the Moon.

The Second New Moon

An Annular Eclipse

The miller's daughter's troubles are far from over:

> At sunrise came the king, and when he saw the gold he was astonished and very much rejoiced, for he was very avaricious. He had

the miller's daughter taken into another room filled with straw,
much bigger than the last, and told her that as she valued her life
she must spin it all in one night. The girl did not know what to
do, so she began to cry, and then the door opened, and the little
man appeared and said,
    "What will you give me if I spin all this straw into gold?"
    "The ring from my finger," answered the girl.
    So the little man took the ring, and began again to send the
wheel whirring round, and by the next morning all the straw was
spun into glistening gold.

The ring represents another phenomenon of the solar eclipse. Sometimes when the moon passes in front of the sun, its shadow does not reach the earth. In such instances, an annular eclipse occurs, in which observers see an annulus or bright ring of the solar disc surrounding the black disc of the moon.[25] This happens because the moon's orbit is elliptical and sometimes the moon is farther away from the earth and therefore appears smaller and is unable to completely cover the disc of the sun.

In the Greek myth of Prometheus, that stealer of the sun's fire who brought fire and language to humans, Hercules frees him on the condition that he wear an iron ring on his finger. The ring is set with a piece of rock to remind him of the rock of the Caucasus to which he has been chained and to remind him of his submission to Zeus.[26] The iron must have been made red hot in the forge of the heavenly blacksmith, Hephaestus (Vulcan). This is a description of an annular eclipse as well.

As with the necklace, two common themes in myth are the stealing of a ring and the retrieving of a ring from the underground. There are many stories of rings being carried off by birds or otherwise being stolen. There is a Hindu story of a lover who removes the ring from his mistress's finger. A bird carries it off, and the two youths become separated. Often a ring is cast into the water only to be found later inside a fish. Sometimes a hero retrieves the ring from the sea. A Hindu tale tells of a magic ring that works when the sun's rays shine upon its gemstone.[27] (There is a very brief phenomenon just after Bailey's Beads and just before totality known as the "diamond ring," in which the last solitary bead burns like a brilliant flare on the rim of the moon.)[28]

The Ring of the Nibelungen, who were dwarfs of the underworld, was a magic ring. The German god Woden (Odin) snatches the ring from the Nibelungen with a thrust of his spear. However, he returns the ring, which he created, to humans. Later Siegfried and Woden's daughter, Brunhild, throw the ring back into the Rhine to end the corruption that comes with its power.[29] Often the ring makes the wearer invisible, as in *The Lord of the Ring* trilogy by J. R. R. Tolkien.

All of these myths are allegories for the annular eclipse. As with the necklace, the stealing of the ring is the dark moon taking the ring as it disappears from the sky after the eclipse. The ring tossed into the sea is the light of the sun taken by the moon into the underworld of the night sky. Woden's spear thrown through the ring is the black moon's shadow thrust into the center of the sun. Woden, like Hephaestus, is a smith god and therefore is connected with the moon. The corruption that comes with the ring is the wounding power of the sun, which is so intense that it cripples whoever possesses it. The power of the ring to make its wearer invisible is the fact that the moon, which created or stole the ring, is again invisible in the daytime sky as soon as the eclipse has completely ended.

The ring symbolizes bondage to another person, including the marriage bond. The miller's daughter is forming a tighter bond with the little man. The ring is a pledge of loyalty to the lord of darkness and even a marriage to him. This is similar to the "Woman Who Married a Bear" motif, which we have already encountered.

The Third New Moon

The Corona

The girl will soon discover just how strong this bond has become:

> *The king was rejoiced beyond measure at the sight, but as he could never have enough of gold, he had the miller's daughter taken into a still larger room full of straw, and said,*
>
> *"This, too, must be spun in one night, and if you accomplish it you shall be my wife." For he thought, "Although she is but a miller's daughter, I am not likely to find any one richer in the whole world."*
>
> *As soon as the girl was left alone, the little man appeared for the third time and said,*

"What will you give me if I spin the straw for you this time?"

"I have nothing left to give," answered the girl.

"Then you must promise me the first child you have after you are queen," said the little man.

"But who knows whether that will happen?" thought the girl; but as she did not know what else to do in her necessity, she promised the little man what he desired, upon which he began to spin, until all the straw was gold.

The girl has gone from the loose bond of a necklace to the tighter bond of a ring to the tightest bond of all—that of her own flesh and blood. What the little man was really after was the crown prince or princess.

During the minutes of a total solar eclipse, the sun's corona or "crown" becomes visible. It is made up of the sun's outermost atmosphere, which is not usually visible. It is the corona that gives off the dim eerie light of the black sun.[30] Rumpelstiltskin wants to steal that crown, just as he has stolen the necklace and the ring. It is his "crowning" achievement to reach totality. Here in one story are represented three of the most interesting phenomena of the sun during an eclipse: Baily's Beads, the annulus, and the corona. There are other stories besides "Rumpelstiltskin" in which the necklace and the ring appear together. For example, as we have seen in a French version of "Snow White," "The Mirror That Talks," a poisoned necklace, ring, and apple are used to try to kill the heroine.

The kidnapping of children is a common theme in tales about the bear. The Mistassani Cree tell a story, "The Boy Who Was Kept by a Bear," that describes a benevolent bear who finds a boy in the woods and keeps him. He teaches the boy many bear skills but is ultimately killed by the boy's father.[31] However, not all bears are as kind with the children they kidnap.

The Fourth New Moon

The First Child

The miller's daughter has a promise to keep:

And when in the morning the king came and found all done according to his wish, he caused the wedding to be held at once, and the miller's pretty daughter became a queen.

In a year's time she brought a fine child into the world, and thought no more of the little man; but one day he came suddenly into her room, and said,

"Now give me what you promised me."

The queen was terrified greatly, and offered the little man all the riches of the kingdom if he would only leave the child; but the little man said,

"No, I would rather have something living than all the treasures of the world."

Then the queen began to lament and to weep, so that the little man had pity upon her.

"I will give you three days," said he, "and if at the end of that time you cannot tell my name, you must give up the child to me."

Like a true lord of darkness, he insists on a living sacrifice. The queen begins the traditional lament at the beginning of an eclipse, and she moves him with her prayers. Since the new moon lasts for three days, he has three opportunities to eclipse the sun. Therefore he gives the queen three days to save her baby by guessing his name.

The Power of Names

The Sanskrit *naman* means "name" and is found in all of the Indo-European languages in its cognate forms such as *nomen* in Latin and *onoma* in Greek.[32] It also occurs outside the Indo-European group, such as the Lapp *namma,* the Finnish *nime-,* and the Hungarian *nev.*[33] All over the world, knowing and invoking a person's name gives one power over that person. There is a widespread taboo against revealing one's name for fear of giving away power over one's soul. Many cultures give secret names in order to protect the spirit from being cursed by one's enemies. In India, one's secret name is entered into one's horoscope in such a way that it cannot be discovered if it falls into the wrong hands.[34] Also, in Egypt, Babylonia, and India, humans commanded power over the gods just by naming them.[35] In addition, there is a taboo against naming either a good for fear it will be taken away or an evil for fear that it may come true. In our culture we use terms such as "God forbid" when naming an evil and "knock on wood" or "touch wood" when naming a good.

In keeping with the bear's son theme, it is worth noting that Ural-Altaic peoples of Siberia never speak the name of the bear. They call him "Grandfather," "Dear Uncle," and "Wise One"; but most interesting of all is that they called him "Little Old Man," almost the same description as that of Rumpelstiltskin! Baltic peoples call him "Beautiful Honey-paw," "Broadfoot," or "Grandfather." The Tête de Boule tribe of Quebec also call the bear "Grandfather." The North American Kiowa say that unless you are named Bear, you must not use its name. Bears can drive people crazy just for saying their name.[36]

Sometimes using the name of a powerful spirit is believed to transfer that power. There is a Gnostic belief that souls that know the names of demons can control them.[37] Similarly, in witchcraft, saying the name of a devil or evil spirit calls it up and puts it under the witch's power.[38]

The Fifth New Moon
The Common Names
Then the queen spent the whole night in thinking over all the names that she had ever heard, and sent a messenger through the land to ask far and wide for all the names that could be found. And when the little man came next day, (beginning with Caspar, Melchior, Balthazar) she repeated all she knew, and went through the whole list, but after each the little man said,

"That is not my name."

The messenger is like Mercury, the messenger of the gods, who seeks not only on land but also in the heavens for the secret of the little man. But the shadow of the solar eclipse is getting closer.

The Sixth New Moon
The Uncommon Names
The queen tries again:
The second day the queen sent to inquire of all the neighbours what the servants were called, and told the little man all the most unusual and singular names, saying,

"Perhaps you are called Roast-ribs, or Sheepshanks, or Spindleshanks?" But he answered nothing but

"That is not my name."

Again the shadow gets closer.

The Seventh New Moon

The Secret Name

The new moon is about to engulf her child:

> *The third day the messenger came back again, and said,*
>
> *"I have not been able to find one single new name; but as I passed through the woods I came to a high hill, and near it was a little house, and before the house burned a fire, and round the fire danced a comical little man, and he hopped on one leg and cried,*
>
> > *"To-day I bake, to-morrow I brew,*
> > *The day after that the queen's child comes in;*
> > *And oh! I am glad that nobody knew*
> > *That the name I am called is Rumpelstiltskin!"*
>
> *You cannot think how pleased the queen was to hear that name, and soon afterwards, when the little man walked in and said, "Now, Mrs. Queen, what is my name?" she said at first,*
>
> *"Are you called Jack?"*
>
> *"No," answered he.*
>
> *"Are you called Harry?" she asked again.*
>
> *"No," answered he. And then she said,*
>
> *"Then perhaps your name is Rumpelstiltskin!"*
>
> *"The devil told you that! the devil told you that!" cried the little man, and in his anger he stamped with his right foot so hard that it went into the ground above his knee; then he seized his left foot with both his hands in such a fury that he split in two, and there was an end of him.*

The messenger was traveling in the woods, which means that he was in the underworld of the night sky, when he came to a high hill. The high hill in the night sky is the hill created by the moon as it progresses higher and higher each night until at the full moon it has reached the top of the midnight sky. The little house is the lair of the lord of darkness—it is the shadow of the earth near but not touching the full moon. The fire is the light of the full moon, and the little man is hopping on one leg because he is the lame Man in the Moon. In ancient China one-footed dances were performed to bring on rain.[39] Traditionally it is said that the moon controls the rain. We will learn more about the moon and one-footedness in "Goosey, Goosey Gander."

Rumpelstiltskin sings about baking and brewing because the moon is thought of as food and drink. The full moon looks like a round loaf of bread, and the thin crescent moon, with its cusps pointed approximately upward, looks like a cup filled with brew. If we look at each visit to the heroine as a full lunar cycle rather than a day, then "Today I bake" means that he is at the full moon. "Tomorrow I brew" means that he will be at the new moon, ready to eclipse the crown prince or princess, when he visits the queen. (For more about food and the moon, see Chapter 13, "There Was a Man Lived in the Moon.")

The Man in the Moon

In his rage Rumpelstiltskin says, "The devil told you that." This is literally true in the sense that indirectly the little man told her, and he is a devilish person, a dweller of the underworld, who resides in the moon. The "underground people" of folklore can also be residents of the moon, because the full moon is in the underworld of the night sky. He stamps his right foot deep into the earth and pulls on his left foot till he tears himself apart. The left is associated with the moon because its phases follow a retrograde motion from right to left across the sky through their monthly cycle—they travel counterclockwise as opposed to the sun, which travels from left to right. Many folk dances are still danced "widdershins" or counterclockwise, even though dancing widdershins was associated with the Devil and resulted in death for many supposed witches.[40]

The moon has traveled from the winter solstice, when the full moon is at its peak, high in the midnight sky, to the summer solstice, when the full moon is low in the midnight sky. During the same time, the sun has grown from being low in the winter midday sky to being high in the summer midday sky. Similarly, the heroine's child has gone from being nonexistent to being on the way to power, while Rumpelstiltskin has gone from being in power to being nonexistent.

The Seven Days of the Week

The seven days of the week, which the moon passes through on its trip from the horizon to the height of the sky, are associated with the seven planets and with the journey of the soul.

The miller's daughter travels through the days and planets as follows, beginning from the bottom:

Weekday	Planet	Episode
Sunday	Sun	Secret name
Monday	Moon	Uncommon names
Tuesday	Mars	Common names
Wednesday	Mercury	Child's birth
Thursday	Jupiter	Promise
Friday	Venus	Ring
Saturday	Saturn	Necklace

Saturn is often described as rich because of the precious gems and minerals under the earth, which he controls. A necklace can be made of jewels or it can be made of children's beads. The first stage of development is the stage of childhood. In the second stage, the ring symbolizes love and betrothal. Although against her will, the girl is forming a bond with the little man. In the third stage, she makes a promise to the man, which she cannot break. This is the stage of Jupiter, the stage of morality and obligation. She has indebted herself to old Father Time and cannot get past his hold. In the fourth stage, her child is born. This is the stage of transition from the world of time to the world of the eternal. It is the age of hope and the heart, which are represented by the child. As Jesus said, "Whoever does not receive the kingdom of God as a little child will never enter it" (Luke 18:17, Mark 10:15).[41]

The next three stages are spent seeking names. Mercury, the god of the fourth level, is the messenger who wanders the upper realms is search of the truth. Platonists and Gnostics believe that through knowledge of the world of ideas—the really real world—the absolute truth can be reached. Ultimately, the miller's daughter is able to thwart the little devil by knowing and naming what he really is, that is, the shadow of the new moon. It is interesting that she never gives to him her name throughout the story, thus preventing him having further power over her. Finally, at the level of the sun, the light of the sun conquers the lord of darkness; the absolute is reached; and, as in most fairy tales, there is a happy ending.

Other Versions and Other Names

A Working Girl

Rumpelstiltskin had many other sobriquets in stories throughout Europe, including Titeliture, Doppelturk, Purzinigele, Batzibitzili, Panzimanzi, Whuppity Stoorie, Ricdin-Ricdon, and Tom Tit Tot.[42] The stories all involve a young woman expected to work miracles spinning, and they all deal with guessing the name of a devilish person. In the versions where she has to produce mountains of flax, she is usually a lazy and often gluttonous girl. In Italy she consumes seven pots of noodles, in England she downs seven dishes of pudding, and in Russia she finishes seven loaves of bread.[43] Here, again, we find the number seven, which tells the number of days the waxing moon must grow in the midnight sky to become the full moon. The girl literally waxes with the moon, thanks to her voracious appetite. Both her gluttony and her laziness are traits of the bear, which must consume ample amounts of food before its long sleep. Both in the tales of women who marry bears and in the tales of children kidnapped by bears, the humans become more bearlike the longer they remain with the bear.[44] In some variants of the "Rumpelstiltskin" story, the girl's mother or mother-in-law acts like a bear toward her.[45]

In the tales where the young woman must spin gold, she is often described not as lazy but instead as beautiful. This shows the deference afforded those who spin golden and other precious threads, for such women were ultimately of the ruling class. Jack Zipes sees folk tales such as "Rumpelstiltskin," and "Snow White" as narratives that begin with seemingly hopeless situations and that sympathize with the exploited heroines. For the agrarian lower classes, the only hope of escape was through an idealized utopian image. In folk tales this was achieved by means of enchantment.[46]

The majority of German folk still labored under the injustices of medieval feudalism even in the early nineteenth century. People elsewhere in the world have also labored endlessly, and they have seen in the moon that same unceasing cycle of work. A good example is the story of the Iroquois woman who can be seen in the moon with her hominy pot. She is continuously weaving a forehead strap, but once a month she sets it down in order to stir her pot. A cat that is always by her side unravels the strap, and the woman must start all over again.[47]

Variants of the Grimms' "Rumpelstiltskin"

As to the story's immediate source, the Brothers Grimm said that they derived the story from four complementary versions that they collected in Hesse. As to the name Rumpelstiltskin, it can be found as early as 1575–90 in a list of games and pastimes in Johann Fischart's adaptation of Book I of Rabelais' *Gargantua*, entitled *Geschichtklitterung*. The 363rd amusement is "Rumpele stilt oder der Poppart."[48]

In the Grimms' 1810 manuscript, prior to their first edition, the young woman in the story is sad and can only spin flax into gold, which she does for three days, sitting on her roof. A tiny man appears and offers to help her out. He says that a prince will marry her but that she must turn over her first child. The young woman agrees. At the end of the story her maid comes across the tiny man in the woods riding a cooking ladle around a fire. She discovers that his name is Rumpenstunzchen. When the princess later tells him, he says, "The devil must have told you," and out the window he flies on the cooking ladle.[49] The cooking ladle is the crescent moon.

The Spoon of the Moon

In the story "The Man Who Married the Moon," the dipper of pearl is also the crescent moon. The pearl is the gem of the moon, and only the moon's cornmeal would stick to its surface. In stories of Coyote's-son by the Coeur d'Alene Native Americans, Spider Woman helps him get to earth by dropping him in a box. Sometimes, however, he is dropped in a spoon.[50] Coyote's-son, like Coyote and other canines, is a lunar character. The box is the dark of the new moon and the dark of the eclipse. The spoon is the waning crescent moon just before the new moon.

At the royal graves of Alaca Hoyuk in central Turkey, which date to about 2500 B.C., one prominent lady has near her hands a large silver spoon and a silver spindle with a golden head.[51] (*Spoon* and *spindle* are etymologically related. A spoon is a "stretched out" piece of wood.)[52] Besides standing for domestic activities related to food and clothing, the spoon represents the crescent moon and the spindle the full moon.

Rumpelstiltskin's riding on a spoon fits with Pope John XII's accusation, in the tenth century, that witches rode with Diana, the moon.[53] It reveals that Rumpelstiltskin is a devilish person, and like the Devil, who wears crescent horns, his home is in the moon.

In a Slav folktale about a lazy girl who is forced to spin hemp into gold, it turns out that the little man with a red cap who helps her is named "Kinkach Martinko." She not only has to guess his name, which she does, but she has to guess what his boots are made of as well. She discovers that they are made of "doggies' skin."[54] This is another clue to the little man's lunar origins. The dog, wolf, and other canines are all animals of the moon, as we shall see in "Little Red Riding Hood."

The master spinner of fate, the dark of the moon, who attempted to steal the necklace, ring, and crown of the sun, has been foiled by the knowledge of who he is. He is the waning and new moon, whereas our heroine is the waxing and full moon. She waxes during her pregnancy and brings new life into the world. Rumpelstiltskin is the nothingness of death and darkness that fades in the light of the creation of new being.

Chapter 6

Goosey, Goosey Gander:
The Sacred Foot I

Goosey, goosey gander,
　Whither shall I wander?
Upstairs and downstairs
　And in my lady's chamber.
There I met an old man
　Who would not say his prayers.
I took him by the left leg
　And threw him down the stairs.[1]

The Moon Is a Goose

This familiar rhyme has many intimations of the moon. Like birds in general, the goose is closely allied with the moon. Anyone who has seen a V-shaped formation of geese flying across the face of the full moon and heard their calls on a clear night can understand how they became associated with the moon. Even in the seventeenth century birds were believed to fly to the moon when they migrated, and geese are the most ubiquitous of migrants. Even the plump white bodies of domesticated geese recall the moon's fullness. Because of their snakelike necks and because of their migration, geese became connected with regeneration.[2] As early as the Ice Age period in Europe, geese were painted on cave walls and engraved on bone objects

Goosey, Goosey Gander

marked with *V*'s or chevrons. The *V*'s or chevrons were female sexual symbols and signs of the bird goddess.[3]

The Sun Is a Goose

But the annual journey of geese has also linked them very closely with the sun and its annual sojourn to the winter solstice and back. In Egypt, Amon-Re, the sun god, was said to have taken the form of a goose and flown over the waters, his honking being the first sounds ever made. The sun's disk was sometimes called the "Goose Egg."[4] In northern Asia, shamanism related the goose to the sun.[5] In North Africa a goose is still sacrificed at the winter solstice because of the goose's connection with the sun.[6]

The eating of the goose is related to the sun and to the winter solstice and fall equinox. In ancient Britain the eating of goose flesh was forbidden, and geese were raised as pets.[7] In medieval Europe killing a goose was not allowed near the winter solstice. But this tradition reversed itself. By the time of Charles Dickens's *A Christmas Carol*, the goose is the center of the Christmas meal.[8] In England, eating a goose at Michaelmas (September 29) also became a tradition that is still practiced today.[9] Just as the goose travels south for the winter (in the Northern Hemisphere), so the honoring of the goose at midwinter is in hope of its return with the sun in the spring. The Feast of Saint Michael the Archangel celebrates the fall of Lucifer from heaven into the underworld. It occurs near the fall equinox, when other winged creatures, including geese, also leave this world. In Prussia, another fall equinox belief was that a woman's spinning on Saint Matthew's Day (September 27) would be bad for the geese.[10]

The Uralic peoples of northern Asia believe that the Land of the Birds, beyond the horizon, is the land of the dead. They say that birds die there but come back to life each spring and fly back to their summer home.[11] In the Altai Mountains of central Asia, a shaman mounts a goose after the sacrifice of a horse and pursues the spirit of the horse. A shaman also uses a goose to return from the underworld after visiting the King of the Dead.[12] Geese were often the familiars of witches in medieval Europe, and witches rode geese to their sabbat.[13]

Who Is Mother Goose?

Sometimes Mother Goose is pictured as a goose wearing the traditional outfit of the witch/midwife: black cloak, pointed hat, and magic wand.[14] She is also sometimes shown as an old woman busily spinning while she tells her tales to a group of children. Her name was made synonymous with nursery rhymes by John Newbery, who published *Mother Goose's Melody; or, Sonnets for the Cradle* in the 1760s in England.[15] Charles Perrault had already connected Mother Goose with children's literature in 1697, when he published a book of fairy tales and described them as "stories of my Mother Goose."[16] Prior to that, there was a reference to Mother Goose in a line in Loret's *La Muse Historique*, published in 1650, which says, "like a Mother Goose story."[17]

An even older connection of a goose with children's stories is "Goose-footed Bertha" or "Queen Goose-foot," who was the wife of Pepin and the mother of Charlemagne and who died in 783. She is represented as spinning, with lots of children sitting nearby and listening to her tales. French tales were often said to have been told "at the time when good Queen Bertha spun."[18] In Langue d'Oc, the medieval language of southern France, *bertel* means "distaff."[19]

Other Goose Mothers

In Germany, Berchta or Bertha or Perchta is an unkempt, stringy-haired old woman with beady eyes, a long hooked nose, and one foot large and flat (like a goose's foot) from using the treadle on the spinning wheel. Although she does not care for herself, she demands that others clean both themselves and their household, especially between Christmas and her special night, Twelfth Night or Epiphany. The stable threshold must have fresh straw, and there must be no flax or wool on the distaff. If she is offended, she will send a plague on the cattle or do bodily harm; but she is gentle toward children who obey her and will steal into the nursery to rock the cradle of a lonely baby. She is sometimes seen with a trail of children following her like a flock of goslings. There are rituals, dances, and masquerades of good and evil spirits at Epiphany in her honor.[20]

In northern Germany, Holde, Hulda, or Holl fills a similar role. Both Berchta and Holde rule limbo, where the souls of unbaptized children go, and both are used by parents to threaten unruly children. They are both also patronesses of the hearth and spinning, and they both have at times been called the "White Lady." Throughout Europe the White Lady is either the messenger of death or the dispenser of death.[21] In their malevolent manifestation Holde and

Berchta lead wild rides of the ghosts of the unbaptized. When Holde's procession rides over a field, the grain harvest is doubled. Additionally, Holde can be reached by traveling down a well. Snow is said to be feathers that fly from her bed when she is making it.[22]

Holde's feathers are like the feathers of Tomam, the mother goddess of the Ostyaks of northwestern Siberia. In the spring she shakes feathers out of her sleeves, and they fall to the earth as geese.[23] In North America, among the Mandans and Minnatarees, the Old Woman who Never Dies lives in the south and causes the crops to grow. Each spring she sends her birds as messengers: the wild goose for the corn, the wild swan for the gourds, and the wild duck for the beans. A corn-medicine festival was held in the spring when they arrived and again in the fall when they departed. In the spring she was asked for a good crop, and in the fall the birds were sent back to her to ask for a mild winter and adequate game till spring.[24]

This goddess of last year's harvest is the same worldwide. She is gentle when she is propitiated, but she is cruel to those who offend her, sending pestilence and draught. Berchta and Holde were patronesses of weavers, and this symbolizes the underworld and lunar nature of the goddess of fertility and death.[25] The goose-mother aspect of these two figures can be understood better when we consider that geese were believed to contain the souls of the unbaptized.[26] Another name for the leader of the host of souls is Dame Gauden.[27] Under the name Fru Gode or Fru Gosen she has been mentioned as a possible predecessor of Mother Goose.[28] (The Old English for goose is *gos*.) The goose's connection with spinning derives from its association with fate and the souls of the dead. Through spinning the goose becomes related to the telling of tales, especially fairy tales, since the word *fairy* originally meant "fate."

Inanna, the Sumerian mother goddess, visits the underworld and returns with a band of specters, with whom she wanders the earth. (See Chapter 13, "There Was a Man Lived in the Moon.") Like Berchta and Holde, Inanna is both kind and cruel, being the goddess of both love and war. Today we see the kindlier aspects of these goddesses. The goose signifies the hearth because it is associated with nurturing and because it is said to mate for life.[29] The Ice Age goddess of geese and birds survives in Mother Goose, and in many kitchens today the protector of the hearth and home is recalled in the use of the goose motif.

Upstairs Downstairs
The lofty flight of the wild gander is a model for the spiritual efforts
of the faithful Hindu to reach Brahman and, like the gander, reach a
balance between heaven and earth.[30] In the nursery rhyme we can
picture a gander walking up and down the stairs of a house. Similarly,
a gander flies high into the sky and then back down to earth again.
"In my lady's chamber" implies upstairs again, but the lady is not
there because the lady moon cannot be seen upstairs in the daytime
sky because of the effulgence of the sun. Instead there is a strange old
man who would not say his prayers. Actually, the old man comes
from another rhyme, which became amalgamated with the original
"Goosey, Goosey Gander." The earliest recording of the rhyme,
which appeared in 1784, goes like this:

> Goose-a, goose-a, gander,
> Where shall I wander?
> Up stairs, down stairs,
> In my lady's chamber;
> There you'll find a cup of sack
> And a race of ginger.

Here sack is a dry wine and a race of ginger is a root of ginger.[31]

The Man in the Moon
The other rhyme is about the daddy longlegs, harvestman, or crane-
fly:

> Old father Long-Legs
> Can't say his prayers:
> Take him by his left leg,
> And throw him down stairs.
> And when he's at the bottom,
> Before he long has lain,
> Take him by the right leg,
> And throw him up again.[32]

Children sang this chant, first printed in 1780, while cheerfully pulling the legs off these little creatures.

The reference to an old man who would not say his prayers calls up an old story about the Man in the Moon. According to the medieval myth, there is a man with a bundle of sticks on his back who was exiled to the moon and is beyond the reach of death. In the Christian version he is identified as the man brought before Moses for gathering sticks on the sabbath.[33] That man was given the typical punishment for his crime: he was stoned to death (Num. 15:32–36). This story has merged with a fifteenth-century tale about a man who stole his neighbor's thorns:

> *A man which stale sumtyme a birthan of thornis war sett*
> *in the moone there forto abide for euere.*[34]

These stories combined to make the man in the moon an old man who instead of saying his prayers on Sunday preferred to gather sticks; and for his punishment he was thrown up to the moon where he can still be seen carrying sticks along with, some say, his dog. The myth is also found in the classical story of Apuleius's journey into the underworld where he meets a lame man with a bundle of faggots on his back and an ass as lame as he.[35]

The Man in the Moon is an old man who, in the dark of the new moon, has stolen into heaven (the daytime sky) and battled with the sun in an attempt to eclipse it. In trying to steal fire or kidnap a woman or a child, he is wounded or else he becomes lame because of his fall from the upper world to the full moon in the lower world, where he becomes the spots on the moon. The moon is often depicted as old. In Australia, Aborigines describe the curved crescent of the last waning moon as a frail stooped old man.[36] Henry Wadsworth Longfellow's *Song of Hiawatha* tells of a grandmother in the moon.

> Once a warrior very angry
> Seized his grandmother, and threw her
> Up into the sky at midnight;
> Right against the moon he threw her;
> 'Tis her body that you see there.[37]

The Man in the Moon is a thief. In Luxembourg he is a turnip thief. One night as he was stealing a turnip, he was grabbed by the moon and pulled up to the sky. He grabbed a thorn bush, which can now be seen in the moon along with the man and his turnip.[38] In northern Holland and northern Germany a peasant who stole cabbages was taken up to the moon.[39] In Sylt, off the coast of Germany, he is a thief who stole sheep, enticing them with cabbages.[40]

The Moon's Foot

The most critical aspect of the Man in the Moon is that he is lame. Lameness or the lack of a hand or foot or eye is the sign of a person or god that represents the moon. Goose-footed Berchta is an example of this. Mani, the Scandinavian moon god, was lame.[41] Carl Hentze shows that figures with one arm and one leg symbolize the rain, lightning, and the moon, all at the same time. For example, among the Samoyeds of northern Asia, storm makers have only one hand, one foot, and one eye, and lightning coming from their mouths.[42]

In China, K'ouei, who was linked to thunder and the moon, had only one leg. Another K'ouei, who was a monster, took the form of an ox with one foot and no horns. Another figure connected to thunder and the moon was Yu. He was a man disguised as a bear, which could only use one leg and had to hop around. In Australia, Daramulan, who also was related to thunder and the moon, was one-legged. The Dyaks of Borneo told of a moon man who was connected with lightning and rain and who only had one eye, one arm, and one leg.[43]

In Mexico, the Mayan god of lightning and agriculture had a serpent in place of his missing foot.[44] Also in ancient Mexico, the plumed serpent, which was related to the moon, was sometimes provided with a single paw. Among the Miwok of the Sierra Nevada, a spirit associated with the moon also has a single paw.[45] In Peru, the thunder god becomes lame after combating the underworld fire god.[46] Throughout the world the moon's changes are associated with water, the tides, and rain, but why is the moon associated with a missing foot?

The Left Foot

The old man is taken by the left leg. The Latin word for left is *sinister*. In the Northern Hemisphere, as the phases of the moon move monthly from right to left across the southern sky at night, the waning moon is to the left of the waxing moon. (See Figure 7, p. 32.) Thus left has taken on a negative connotation.[47] The left leg could also refer to the last narrow crescent before the new moon. If the new moon is facing toward us, then the last crescent is on its left side. The root of the prejudice against left-handedness may be that the majority of people are right-handed, but it is fair to say that the moon can be partially to blame.

The last crescent could be a shoe—as we will see in "Cinderella"—a leg, an arm, or a cupped hand, as for holding water. As to how the moon relates to a missing eye, we will learn about that in "Three Blind Mice." We still have a lot to learn about the foot and the hand and how they relate to the moon. In the process we will unravel an Ice Age mystery that has been frozen in time.

Bonfire of the Vanities

The Man in the Moon had a broken limb, but he also was gathering broken limbs from trees. Another meaning of *limb* is the outer edge of the visible disk of a celestial body such as the sun or the moon. Therefore, the lighted limb of the disappearing crescent just before the new moon is also the limb of the Man in the Moon. The word *limb* comes from the Indo-European root *lei-* meaning "to bend, be movable." The sense of an outer edge comes from the bending line of a boundary. Words related to *limb* include *limp, limit, sleep, subliminal,* and *limbo.* The lameness of the Man in the Moon is explained by his being thrown down the stairs, that is, his declining farther each night out of the daytime sky and into the night sky. Each day is another step of the stairs, until he lands in the underworld of the full moon. He had a limp limb after his fall.

If, instead of falling down stairs, the Man in the Moon fell from the new moon through the branches of the tree of heaven, then the old man would have broken the branches as he fell and now carries them on his back in the full moon. With his branches he fuels the bonfire's red flames at the eclipse of the full moon. Sometimes the Man in the Moon was said to have carried a thorn bush or brambles instead of sticks. In northwestern Germany, people used to say that a man and woman stood in the moon—the man because he strewed brambles in the path of churchgoers to prevent them from getting to church on Sunday and the woman because she churned butter on Sunday.[48]

The word *bramble* is etymologically close to *broom.* A broom is a bundle of firm twigs bound together on a handle, just as the man's bundle of sticks is bound together. Like the burning bush of Moses and the brambles containing the ram in the story of Abraham and

Isaac, the brambles of the Man in the Moon and the witch's broom symbolize the interlacing branches of the path of the moon. The thick mat of twigs or fibers can be seen as the dark spots on the moon. After the bundle is complete and the moon has finished its course, the branches will be consumed in the fire of the moon so that the moon can begin anew.

When a broom is held upside down it looks somewhat like a distaff with its tangle of fibers at the top. Both spinning and sweeping are activities related to the winter solstice. In England, spinning was not allowed on "Saint Distaff's" Day, which was shortly after Twelfth Night, and sweeping was a part of New Year festivities around the world.

Both Mother Goose and the Man in the Moon are the old year and the old harvest, as well as the waning moon. They are reminders of the punishment that comes from not doing one's duty, but they are also both the source of renewal and the regeneration of life.

Chapter 7

Diddle, Diddle, Dumpling:
The Sacred Foot II

Diddle, diddle, dumpling, my son John,
Went to bed with his trousers on;
One shoe off, and one shoe on,
Diddle, diddle, dumpling, my son John.

Hot Dumplings
"Diddle, diddle, dumpling!" was the cry of the hot dumpling ven-
dors. The rhyme first appeared in print in this version in *The Newest
Christmas Box* around 1797.[1] It is a perennial favorite because it so
perfectly captures the image of the tired tyke falling into bed ex-
hausted after a day of expending boundless energies. Can this brief
piece fit a description of the moon's activities? We will see.

Although it doesn't say, it is possible that John is sleepy after eating a dumpling. A dumpling is a dessert made by wrapping fruit in
biscuit dough and baking it. The white round pastry resembles the
full moon, just as the French *croissant* resembles the crescent moon.
Like fruit dumplings, Chinese mooncakes are pastries filled with fruit
and nuts.[2] Just as the dumpling is eaten bite by bite, growing smaller
and smaller until it is gone, so, too, the moon wanes each day from
its wholeness in the full moon to its disappearance in the new. (For
more about the moon as food, see Chapter 13, "There Was a Man
Lived in the Moon.")

Diddle, Diddle, Dumpling

My Son John
The name John implies Everyman in English. Although today in the United States it no longer is among the top ten names for male children, at one time it was the most common name for boys. Coming from Hebrew, it means, "The Lord is gracious."[3] John the Baptist was one of the well-known saints after whom boys were named. He was very closely tied with the sun and the moon. His birthday and feast day (June 24) is near the summer solstice opposite the birthday of Jesus (December 25), which is near the winter solstice. John's conception is celebrated near the fall equinox on September 25, which is opposite the celebration of Christ's conception near the spring equinox at the Annunciation on March 25.

At Advent in December, Christians remember John the Baptist going into the desert to proclaim the coming of Christ. John wore animal skins and long hair and he ate locusts. He represents the Old Testament and the prophets. He also represents the old year, as his attire attests. Adam before the Fall is depicted as clean-shaven, while after the Fall he is shown in animal skins with a beard and long hair.[4] John is the Old Adam, whereas Jesus is the New Adam. Christians also celebrate the baptism of Jesus by John near the beginning of the New Year. As John is the old year, so Christ is the new. John said of Jesus: "He must increase, but I must decrease" (John 3:30).[5] This is an excellent description of the relationship between the sun and the full moon at the winter solstice. At that time the full moon is out the longest and makes the highest arc in the night sky. The sun on the other hand is out the shortest and makes the lowest arc in the day sky. Each month after December the sun increases and the full moon decreases, until, at the summer solstice, the sun is at its highest point and the moon is at its lowest.

The New Moon and the Shoeless Foot
Just before the moon becomes dark, there is the thinnest crescent still left in the sky. This crescent is the uncovered foot of our tired boy. Wearing dark trousers and one dark shoe, John becomes the waning moon with his white foot sticking out. The image of the white crescent is striking. Another image of the feet as white crescents near the new moon is found in versions of the English and Welsh tale "The Buried Moon." It is a story about the Moon and how she came to earth to see what occurred in the bog during the dark of the moon.

At the end of the month she wraps herself in a dark cloak and covers her golden hair with a dark hood. "Before her, all was dark—all dark but the glimmer of the stars in the pools and the light that came from her own white feet, stealing out of her black cloak."[6]

Two other one-shoed characters who stand out in literature are Cinderella and Jason. Cinderella is dark and sooty in her place by the fire, but when the bright slipper is placed on her foot, she is recognized for who she is—the queen of heaven—the bright moon. (See Chapter 15, "The Grimms' Cinderella.")

Jason, famed in Greek legend as the leader of the Argonauts, is also recognized by his shoeless or, specifically, sandal-less foot. When Jason is young his father has him hidden away so that he will not be harmed by his wicked cousin Pelias, who has usurped the throne from Jason's father. An oracle has told Pelias that he will be killed by a relative and that he should beware of anyone shod with a single sandal. So into town strolls Jason, making a spectacle in the marketplace. His super-hero body is clad in a well-fitting garment, and around his shoulders is a leopard skin. He has not cut his long hair, which flows rippling down his back. As for his feet—of course—he wears but one sandal. When he confronts Pelias, the evil cousin is able to put him off by saying that if Jason brings back the Golden Fleece to Greece, then Pelias will relinquish the throne. Thus begins the famous voyage of the Argonauts.[7]

Lame Heroes and Villains

We assume that walking with one sandal would cause Jason to limp. Many heroes and villains in literature and myth had wounds that caused them to limp as well. In Greek myth both Zeus and Odysseus had wounds in their thighs, and, similarly, in medieval romance the Fisher King who lived in the Grail Castle had a wounded thigh, as did Tristan, the lover of Iseult.[8] In the Bible, Jacob was crippled when he wrestled with an angel; and, in Egypt, Horus, the son of Isis and Osiris was born crippled.[9]

The Greek Prometheus was made lame as punishment for stealing fire from the gods.[10] Other thieves of fire were also lame. In Benin, the Fon god Arui, who brought fire to humans, is a tiny man with one arm, one leg, and one eye. The Ekoi in southern Nigeria call the stealer of fire the "Boy-on-sticks" because he was made lame as punishment for his crime.[11]

There are many underworld figures who are lame. Hephaestus, the smith of the Greek gods became lame when he fell from heaven. The Amazons, Greek women warriors, crippled the men who were their smiths so they would not escape. Other lame smiths include the German Wayland and the Devil, who, like Hephaestus, was injured falling from heaven.[12]

The Sacred Paw

Two famous heroes who were killed by being wounded in their only vulnerable spot—their heels—were the Greek Achilles and the Hindu god Krishna.[13] The Norse god Tyr sacrificed his arm in order to save the other gods.[14] More recent characters who were missing appendages include Captain Ahab, who lost his leg to the whale in *Moby Dick*, and Captain Hook, who lost his hand to the crocodile in *Peter Pan*. There is something very special about the hand and the foot that is also very ancient.

Black and red silhouettes of hands were painted on European cave walls throughout the period from 20,000 to 10,000 B.C.[15] This was a worldwide practice, appearing even in Australia during this same period.[16] The sacredness of footprints is also widely held. They can be seen on a shrine at Catal Huyuk in Turkey, dating about 6000 B.C. Handprints and footprints convey the sanctity of the place where they appear.[17]

The Mistassini Cree have a tale about a bear who found a boy and kept him as a son. He taught the boy to hunt and fish and gather berries, and the boy learned all the ways of the bear. Eventually the boy's father tracked the bear; and despite all the bear's use of magic, including thunderstorms, to distract him, he made straight for the bear's cave. The bear loved the boy, and, knowing the end was near, he gave the boy his foreleg and told him to wrap it and hang it in his tent over the place where he sat. The father killed the bear, and the boy went home and grew up to be the greatest of bear hunters. One woman, who was jealous because the other husbands could not kill bears, stole into the bear's son's tent and unwrapped the foreleg. When the bear's son returned, he discovered who had disturbed his tent, and he told her where her husband could find a bear. Afterward, he sat under the foreleg as usual, but it fell down, and they both disappeared underground. It was rumored that he became a bear.[18]

The bear's paw has been sacred from time immemorial. Today, among the Ket, an Ostyak tribe of Siberia, the bear's right forepaw is cut off ceremonially after the bear is killed and is tossed in the air as a form of divination. The paw is the last part of the bear to be eaten, and it is given to a privileged person for his protection.[19] In Iceland a boy would cut the paw off a bearskin to symbolize his transition to manhood.[20]

The hand, the foot, and the bear's paw, as well as the rabbit's foot, all carry a special message, a secret that we will discover. It is revealed in the story of another bear's son, "Jack and the Beanstalk."

The Bear's Son
There is a cycle of tales told around the world known as "The Bear's Son" story. A boy of superhuman strength is either the son of a bear and a human mother, or the son of a woman who was abducted by or married to a bear while she was pregnant by a human husband. In either case, the boy acquires bear characteristics. The mother and son usually return home, and the boy often avenges his mother by killing the bear. In Germany and Croatia, there is a version in which the child is stolen by a she-bear that suckles the child, thus giving it bear qualities. These include bear's teeth or ears or hair as well as bear's strength.[21]

In its European form, the young son acquires some miraculous weapon and a group of companions. They set out on an adventure and enter an empty house. The monstrous owner arrives and mistreats each of the companions. The Bear's Son wounds the monster and tracks it to the underworld, following a trail of blood. There he kills the monster and either saves a maiden or retrieves a treasure or both. Due to the fault of his companions, the Bear's Son is delayed in returning home and often returns just in time to prevent the marriage of a maiden to a treacherous companion. He then marries the maiden himself. The main features of this tale can be seen in the Grimms' fairy tale "The Gnome" (#91), as well as in *Beowulf*.[22] A similar pattern can be seen in Homer's *The Odyssey*.[23]

Jason Is the Bear's Son
Jason fits the image of the Bear's Son. He is the true inheritor of his kingdom who must be hidden away as a child and raised by foster parents just as the Bear's Son was raised by a bear. His leopard skin

and long hair belong to a hero who has learned the ways of the king of beasts, which is the bear in northern climes. His wearing of one sandal is symbolic of the lameness of the wounded beast. His entering into a quest that will take him into the perils of the underworld before allowing him to regain his rightful kingdom is another part of the archetypal hero's role.

In *The Quest of the Golden Fleece,* Jason and the Argonauts seek to capture the fleece, which hangs on an oak tree guarded by a dragon in a dark grove protected by the war god Ares (Mars) in the foreign land of Colchis across the Black Sea. After many adventures Jason and his companions reach Colchis, and with the help of Medea, daughter of the King of Colchis, the dragon is put to sleep so that Jason can obtain the Golden Fleece and return to Greece. Again with Medea's help, Jason arranges the death of Pelias, who has in the meantime brought about the death of Jason's mother and father.[24]

Just as the bear is the moon, so Jason is the son of the moon. In terms of the cycles of the moon, as soon as Jason is born, he is delivered into the care of foster parents, who live hidden away in the underworld of the night sky, where he resides in the full moon. As he grows older, he breaks away from his temporary home in the underworld and begins his journey back to his own kingdom in the day sky. Since birth, his journey daily circling the earth as the moon has created long ringlets of hair, which are never cut but which spiral longer and longer each day. As he approaches his kingdom he dons an animal skin to disguise his true identity, just as the moon gets darker as it approaches the sun.

However, his one sandal gives him away. His bare foot is the final crescent before the new moon, and the brightness of his foot reveals the moon's presence. He has returned to his kingdom to eclipse the old sun, Pelias, and to take his rightful place. But first he will have to complete a cycle of adventures with his comrades. Instead of killing a bear, Jason, through Medea, will put to sleep the dragon, a relative of the serpent, which hibernates like a bear. The story of Jason is also an allegory of the journey of the sun through the year, where Jason, disguised as the old year, is really the new sun, who will usurp the throne. These sojourns are harmonized in one tale.

"Diddle, Diddle, Dumpling," with the little boy sleeping as deeply as a hibernating bear, fits the image of the heroic moon, the heroic sun, and the Bear's Son. However, we should not lose sight of the fact that the hand and foot are symbols of the mother goddess. The majority of hand silhouettes painted on cave walls in Europe are women's hands.[25] Also, there are many heroines who portray the Bear's Daughter, including Snow White, and, as we shall see, Little Red Riding Hood and Cinderella.

Chapter 8

Jack Be Nimble:

The Sacred Fire I

Jack be nimble,
Jack be quick,
Jack jump over
The candle stick.[1]

Leaping the Flames

Although this rhyme was first published in 1815, candlestick jumping had already been a game and a method of fortune-telling in England for centuries. For instance, in Wendover in Buckinghamshire, the lacemakers used to perform many traditions on Saint Catherine's Day and concluded with "jumping the candlestick for luck."[2] A candle was lit and placed on the ground in a candlestick. If it could be jumped over without extinguishing the candle, then good luck would ensue for the coming year.

Saint Catherine's Day, November 25, was just before the beginning of Advent and the new liturgical year in the Christian calendar. Leaping over bonfires also took place at important turning points in the seasonal calendar of the Indo-European and North African world. In India, at the spring festival of Holi, jumping over bonfires and putting ashes from the fire on one's forehead the next morning is part of the exuberant celebration that includes the telling of lewd jokes and the throwing of colored water and colored powder.[3]

Jack Be Nimble

In *The Golden Bough*, Sir James Frazer catalogues many of these festival fires. The first Sunday in Lent was the prevalent time in Belgium, northern France, and Germany. A pole called a "witch" or a straw man was set in the middle of the bonfire, and when the fire had died down young people leapt over the embers to ensure good crops and happy marriages for the coming year. In eastern France it was known as the Sunday of the "Firebrands." After the Angelus the young folk would rush out shouting, "To the fire, to the fire!" They would dance around the flames and whoever jumped over the glowing embers without singeing his or her clothes, it was said, would be married within the year.[4]

This tradition of leaping over the midsummer fire on Saint John's Eve (June 24) was widespread in Europe and Northern Africa. In southern Germany it was believed that whoever leapt over the fire would not suffer backache at harvest time and that the height that the young people leapt determined the height of the crops in the field. In Sweden, Austria, and Greece the custom was the same, and in Lower Austria and western Czechoslovakia the young had to leap *three times* across the flames to be free from aches and fever. In Russia young couples leapt over a bonfire carrying an effigy of the hero/god Kupalo. In Morocco and Algeria jumping over midsummer fires was common. In some places participants were expected to spring *seven times* over the fire.[5]

Sir James Frazer considered the possibility of the "solar theory"— that these customs mimic the activity of the sun and that leaping over the fire is a sun charm to strengthen the sun's influence through the year. However, he put more stock in the "purificatory theory"—that the smoke and ashes from the fires are believed to purge and cleanse everything that they touch.[6] By adding the moon into the equation, we will see that the bonfire portrays the behavior of the sun and the moon and that the smoke from the bonfire has a beneficial effect on participants.

The Hare's Fire

In certain instances the young were encouraged to leap three or seven times over the flames, both of which numbers are indicative of the moon. In one example Frazer provides, the people of the Greek Island of Lesbos lit three fires and jumped over them three times. Each person held a stone on his or her head and said, "I jump the hare's fire, my head is a stone!" In Calymnos in Greece, people sang and danced around the fires with stones on their heads. When the fire was low they threw the stones into it.[7]

There is a Greek myth about a stone. Cronus (Saturn) swallows five of his children because it was foretold that one of his offspring would overthrow him. Cronus's wife, Rhea, however, wraps a stone in a blanket and gives it to her husband to swallow instead of their sixth child, Zeus (Jupiter). With the help of his grandmother, Earth, Zeus ultimately causes Cronus to disgorge the other five children as well as the stone, which is placed at Delphi for pilgrims to view.[8] Swallowing is often used as a metaphor for an eclipse, while disgorging represents the return of the sun or moon. The moon looks like a round stone in the sky. The Aleuts believed that the moon threw rocks down on those who offended him.[9] Samoans said that thunder was stones crashing in the moon.[10] As the devourer of children, Cronus depicts the shadow of the earth swallowing up the moon. Similarly, the stone thrown into the midsummer fire also signifies the moon being engulfed in the red flames of the lunar eclipse.

In Lesbos, as throughout Europe, Hare was a common name for the grain spirit. The last sheaf to be cut was called the Hare.[11] "The hare's fire" also refers to the rabbit as one of the oldest and most ubiquitous symbols of the moon. There are many reasons why the hare or rabbit is associated with the moon, of which the most outstanding is that the gestation period for the rabbit is thirty days, the same length as the cycle of the moon (twenty-nine and one-half days). The rabbit's head and V-shaped ears depict the uterus and connote fertility.[12] Its reputation for abundant reproduction fits with the moon's monthly pregnancy during its waxing. Also, the rabbit's vaulting ability mimics the moon's capacity to bound over the day and night sky; and the rabbit's silence and ability to hide are the same as its heavenly relative. Furthermore, the rabbit, like the moon, is nocturnal; and, finally, since prehistory, throughout the world the rabbit has been seen in the markings of the full moon. (See Figure 1, p. 3.)

A Hare in the Moon
Like the moon, the hare or rabbit has a dual personality. On one hand, he is a trickster (as in Bugs Bunny) and a ne'er-do-well known

for his idleness and drunkenness, and on the other hand he is a hero and martyr who intervenes with the heavens on behalf of humans, teaching them all that they know.[13] In China he is seen standing under the cassia tree, pounding out his herbs with his mortar.[14] In India, the hares fool the elephants and prevent them from spoiling the lake of the moon high on the mountain.[15]

The Aztecs told of how the moon shone too brightly at one time, and how the gods struck the moon with a rabbit to dim its light. The markings of the rabbit can still be seen in the moon.[16] Joel Chandler Harris tells a story about the rabbit and the moon that originated in Africa. The moon wanted to assure humans that after they died they would come back to life again. The moon was tired and so the rabbit delivered the message instead. However, the rabbit got the message wrong and so now humans must die. The moon was upset and fought with the rabbit, thus causing the marks on the moon and the rabbit's split lip.[17] In North America, the Delaware and Iroquois sacrificed to the rabbit in the moon and gave the rabbit's name to their first ancestors.[18]

In European tradition, the relationship between the hare and the moon is less obvious. Today, we know the hare or rabbit as the Easter Bunny. He became associated with Easter because he was the consort of the Saxon Oestre and the German Ostara, goddess of spring and the dawn, for whom Easter was named.[19] In southwest Germany children were not allowed to make a shadow of the hare with their hands, and in Roman times, Britons were not allowed to eat the hare.[20] The moon can be seen in the superstition that a lucky rabbit's foot must be taken in the dark of the moon.[21] The hare is also the companion of Hecate, who is the Greek goddess of the new moon, and of Harek, the German equivalent of Hecate.[22]

The Theft of Fire

In the New World the rabbit is often associated with eclipses. The Maya described the solar eclipse as a rabbit eating the sun.[23] In the western Rocky Mountains, Native American lore tells of a three-legged rabbit that fights with the sun, scorching the rabbit's fur in the process.[24] Cottontail, an important figure in Great Basin Native American mythology, steals the sun for humans.[25] A Canadian myth tells of how Rabbit captures the moon for stealing from his traps. He finally unties him but is scorched in doing so.[26]

From North America comes a Chippewa tale entitled "The Theft of Fire." It is about Manabozho, the great helper of humans whose favorite disguise was that of a rabbit:

When Manabozho is still a young man, he asks his grandmother, Nakomis, about fire, since he has never seen it. She tells him that once all humans had fire, which gave people warmth and light, but that now only a crippled blind old man who lives with his two daughters across the frozen ice still has it and he will not share it.

When it becomes bitter cold and dark, Manabozho determines that he is going to steal fire from the old man. He sets out across the frozen lake; and, when he comes near the lodge, he turns himself and his rabbit-skin cloak into a rabbit, which he can do since he was a Manitou (miracle worker). He waits till a daughter comes out and then throws himself into a hole in the ice and pretends to drown. The girl takes him inside and dries him off. She shows him to her sister, who agrees to ask their father whether they can keep him. While the girls badger their father after he awakes, Manabozho rolls over into the embers and catches a spark in his fur. He races out the door and streaks across the ice. The old man is too slow to follow. By the time Manabozho nears home he is in pain from the fire that reaches from his back to his tail, but he keeps the flame alive until Nakomis can catch the spark in her tinder and start a fire. Then, he turns himself back to Manabozho with his now burnt rabbit-skin cloak.[27]

The Fire Is the Full Moon

Manabozho, like the Greek Prometheus and other fire-stealers, brought fire and other skills of civilization to humans. Unlike Prometheus and others, Manabozho does not steal fire from heaven but from here below. Prometheus is the new moon, which rises high in the daytime sky to steal a piece of the sun's fire in a partial eclipse. He takes it as a piece of kindling in the small crescent moon that appears after the new moon, and then he descends each day toward the night sky, the fire growing until at the bottom of his journey it is the blazing full moon. Manabozho, however, is the partial eclipse of the moon. He steals a piece of the full moon's fire flaring in the bottom of the underworld and takes it back up through the phases of the moon to the upper world, saving the world from darkness. His burnt and blackened fur coat is the blackness of the new moon at the top of the daytime sky. Like Prometheus, who is made lame, and like the three-legged rabbit that fights with the sun, Manabozho is injured in his encounter with the fire of the moon.

It is interesting that the word *Manitou* contains *mani* and *Manabozho* contains *mana*. Both *mani* and *mana* are Indo-European words for the moon. Manabozho is sometimes called "Nanabozho." As we will see in "Little Red Riding Hood," *Nana* is also a name for the moon. The syllables *ma* and *na* are both infantile imitative sounds that become linked in languages around the world to *mother, grandmother, aunt,* and *nurse*.[28] For example, the Inca word for "mother" is *mama*.[29] The word can also be transferred to the moon. On the northwest American coast, the Tsimshian tell the story "The Theft of Light." Raven the Giant becomes a little child in the house of the chief of the sky and cries, *"Hama!"* The chief is told that the child wants the *ma*, which is the box that contains daylight and which hangs in the corner of the house. When they give it to Raven for play, he runs away with it and brings it to this world.[30] The box containing light is comparable to the new moon during a solar eclipse, which is often compared to a box or a jar. Being archetypal images, the sounds *ma* and *na* naturally suggest mother and, by association, the moon.

The Sacrificial Fire
From India comes "A Hare in the Moon":

A hare, a monkey, a fox, and a coot (a water bird) all lived good lives. The god Sakkira decides to test them and takes the form of a Brahmin or priest and visits them begging for alms so he can eat. The monkey gives him mangoes, the coot gives him fish, and the fox gives him milk and rice. However, the hare apologizes to him saying that since the Brahmin cannot eat grass, he has nothing to give him. To test him further, Sakkira asks him to offer his own flesh to eat. The hare obliges, and Sakkira further asks the hare to climb a large rock while the fire is being kindled so that he can leap into the fire. Again the hare agrees, and, as he is leaping into the fire, the fire disappears. Sakkira takes him into his arms and traces his figure on the face of the moon, as a lasting reminder to everyone of the meaning of true generosity.[31]

Like Manabozho, the rabbit in the Hindu tale throws himself into the fire as a sacrifice for the benefit of a human. Just as the full moon is sometimes blackened during a total lunar eclipse, the rabbit too would have been blackened had he not been rescued. The custom of leaping three times or seven times over bonfires stands for the three days of the full moon and the seven days from the time the half moon is at the western horizon at midnight to the time the full moon is at the top of the night sky at midnight. Seven can also stand for the seven new or full moons between the summer solstice and the winter solstice. The bonfires themselves are the full moons that burn brightly in the night sky giving hope in the darkness. Sometimes seven bonfires were lit, attesting to the seven full moons.

The word *bonfire* originally meant "bone fire," implying a fire hot enough to burn bones, such as a funeral pyre. As Sir James Frazer points out in detail in *The Golden Bough*, the straw men and other effigies that were placed in the bonfires were replacements for what were originally human sacrifices. Primitive societies took their metaphors very seriously. Often people willingly sacrificed themselves in order to ensure that the fire of the full moon would be fed and that the fertility of the fields would be renewed. At the hare fires of the Greek isles, the dancers identified themselves with the stones that they then threw into the fire to take their places as victims.

The Flaming Red Portal

The sacrificial bonfire does not represent just any full moon, but, rather, the shadowy smoke, the red flames, and the black ashes specifically stand for a total eclipse of the full moon. In Babylonia, a large fire was lit during the eclipse of the moon.[32] At the lunar eclipse, the red flames are the red portals that souls pass through, both into and out of this world. Jumping over the smoky embers ensures fertility because it represents entering the shadowy path of the shadow of the earth, down which new life travels into this world, and up which sacrificial victims are being wafted, to satisfy the hunger of the dark forces of nature.

The smoke represents the path through which souls leave the world. In the early Hindu teaching of the Upanishads, there were two roads that souls traveled from this world—the road of flame, which leads to the sun and the gods, and the road of smoke, which leads to the moon, to the ancestors, and to reincarnation.[33] People of the Tonga Islands believed that during an eclipse a thick cloud passes over the sun or the moon.[34]

In Mexico, hunchbacks and dwarfs were sacrificed during eclipses.[35] The story "The Princess of the Full Moon," from the African Mossi of Burkina Faso, describes how a monster tried to eclipse the full moon in a sacrificial bonfire. The Princess of the Full Moon ignores a hunchback, who is in love with her, and marries a perfect prince. The couple travels for fourteen days back to his kingdom. Each day he discards either a part of his retinue or an article of clothing, until, on the fourteenth day he reveals himself as a hairy monster living in a mountain cave. He tells her that after fourteen days he will roast her over a fire and feed her to his giant fish that lives in a lake under the mountain. In the end, with much effort the hunchback destroys the monster and marries the princess.[36]

The hunchback is the thin, stooped crescent of the waning or waxing moon. The hairy monster is the Lord of Darkness, both of the new moon, which occurs fourteen days after leaving the Palace of the Full Moon, and the shadow of the eclipses. His home is the shadow of the solar eclipse in the mountain of the moon's path across the daytime sky. The roasting of the Princess of the Full Moon fourteen days later is the full moon being engulfed by the red flames of the total eclipse and being consumed by a fish is the darkness of the eclipse. This is a story about a lunar eclipse that almost occurs, just as is the story about the hare and the Brahmin. In that story, the rabbit is the moon about to be consumed.

Jack the Rabbit

Sacred fires and candles are lit at times when the normal measure of time has come to a stop—times such as midsummer and midwinter, New Year's, and eclipses of the sun and the moon. The Chinese used to light red candles at the lunar eclipse.[37] At midsummer in Poland and Hungary, all fires in the village were extinguished, and the new fire was kindled by rotating a wheel to create friction.[38] Today, in the Roman Catholic rite, the new fire is lit at the Easter Vigil and is used to light the Easter candle. Candles are an important part of Christmas and Hanukkah celebrations, as well as Candlemas on February 2.

So we have traveled from jumping candlesticks to leaping into sacrificial fires and back to candles again. People leapt over fires in order to reassure their community that there would be sunlight and food for the coming year. Jack, like the rabbit, brings fire to humans, ensuring the continuation of civilization and the renewal of life.

Chapter 9

There Was a Man
and He Had Nought:
The Sacred Fire II

There was a man and he had nought,
  And robbers came to rob him;
He crept up to the chimney top,
  And then they thought they had him.

But he got down on the other side,
  And then they could not find him;
He ran fourteen miles in fifteen days,
  And never looked behind him.[1]

The Man in the Moon

Here is an early nursery rhyme in which there are many clues that the travels of the moon are being described.

The man who has nothing is the moon, which, when it is new, has no light and therefore no silver or gold. The chimney top is the top of the house. The new moon is at the top of the sky at midday. By the time the robbers get to him the new moon is already past, and the man has hidden on the other side of the chimney. The fourteen miles in fifteen days is the clincher. There are fourteen days (a fortnight) between the new moon and the full moon, and fifteen days is half of the traditional thirty-day month of the Egyptians and Babylonians. The full moon is opposite the new moon in the circle that the moon travels through the month, so therefore the full moon is as far from the top of the house as it can get.

Saved by the Eclipse

By adding eclipses to the equation, the rhyme becomes even more interesting. Solar eclipses can happen only during the new moon. The chimney is a metaphor for the shadows of the solar and lunar eclipses. (See Figure 7, p. 32.) The black soot and smoke in the chimney equates to the black shaft of the eclipse's shade. The robbers are the three days of the dark of the moon. Just as they dress in black to avoid being seen, so too the new moon is dressed in black.

Only while the moon passes across the face of the sun is it visible in the midday sky. Otherwise, the sun is too bright for anything else to be seen. In the same way, the robbers cannot see the man until he is at the chimney top, that is, during the eclipse, and they cannot find him when he gets down the other side of the chimney. So the man flees his home and goes into the foreign land of the night sky. Fifteen days later, if there is a lunar eclipse, he can be hidden by the umbra of the earth as it passes between the sun and the moon.

The Woman in the Moon

This rhyme first appeared in print in 1805 in *Songs of the Nursery*. In 1810 a related verse was published in *Gammer Gurton's Garland*:

> There was an old woman had nothing,
> And there came thieves to rob her;
> When she cried out she made no noise,
> But all the whole country heard her.[2]

Although this piece seems to be nonsense, it could tell of the moon's exploits. She begins as the new moon. Her crying out could be the appearance of the first crescent, which looks like an open mouth. And even though she was silent, the entire country would be able to see her shouting.

In the 1901 edition of *Folklore* another version of this rhyme was recorded from the oral tradition:

There Was a Man and He Had Nought

There was an old woman lived under a hill,
   And three thieves came to rob her,
      She cried out,
      And made a great rout,
   For the thieves had a mind to stab her.

She ran fourteen miles in fifteen days
   And never looked behind her.
      She got in a wood,
      And there she stood,
   And the thieves could never find her.[3]

Again we see here the moon. This time she lives under a hill. The moon in its monthly path across the midday sky creates an arc or a hill. The three robbers are the three dark days of the new moon. Afraid of being stabbed, she gives the alarm. Stabbing relates to the shadow of the solar eclipse, which occurs at the new moon. The woman avoids this fate by fleeing to the underworld of the night sky, where the full moon dominates a fortnight later. The darkness of the deep wood represents the night sky. The three thieves of the new moon cannot reach her there because the new moon has dominion only in the day sky.

Chim Chim Cher-ee

The smoky odor of those who jump over festival bonfires makes them pleasing to the gods and brings good fortune for the coming year. How much more pleasing must be those who spend their lives in soot and smoke—the chimney sweeps, whose reputation for bringing good luck is recalled in the song "Chim Chim Cher-ee" in Walt Disney's *Mary Poppins*.

Before the invention of chimneys, either fires were made outside or smoke holes were used for indoor fires. From time immemorial, smoke and smoke holes, like the shadows of the eclipses, have been the passageways to the sun and the moon. The Toba of Argentina tell how Thunder falls out of the sky during a storm. He is stuck to a tree and unable to return to heaven. He begs a man to build a fire with much dry wood and green leaves so that it will make a lot of smoke. Then Thunder is carried up to heaven on the thick smoke. In payment he sends rain and makes sure the man never wants for anything.[4] In the Americas, thunder and rain are closely associated with the moon.

In northwest Canada, the Loucheux tribe relates the story "The Boy in the Moon." A boy with magical powers hunts much game for his people, but when they refuse to give the best pieces to his father, he decides to go to the moon. He goes up through the smoke hole of his tent at night, but he catches his pant leg in the hole, and so he can still be seen in the moon with one pant leg missing.[5] This story fits with the idea of the Man in the Moon being lame and with various moon gods with missing limbs. It also fits with a lunar eclipse, which happens at night, and which provides a path, like the smoke through a smoke hole.

In *The Door in the Sky,* Rama P. Coomaraswamy compares the sun door or smoke hole at the top of a building with the passageway from this world to a higher world. In *The Hymns of the Rgveda,* it says, "like a builder hath Agni upheld his pillar of smoke, upheld the sky."[6] Agni is the Hindu god of fire. In Hindu tradition, the sun door can be either the Gate of Life or the Jaws of Death, depending on the heart and mind of the person making the sacrifice.[7] The eye of a dome is an opening that serves as both an entrance for light and an exit for smoke. In a Buddhist domed temple it serves as the hole for the mast that stands over the dome. The eye symbolizes the sun and the moon.[8]

Native North American stories describe entering a hole in the sky in order to capture the sun. The Slavey of British Columbia recount how seven animals found a hole in the sky and stole heat, which was kept in a bag in a bear hut.[9] The Snoqualmie in the Pacific Northwest tell how Blue Jay made a hole in the sky and Spider made a rope so that Fox could climb to the sky and steal the sun and fire from the moon. The Tsimshian of British Columbia relate how Giant put on his raven skin and flew through the hole in the sky and stole the box containing daylight from the chief of the sky.[10]

Smoke, the smoke hole, the sun door, and the hole in the sky are all paths to the sun and the moon, just as the chimney also becomes such a path. Santa Claus uses the path of the chimney to enter and leave a house. Another gift-giver is Befana, whose name derives from Epiphany. She is a frightening old woman, who visits Italian children's houses on Twelfth Night and leaves presents for the good children and coal for the bad. She is very much like Berchta and Holde in Germany. Befana eats food that is left for her and travels up and down the chimney with her broom.[11] Similarly, witches ride their broomsticks up and down chimneys rather than using doors or windows.[12]

The New Year's Broom Sweeps Clean

The coming of the New Year is a time for sweeping out the old and making way for the new. The Hmong of Southeast Asia sweep up all the dust, dirt, and soot from their homes at New Year's. They dump the debris by a tree that has a rope looped around it. They then jump in and out of the loop, and the evil spirits in the dust try to follow, but they soon give up the chase.[13] At the winter solstice, on the Dutch Wadden Islands, the Sunderums dress in costumes made of heather, dune grass, shells, and chicken feathers and attempt to frighten everyone. Some blow ten-foot-long *buffelhorns* and talk through them in scary voices. Others, called *baanvegers* or "trail-sweepers," both dance with the girls and frighten them. Finally all the women and children are chased back into their homes.[14]

It is appropriate that the trail-sweepers should wipe clean all the old trails, just as all the old paths of the sun and the moon are wiped clean from the sky when the new sun begins its rounds. In North America, at the New Year festival of the Munsee-Mahican Delaware, sweepers using turkey or eagle feathers sat at each door of the Big House, regularly sweeping away evil forces during the ceremonies.[15]

Spare the Rod . . .

Another winter solstice custom involves a bundle of twigs, but they are not used for sweeping. In nineteenth-century illustrations from Europe, Father Christmas is sometimes shown carrying a bundle of sticks. In the Netherlands in the twentieth century, Santa Claus's assistant, Black Pete, is depicted carrying a bundle of sticks, and bundles of switches are sometimes shown on Christmas wrapping paper.[16] This hearkens back to early German traditions about Saint Nicholas and his assistant, Knecht (Knight) Rupert.

In the seventeenth century, Knecht Rupert took the place of Saint Martin or Saint Nicholas as the companion of Christ and the giver of gifts. On Christmas Eve or Saint Nicholas Eve or Day (December 5–6), a man of the village would dress in high boots, white robe, blond wig, and a mask and would deliver presents that parents previously had given him. He would carry a bundle of sticks or whips, and if a parent said that a child had been bad, the child received no present and the father was given a stick and encouraged to use it on the child. The custom of gift giving on Saint Nicholas Day is very old and originated with Martinmas (November 11), when Saint Martin gave sweets to good children and whipped bad ones.[17]

This puts the candy cane in a new light. It is not only Saint Nicholas's bishop's crosier but also a punishing rod for caning a naughty child. The stripes on the candy cane, like the stripes on a barber's pole, are the red and white spiraling paths of the sun and the moon in their journey to the solstices. The bundle of sticks associates Santa Claus with another man who carried a bundle of sticks—the Man in the Moon.

Another winter solstice custom involving sticks is the "rods of life." In southern Germany and southeastern Europe, on or about Holy Innocents' Day (December 28), young people beat one another with green branches from certain trees. The boys beat the girls and vice versa to bring good health and fertility for the coming year. The fool's whip of the European Carnival and Santa's whip are descendants of the rods of life. Stick dances performed as combat dances, such as the English Morris dances, are also prevalent at the winter solstice. In Portugal stick dances are very popular at Epiphany and on Saint John's Day.[18]

The World Tree

Chimney sweeps had a tradition on May Day (May 1) of traveling in a small, outlandishly dressed band. A woman would attend them dressed in spangles, and one man, dressed as Jack in the Green, was concealed in a very tall frame of branches and flowers with a flag sticking out of the top.[19] The chimney sweep dressed in branches is like the hunter and Lord of Death, who is camouflaged in greenery in order to catch his prey. He is the dark new moon or the dark eclipsed moon, while the girl dressed in spangles is the bright full moon.

May Day and May Day Eve hold some clues to the significance of brooms and chimneys. Walpurgis Night (May Day Eve) in German folklore was the witches' annual sabbat, to which they traveled by way of a chimney and by means of a broomstick. Beltane, which begins on May Day Eve, is still celebrated in Ireland, Scotland, Wales, northern France, and the Isle of Man. It is thought by some to be the halfway point in the Celtic year. Cattle and humans both pass through the smoky embers of bonfires to ensure fertility for the coming year. In the Scottish highlands farmers carry pitchforks of kindled fire into the field crying, "Fire! Fire! Burn the witches!"[20] In Ireland the rowan (mountain ash) branch is placed over the hearth fire on May Day to preserve the fire from bewitchment.[21] It is also a concern that the first smoke from a chimney on May Day could be used by witches to bring bad luck, so rowan leaves are the first thing burned that day, because witches can do nothing with their smoke.[22]

Throughout Europe May Day is a time for erecting Maypoles and May bushes. These, along with the chimney sweeps' Jack in the Green, are representations of tree spirits.[23] Maypoles are painted with spiraling stripes representing the spiraling paths of the sun and the moon from winter to summer solstice. Many maypoles have bushes or branches at the top of them, and in Denekamp, the Netherlands, the Maypole has a bundle of sticks tied to the top of it like an upside-down broomstick, and every year it is burned. Up into the seventeenth century in the Baltic and eastern Siberian regions, trees hung with sacrificial slaughter were burned near the winter solstice.[24]

Trees and poles were an integral part of solstice festivals. Yule logs and Christmas trees mark European midwinter festivals. Burning the Bush at Brough is a contest between two crowds, each of which tries to gain possession of a holly bush with torches tied to it.[25] At the sun dance held at the summer solstice among the Great Plains nations, a pole was painted, and men volunteered to be suspended from the pole by ropes fastened to gashes in their skin.[26]

Solstices, Eclipses, and the World Tree
The months of the winter and summer solstices are of particular importance for the moon, because during each of those months the new and full moons inscribe their lowest and highest arcs in the sky for the year. Furthermore, these arcs follow in one month the same highest and lowest paths that it takes the sun a year to achieve.

Additionally, a line drawn between the new moon in the midday sky and the full moon in the midnight sky creates the same north-south axis (meridian) as drawing a line between the midday sun at the summer solstice and the midday sun at the winter solstice. This north-south line is known as the *axis mundi* or axis of the world. It is the World Tree.

The shadows of eclipses are also the World Tree, whether or not they follow a north-south line. The shadows cut through the center of the earth and provide a pillar to hold up our world.

But the sacred fire contained in the sun and the moon and the World Tree is also contained in every tree. How do we know this? Because, by using two sticks of wood as a fire drill, and by turning one stick the way that the sun and the moon turn around the earth, we create friction, which brings forth the sacred fire.

Not only was the fire sacred to the ancients, but so also were the wood, the smoke, and the ashes. An example of sacred smoke and flame is found in the Exodus of the Israelites from Egypt. "The Lord went in front of them in a pillar of cloud by day, to lead them along the way, and in a pillar of fire by night, to give them light, so that they might travel by day and by night" (Exod. 13:21).[27] Like the shadows of the eclipses, creating the dark smoke of the solar eclipses and the bright flame of the lunar eclipse, so God's pillars showed the way for his people.

The fire sticks, the broomstick, the Maypole, the barber's pole, the candy cane, the Christmas tree, the Yule log, the chimney, and the pillar of smoke are all the World Tree here on earth—a gift from the heavens, a reminder that the sacred is in this world waiting to be ignited. We do not have to live in the upper or the lower world in order to possess fire. It travels to us through the World Tree and is present in things around us.

Knock on Wood

The woman who lived under a hill got in a wood, and the thieves could not find her. The Latin word *materia* means both "timber" and "matter" and derives from the word for "mother" and for "moon." Myths from every inhabited continent tell us that fire was stolen from the gods or from a previous owner and was hidden in trees or in a particular tree and could be coaxed from the tree's wood by the use of friction. Maui, the hero god of the Maori, asked his grandmother, Mahuika, for fire. It sprang from her fingers and her toes and burned everything until rain put it out. However it still remained in the trees. The Tembe of Brazil say that an old man stole fire from the vultures and put it in the trees.[28] Fire, which the moon stole from the sun and brought to earth during the eclipse, can be found in timber and in other matter.

Odin in the Norse tradition hanged on a tree to gain the wisdom of the Runes, and, in the Christian tradition, Christ hanged on a wooden cross to save humankind. The column of the solar eclipse in the day sky and the lunar eclipse in the night sky together form Odin's tree and Christ's cross. Knocking on wood or touching wood is one of the most prolific of superstitions, found in all lands and cultures. Even among the educated, most people still hold onto this superstition when others are abandoned.[29] People do it when they find themselves bragging about their good health or good fortune. It is in recognition that fire, which is life and civilization and all good fortune, resides in the World Tree, which brings fire down from the heavens and up from the underworld.

A nonsense verse that appeared as early as 1714 in *The Academie of Compliments* still evokes some of these images of the moon:

> There was an Old Woman
> Liv'd under a Hill,
> And if she isn't gone,
> She lives there still.[30]

Chapter 10

Little Polly Flinders:

The Sacred Fire III

> Little Polly Flinders
> Sat among the cinders,
> Warming her pretty little toes;
> Her mother came and caught her,
> And whipped her little daughter
> For spoiling her nice new clothes.[1]

Ashes of Initiation

Polly Flinders was punished for getting too close to the fire; yet throughout the world ashes and cinders have stood for renewal and rebirth. Being daubed with ashes is one of the most common practices for the initiation of shamans worldwide, to show that they have died to their old selves and are born anew in their quest for higher powers.[2]

In Viking times young men were allowed as much as two or three years "among the ashes." Norwegians then lived in long communal houses with a paved fireplace down the middle. The beds were along the walls of the house and cinders were placed between the beds and the fire. In the two or three feet between the ashes and the fire, these young men would lie about, washing neither themselves nor what they ate. From this they obtained the name "cinder-biters." This stage of lethargy, an imitation of the hibernation of the bear, was a form of initiation, which allowed them a time to die to their childhood before taking on their new lives.[3]

Ashes of Regeneration

In Hindu tradition, Kama, the god of love, shot an arrow into Shiva, the great god of destruction and regeneration, in order to distract him from meditation and make him attend to his wife, Parvati, the world mother, so that the world would continue to exist. Annoyed, Shiva used his third eye to turn Kama into ashes. But he soon gave in to pleading from Kama's widow, Rati, goddess of affection and sensual delight, and resurrected Kama, but only as a mental image representing true love and not carnal desire.[4] Just as Kama was resurrected from ashes, so people of India anoint their heads with ashes the morning after the merry spring celebration of Holi in hopes of regeneration. They use ashes from the bonfires that they had danced around and leapt over the night before. (See Chapter 8, "Jack Be Nimble.")

Sir James Frazer in *The Golden Bough* describes many uses of ashes. In Grande Halleux in Belgium, children would punish those who did not contribute fuel to the Lenten bonfire by blackening their faces with the ashes of the extinguished fire. At Delmenhorst, in Oldenburg, Germany, at the Easter bonfire children tried to blacken one another and the clothes of the adults at the end of the fire. In Bavaria a straw Easter Man was burned on Easter Sunday, and on Easter Monday his ashes were spread on the fields as protection against hail.

In Ireland the ashes of the midsummer bonfire were thrown on the fields to fertilize them, and in Northern Africa they were rubbed on the hair and body for their curative benefits. The Berbers of the Rif Province of Northern Morocco made a paste of the ashes and rubbed it in men's hair to prevent baldness. In Bulgaria, in times of want, a need-fire was lit and sick animals were driven through it. When the fire had been consumed the young rushed at the ashes and cinders, blackening one another with them. Afterward they marched through the village with pride and went for days without washing themselves. The ashes were also strewn on the fields and used at home for medicinal purposes. They were applied externally to ailing parts of the body or mixed with water and taken internally.[5]

Little Polly Flinders

In Assam in northeast India, the winter solstice festival involves building huge bonfires and high templelike structures built out of field stubble, dried banana leaves, and green bamboo. They are set on fire and the embers and ashes are spread about the fields. Priests or elders take the ashes and mark the foreheads of the people.[6] In the New World, the Maya-speaking Quiche linked ashes with magic and regeneration. The twin heroes of the *Popol Vuh* turn themselves to ashes before being reborn. Today the Chorti, descendants of the Maya, make a cross of ashes in their fields to protect against evil spirits and mix ashes with seed corn to prevent rotting and diseases.[7]

Ashes of Victims
In Callander in Pershire, England, on May Eve or Beltane, pieces of oatmeal cake were placed in a hat. One of the pieces was blackened, and everyone was blindfolded before choosing a piece. Whoever chose the blackened piece became the "devoted" person who had to jump three times over the bonfire. Frazer believed that this and other bonfire traditions stemmed from earlier customs of burning sacrificial victims chosen by lot to ensure the regeneration of the crops.[8]

Ashes of Purification
Ashes were called the seed of Agni, the Hindu god of fire, and the blood of Shiva, the god of destruction and the dance. Whoever bathed in ashes could wash away all sins. At the Roman New Year in March there was a carnival celebration much like our New Year's. Afterward people would dress in sackcloth and ashes to atone for their sins. The carnival was held on Tuesday because it was Mars's Day and Mars's Month and Mars, the dying god, would take their sins with him into death. Therefore the ashes were applied on Wednesday, giving rise to the Roman Catholic tradition of Ash Wednesday.[9]

Ashes as the Moon
There are many stories explaining why the moon is dimmer than the sun and why it is dark part of the month and has dark spots even when it is full. Many of the explanations involve ashes, soot, or charcoal. The Tsimshian of British Columbia tell how Walking-About-Early, who was not as clever as his younger brother, the Sun, covered his face with charcoal and fat. He rose in the evening sky so that the

light of his brother came through the smoke hole of the tent where he was sleeping and shone on Walking-About-Early's face. His father, the chief in the sky, was pleased.[10]

Many of these stories involve incest. The Inuit or Eskimo tell how the sun was dancing by lamplight when a wind came and blew out the lamps and she was raped in the dark by a man. She thought it might happen again, so she put soot on her hands the next time she danced. It did happen, and she covered her attacker's back with soot. Later, when the lamps were lit, she discovered that the culprit was her brother. She ran away and was carried up to the sky by the wind. He followed but dropped his torch in the snow, putting out its flame and leaving only its embers. That is why the moon shines dimly as it chases after the sun.[11] Greenlanders tell a similar story, in which the sun covers the moon's face and hands with soot. This is the cause of the spots on the moon. The moon rejoices at the death of women and the sun at the death of men, therefore men stay indoors during a solar eclipse and women remain inside during a lunar eclipse.[12]

The Khassias of northeast India say that the moon attempts to make love to his mother-in-law each month, and she throws ashes in his face.[13] In Brazil, the Jamunda reverse the gender of the sun and the moon. The sun was visited in the night by his sister, the moon, but he betrayed her by passing his sooty hand over her face.[14] Around the world the new moon, the lunar eclipse, and even the full moon have been described as sooty.

Taking a Licking

The bear ceremony of the Saami of Swedish Lapland ends with the women of the village throwing warm ashes and coals at their husbands in order to purify them. This is a reminder of the mythical women who covered the moon with soot or ashes. The bear ceremony began with the ritual killing of the bear in its den. The bear was taken out of its place of hibernation and beaten with slender switches, perhaps to encourage revivification.[15] Bear ceremonies were concerned with the placation of the spirit of the bear. Its spirit was strengthened so that it would have a good report to give to its Lord when it returned to its home. The bear, which symbolized the moon, is a new moon at its death. Each night during the bear ceremony it grows like the waxing moon.

Polly Flinders received a licking from her mother. The word licking was first recorded as meaning a "whipping" in 1756. Before that time, to "lick" a child meant to "give shape" to a child. This image comes from Aristotle, who said that a bear sow licks her cubs in order to form and mature them. Shakespeare refers to chaos as "an unlicked bear whelp," and the French call an incorrigible child *ours mal leche*—"a badly licked bear."[16]

Polly Flinders was whipped for having her dress covered with ashes. As for Santa Claus, who at one time doled out whippings, "his clothes were all tarnished with ashes and soot."[17] The ashes are the blackness of the new moon and the winter solstice. The whipping is to impart the life of the young switches to the child and to encourage her to grow like the waxing moon and the strengthening sun. The welts on the child's body are the spiraling paths of the sun and the moon. This concept of corporal punishment has fortunately changed in the twentieth century but has not completely disappeared.

Out of the Ashes

Another connection the moon has with ashes is the story of the phoenix. This splendid Egyptian bird was able to burn itself up every five hundred years and then resurrect itself from its own ashes. The fabulous creature is supposedly the purple heron. Taoists called it the "cinnabar bird," which alludes to its redness.[18] Herodotus described the phoenix as "partly gold and partly red."[19] It can be pictured as the beautiful full moon, which turns red and then black as it is burned and then turns white again, as it is reborn. It could possibly be the solar eclipse as well, where the fiery sun is the red and gold bird and the new moon is the black ashes.

The ashes are the phoenix. Ashes symbolize the depths of despair. They also connote hope and tell us that heaven is found in everyday suffering, that this shore is the other shore.[20] We must mourn and we must die, but ashes are the residue out of which new worlds will be born, just as ashes are used for the consecration of a new cathedral.[21] As the Bible says (Ps. 118:22–23; Luke 20:17):

> The stone that the builders rejected
> has become the cornerstone.[22]

Chapter 11

Jack and the Beanstalk

Secret of the Solstices

Like the twining garland of the Christmas tree or the spiraling stripes painted on the Maypole, so the winding vine of Jack's beanstalk rises to the sky. It is a ladder, which Jack takes to claim his rightful place as the sun in the summer sky. This story contains a secret that helps Jack reach the summer solstice, a secret that has been passed on for more than ten thousand years.

First Month—New Moon
Jack and His Mother

At the beginning of the story Jack is not a very bright boy. The tale starts at the worst of times, in the darkness of the new moon. Here is Joseph Jacobs's rendition of Jack's adventure:[1]

> There was once upon a time a poor widow who had an only son named Jack, and a cow named Milky-white. And all they had to live on was the milk the cow gave every morning, which they carried to the market and sold. But one morning Milky-white gave no milk, and they didn't know what to do.
>
> "What shall we do, what shall we do?" said the widow, wringing her hands.
>
> "Cheer up, mother, I'll go and get work somewhere," said Jack.
>
> "We've tried that before, and nobody would take you," said his mother; "we must sell Milky-white and with the money start shop, or something."

First Month—Full Moon

The Moon Cow

"All right, mother," says Jack; "it's market-day today, and I'll soon sell Milky-white, and then we'll see what we can do."

The cow is the perfect metaphor for the moon. Its curved horns are the crescents before and after the new moon, while its full udder is the full moon. Its coloration from all black or brown to all white, with every variation in between, is the phases of the moon. Its four teats are the four quarters of the moon, and its milk is the Milky Way.

The Greek cow goddess was Europa, whose name meant "broad-faced," which is an epithet of the moon.[2] Mount Sinai is named after the moon god Sin.[3] The golden calf worshipped by the Israelites on Mount Sinai was a representation of the moon god.[4] In Sumer the moon was decorated with a pair of cow's horns, and the cow was pictured as a crescent moon. A bull ruled the starry night, and his fertile cow was the full moon.[5] In Egypt Hathor was a cow goddess who was fertility, wealth, and rebirth, as well as mother and wife of the sun and nurse of the King of Egypt. In Memphis and Thebes she was also "mistress of the mountains of the dead."[6]

In India the cow is still sacred. Just as Christ is called the "Good Shepherd," Krishna is called *Gopala* or "Cow-herd."[7] In Sanscrit, one of the meanings of *gaus* or cow is "moon."[8] The cow is guide to the souls of the dead, and in Vedic tradition a dying person clung to the tail of a cow. Then, when the person died, the corpse was placed on a cart and pulled by cows to the funeral pyre. A black cow chosen to be sacrificed followed the cart, sometimes tethered to the corpse's left foot. (See Chapter 6, "Goosey, Goosey Gander" and Chapter 7, "Diddle, Diddle, Dumpling" for more on the left foot.) The best pieces of the sacrifice were placed on the body, with the kidneys in the deceased person's hands. Then, wrapped in the cow's hide, all was cremated in the fire.[9] The cow's hide was a receptacle for the corpse, just as the moon was considered a receptacle for the soul.

Second Month—New Moon

Magic Beans for Magic Cow

It is evident that Jack's cow is no ordinary cow, for his mother and he are able to survive on nothing more than its milk. Now Jack is

Jack and the Beanstalk

about to make an extraordinary trade for his extraordinary cow, a trade that will appear to lead them back into starvation:

> *So he took the cow's halter in his hand, and off he started. He had n't gone far when he met a funny-looking old man, who said to him: "Good morning, Jack."*
>
> *"Good morning to you," said Jack, and wondered how he knew his name.*
>
> *"Well, Jack, and where are you off to?" said the man.*
>
> *"I'm going to market to sell our cow here."*
>
> *"Oh, you look the proper sort of chap to sell cows," said the man, "I wonder if you know how many beans make five."*
>
> *"Two in each hand and one in your mouth," says Jack, as sharp as a needle.*
>
> *"Right you are," says the man, "and here they are, the very beans themselves," he went on, pulling out of his pocket a number of strange-looking beans. "As you are so sharp," says he, "I don't mind doing a swop with you—your cow for these beans."*
>
> *"Go along," says Jack; "would n't you like it!"*
>
> *"Ah! you don't know what these beans are," said the man; "if you plant them over-night, by morning they grow right up to the sky."*
>
> *"Really?" said Jack; "you don't say so."*
>
> *"Yes, that is so, and if it does n't turn out to be true you can have your cow back."*
>
> *"Right," says Jack, and hands him over Milky-white's halter and pockets the beans.*

Jack thinks it strange that the man knew his name, but *Jack* was synonymous with *boy* or *man* and would have been the same as calling him "Sonny" or "Buddy." Jack was impressed with the beans he was given. Beans have had important significance all over the world, particularly at celebrations near the New Year. One of the European carnival figures was called the "King of the Bean." In England and France, a bean was placed in a plum cake on Twelfth Night, and whoever found the bean was the Twelfth Night king.[10] On February 3, the eve of the Japanese New Year, the head of the house puts on his finest clothes and goes through all the rooms scattering roasted beans and saying, "Out—demons! In—luck!" This practice is related to a widespread belief that beans contain the souls of the dead. On the last day of the old Roman festival of Lemuria, May 9–11, the head of the house walked through the rooms barefoot, throwing beans over his shoulder and saying nine times, "These I give and with these I redeem myself and my family." The ghosts picked up the beans and left till another year. Both Greeks and Romans had taboos about beans because of their association with the dead.[11]

The Hopi Bean Festival takes place in February. Beans are planted in the kivas, and all the males must stay up all night in preparation for the nine-day festival that includes clowns playing games and pranks. If anyone falls asleep while watching the beans grow, he is whipped for slowing the growth of the beans.[12] Like Carnival and the Bean Festival, we not only have beans in our story but also have a clown, played by Jack.

The bean's crescent shape reminds us of the moon. Like the moon, which grows through the month into the full moon in the night sky, the bean grows quickly when it falls into the ground and springs up to be one of the tallest growing plants. It is linked with fertility and and at one time was thrown at weddings to ensure the birth of sons.[13] A method for safeguarding a garden from the evil eye is to plant jack beans around it.[14]

The cow and the bean are linked to both death and fecundity. In some versions of "Jack and the Beanstalk" the man with the beans is a butcher.[15] Saint Martin was the patron of butchers; and his feast, Martinmas, was celebrated on November 11, the end of the liturgical year in early Christianity and the day before the beginning of Advent. On that day an ox or other domestic animal was killed and roasted, in remembrance of the saint, and its blood was sprinkled on the threshold. Martinmas was traditionally the day that cattle were slaughtered.[16] The name *Martin* means "of Mars," the bloody god of war.

When the man with the beans is a butcher, we know that Jack's cow is going to be cut up into pieces, just like the phases of the moon. The Egyptian god of resurrection, Osiris, was killed and cut up into fourteen pieces by his brother Set. Isis collected his body and, according to one version of the myth, placed it in a wooden cow.[17] The fourteen pieces are the fourteen phases of the moon as it descends to its death as the full moon in the night sky. The cow stands for both the horns of the crescent moon and for the death and resurrection of the full moon in the underworld. This is the lunar eclipse of the cow, which has already reached its fullness. It has stopped giving milk and is to be cut down by the red shadow of the eclipse. The cow is sacrificed so that Jack and his mother can have these little beans of death and rebirth. Just as the cow has reached its fullness, the full moon reaches its highest point in the sky and is out the longest in the night sky near the winter solstice. After that, it begins its descent toward summer.

The Five Beans and the Winter Solstice

As we have seen, these beans represent the hopes of new beginnings at the New Year as the old year is cut down. The beans are shaped like little crescents and represent the time of the new moon before the seeds grow to fruition.

But why are there specifically five beans? The number five is significant in other versions of the story as well. In a 1908 version Jack's mother instructs him to ask for five gold pieces for the cow.[18] Gold pieces are symbols for the sun or the moon. Jack is quick to solve a huckster's trick question, but there is a connection between the winter solstice and the number five, and that is that the sun stands still on the horizon for five days. The word *solstice* comes from Latin and means "sun standing still," which is what appears to happen for several days every June and December when the sun reaches its highest and lowest declination in the sky. Instead of moving northward or southward each day on the horizon it rises in approximately the same place for these few days.

To confirm the accuracy of five as the number of days the sun seems to stand still during a solstice, and the number used traditionally since ancient times, I checked *The Old Farmer's Almanac* for 1997. In June the declination of the sun over Boston was at its highest point at 23 degrees 25 minutes north for five days, from June 19 to 23.[19] The summer solstice occurred on June 21. Richard Heinberg states in *Celebrate the Solstice* that the sun appears to rise and set in the same place for about six days.[20] I believe, however, that five days is the average. To verify this for Boston, I checked the number of days that the winter sun was at a declination of 23 degrees 25 minutes south or less and that the summer sun was at a declination of 23 degrees 25 minutes north or greater for eleven years, beginning in 1988. The average was exactly five.[21] The next step was to investigate the significance of the number five in myth and the prevalence of five-day solstice celebrations.

Five in Myth

As we saw in Chapter 4, "Snow White, Persephone, and Eve" in the Tewan story "The Man Who Married the Moon," the hero prays five times over the white flower from the Moon's grave. The number five is found in other New World myths as well.

The Yunca of Peru believed that the creation-heroes, before they became human, were born in the shape of falcons from five eggs laid on top of a mountain. We know that among the native peoples of Peru, as elsewhere in the world, the falcon is a symbol of the sun.[22] The only mountain peak related to the sun would be the peak of the summer solstice, and the five eggs would be the five days when the sun stands still.

Both in Mayan and in Peruvian tradition, the maize shoot sprouts five days after it is planted and a rope draws up the soul of a dead person five days after death. The maize shoot is also called a "rope" or a "soul." The maize-god twins were brought back to life by a river five days after their ashes were thrown into it. The twins became the sun and the moon and the moon god retained the number five. Quetzalcoatl was reborn from the underworld on the fifth day, and the Mayan solar hieroglyph contains five circles. In Peru, previous ages were destroyed, one by a flood that lasted five days and another by an eclipse that darkened the world for five days. The Peruvian god Paryacaca, lord of waters and lightning, was born from five eggs in the shape of five kites. He made the rain fall from five different places and threw lightning from the five corners of the sky.[23] All of these stories of rebirth on the fifth day or from five eggs are metaphors for the sun, which begins moving again after five days.

Five-day Winter Solstice Celebrations

To verify that ancient peoples considered the solstice period as lasting for five days we can look to see whether there are any solstice celebrations that last for five days. There are, in fact, many such winter solstice festivals in both the Old and the New Worlds.

Plutarch explained why it was necessary to add five days at the end of the old Babylonian year of 360 days in order to make a solar year of 365 days. According to him these five intercalary days known as *epagomeneia* had a mythical origin. Helios, the sun, cursed Rhea, the mother goddess, for betraying him. He forbade her to bear her illegitimate child under the rule of either the sun or the moon. Hermes intervened by gambling with the moon. He won a seventy-second part of each day, which in 360 days adds up to five days. These five were ruled neither by the sun nor by the moon, and therefore Rhea could have her child between the old year and the new.[24]

In ancient Rome, the Carmentalia was celebrated on January 11 and 15, over a five-day period. It was a festival to the goddess Carmenta, whose name comes from *carmen*, meaning "song," "incantation," or "prediction." She is the goddess of prophecy and healing and the protector of women in childbirth. She was invoked near the New Year to watch over children born during the coming year.

In India, Diwali is a festival of lights that lasts for five days at the end of October or beginning of November.[25] In China, where it was believed that the five elements made up everything in the world, five is the most common number in religion and myth.[26] At the Chinese New Year festival in old Peking, the end of the fifth day of the festival was known as the "Breaking of the Five." On the sixth day women were allowed to go outdoors again and were allowed to cook rice. Also business was allowed to begin again.[27]

In the New World, the Aztec New Year began on February 2, after five days of lamentation. Among the Seneca, a white dog was strangled and hung up on the first day of the New Year ceremony, and on the fifth day the dog was cut down and burned on an altar, concluding the ceremony proper.[28] In the World Renewal Ceremony of the Munsee-Mahican Delaware, which took place in January, the ritual killing of a bear and the solemn feasting on bear meat took place during the first five days of the New Year festival.[29]

Predicting the Solstices

There is a practical reason why five is a convenient number for the standing-still days, particularly for nomadic tribes that could not use the same landmarks year round to measure the progress of the sun. If a person notes the phase of the moon the day after the five standing-still days, then, when that phase occurs again after six full lunar cycles, it will be the first standing-still day of the next solstice. This is accurate to within one-half day. For example, if there is a full moon on the day that the sun stops standing still after the winter solstice, then on the day of the seventh full moon, it will be the first standing-still day of the summer solstice. Six lunar cycles is exactly 177 days. Adding the five days of the solstice makes 182 days in the half year and 364 days in the whole year, which is only one shy of the actual number of days in the year. No wonder the ancients were fascinated with the number seven. It enabled them to keep accurate count of their calendar without using writing instruments. All that was needed was the ability to count to five and to count to seven.

Measuring the solstices was important for knowing when to follow the herds, when to plant, and when to harvest, but it was also important for religious and social purposes as well. Nomadic tribes, including the Irish Celts, used to reunite at the solstices because these five-day periods could be calculated easily by using familiar landmarks to measure the sun against the horizon. At the summer solstice they would match their marriageable children outside of their family. From this came the tradition of June as the month of marriages.

This brings us to the meaning of the riddle to which Jack answered, "Two in each hand and one in your mouth." The one in the mouth would be in the middle between the other four, and the one in the mouth would also be higher. It would be the actual day of the solstice, which would be in the center of the five days and would be ever so slightly higher than the rest. Also, putting a bean in one's mouth and spitting it at a witch or specter was a way to protect against them.[30]

Second Month—Full Moon

Jack's Ladder

Just as the moon reaches its fullness at the bottom of the underworld of the night sky, so Jack's beans will miraculously grow to fullness in the ground of the despair of Jack's mother:

Back goes Jack home, and as he had n't gone very far it was n't dusk by the time he got to his door.

"Back already, Jack?" said his mother; "I see you haven't got Milky-white, so you've sold her. How much did you get for her?"

"You'll never guess, mother," says Jack.

"No, you don't say so. Good boy! Five pounds, ten, fifteen, no, it can't be twenty."

"I told you you could n't guess. What do you say to these beans; they're magical, plant them over-night and—"

"What!" says Jack's mother, "have you been such a fool, such a dolt, such an idiot, as to give away my Milky-white, the best

milker in the parish, and prime beef to boot, for a set of paltry beans? Take that! Take that! Take that! And as for your precious beans here they go out of the window. And now off with you to bed. Not a sup shall you drink, and not a bit shall you swallow this very night."

So Jack went upstairs to his little room in the attic, and sad and sorry he was, to be sure, as much for his mother's sake, as for the loss of his supper.

At last he dropped off to sleep.

When he woke up, the room looked so funny. The sun was shining into the part of it, and yet all the rest was quite dark and shady. So Jack jumped up and dressed himself and went to the window. And what do you think he saw? Why, the beans his mother had thrown out of the window into the garden, had sprung up into a big beanstalk which went up and up and up till it reached the sky. So the man spoke truth after all.

In Poland and other parts of Europe, it is believed that the heavens open on Christmas night to reveal Jacob's ladder with angels coming and going between earth and heaven.[31]

In English the name Jack is a nickname for John and also a term for a peasant. In French, Jacques, the name for James, is the term for a peasant. The word for James in Latin is Jacobus. So, besides meaning Everyman, Jack refers to both John (including John the Baptist) and Jacob. It is interesting to note that Jack, John, and Jacob are all slang words for the male sexual member.[32] The beanstalk is the spiraling path of the sun climbing toward the summer solstice and the feast of John the Baptist (June 24). It is also Jacob's ladder whose seven rungs are the seven paths of the new or full moon between the winter and summer solstices. (See Figure 5, p. 25.)

Just as John the Baptist was the old year and Jesus was the new, so Esau was the old year and Jacob was the new. Esau, the hunter, was the elder brother of Jacob, but he sold his birthright to Jacob for a bowl of porridge and a few gifts (Gen. 25:19–34). Later Jacob wore the hide of a kid on his hands and neck in order to fool his blind father, Isaac, and receive his blessing (Gen. 27:1–29). Like the bear, Esau is the old year with a long growth of hair. His hunting represents the dispensing of death, which is an aspect of the old year. Jacob, however, is like the Bear's Son and the New Year. Jacob exhibits the characteristics of the bear, such as being hairy, but he is not like his brother who is lazy, gluttonous, and foolish. Jacob is the New Year who will go on to father the twelve months and the twelve tribes of Israel.

In most versions of "Jack and the Beanstalk," Jack is described as lazy.[33] This fits with his role as the Bear's Son. The hibernating bear is gluttonous and lazy, but Jack, unlike the bear, will change his ways and redeem the time. Jack is the New Adam and Jesus and Jacob, as opposed to the Old Adam, John the Baptist, and Esau, all three of whom dressed in animal skins.

A New Year's Whipping

Jack's mother gives him a licking for his troubles. Whipping and beans have an ancient common heritage. Not only do the Hopis ceremonially whip men who fall asleep while watching the bean plant during their New Year rites, but the Pueblos also hold a Whipping of the Children Ceremony at the Kachina initiations, using bean colors to determine the order in which the children are whipped. If the yellow beans were cooled first for the Kachinas (supernatural beings), then the youngest child is whipped with the yellow beans, and so on.[34]

Whipping is associated with the moon. The Central Eskimo tell how the moon adopted an orphaned boy and whipped him therapeutically in order to make him exceptionally strong.[35] In the New World, the Tupi, Creek, Iroquois, Algonquin, and Greenland Eskimo, among others, whipped dogs during eclipses.[36] Dogs are lunar animals, and this may have been done in order to encourage the sun and moon to grow again. The whip was also linked with the thunderbolt and rainmaking.[37] These too are connected with the moon.

Whipping was considered a rite that beneficially influenced the output of the fields.[38] It was not just that the stripes on the victim's back imitated the furrows of the plowed field but that they reflected the path of the sun as it declined farther south each day toward the winter solstice. The stripes also mimicked the scales on the old skin of a snake, which it would slough off at the end of the old year.

So Jack's mother was just helping out the growth of the beanstalk, as well as her son, by giving Jack a few blows. Also, Jack's abstinence from supper is another preparation for new growth, just as Advent was a time of abstinence and purification, which, in the Christian tradition, used to begin on Martinmas (November 11), and last till Christmas.

Climbing to the Moon

So the thrown-away beans become the way to salvation for Jack. How often what is unimportant in one aspect of our lives becomes most important in another. The little things that are overlooked become the things that really count. The beans are things of the soul that are mere leftovers in our everyday existence.

Mircea Eliade points out in his book on shamanism that stories about vines that travel from earth to heaven can be found in native North and South America, Africa, Indonesia, Oceania, India, and Tibet.[39] In many instances, the vine was special to the moon. In China, children would give a bundle of beanstalks to the statue of the Moon Rabbit, because it was his favorite food.[40] A story from China tells of an avaricious man who planted a seed that grew into a vine. He climbed the vine in order to reach the gold and silver of the moon, but when he got there the vine vanished, and he still is there today.[41] The Jibaro of Ecuador say that the reason there is a man in the moon is that a man fled his nagging wife by climbing a long liana or creeper to the moon.[42]

Tales of ladders to the sky can be found in the Cape Verde Islands, Egypt, and Mongolia.[43] In the Gold Coast story of Kweku Tsin, he climbs to the sky by way of a ladder with his father and his friends in order to escape a dragon. Kweku Tsin becomes the sun, his father becomes the moon, and his friends become the stars.[44] There is a South Seas tale of Kereke, a boy who wants to go to the moon. The moon lifts him up to a ladder, which he climbs to get the rest of the way.[45] As we shall see, the moon in our story is the ogre that lives in the sky.

Third Month—New Moon

Jack's Heritage

The beanstalk grew up quite close past Jack's window, so all he had to do was to open it and give a jump on to the beanstalk which ran up just like a big ladder. So Jack climbed, and he climbed and he climbed and he climbed and he climbed and he

climbed and he climbed till at last he reached the sky. And when
he got there he found a long broad road going as straight as a dart.

We have been reading the version of "Jack and the Beanstalk" told by Joseph Jacobs because it is the most popular and accessible telling and because it combines brevity and wit. Yet it diverges from earlier versions of the story in several significant ways. To begin with, it leaves out the story of Jack's heritage. In the earliest published version, of which Jacob's version is a literary retelling, the story of Jack's father is told. In *The History of Jack and the Beanstalk, Printed from the Original Manuscript, Never Before Published,* 1807, edited by Mary Jane Godwin, when Jack reaches the top of the beanstalk he meets up with an old, impoverished woman. She tells Jack that she is a fairy and relates a story, which his mother could never tell him.

Jack's father was rich and kind and lived in a great house in this land in the clouds. He took in the poor and needy, and once he took in a giant who claimed to be a dispossessed gentleman. One day a ship wrecked on a nearby shore and almost everyone in the household went to rescue the survivors. The giant took this opportunity to dispatch Jack's father, Jack's nurse, and the porter, and he was about to kill Jack, who was a baby, and his mother when, responding to her entreaties, he relented and agreed to spare her and Jack if she swore that she would never tell her son what had happened. In return he let her escape. He then stole all of the household treasures and burned the house to the ground. Jack and his mother made their way to the little cottage, where they have lived ever since.[46]

The death of Jack's father is the death of the sun that brightens the upper world. The ogre is the new moon that brought about the death through a solar eclipse. The banishment of Jack and his mother to the lower world is the exile of the full moon to the nether world.

Third Month—Full Moon
Jack Is the Bear's Son
This episode fills in a lot that was missing in the story. It also makes Jack's story fit the Bear's Son motif. (See Chapter 7, "Diddle, Diddle, Dumpling.") The difference with Jack's story is that he was a babe in arms when his mother went to the underworld, rather than being born there. Furthermore, they were exiled rather than abducted. But Jack has taken on the characteristics of the bear. In many versions of the story he is lazy and dim-witted like the lethargic bear coming out

of hibernation. He also is of low birth. These are all disguises that the Bear's Son assumes. Similarly, Jack's namesake, Jacob, disguised himself with the skin of a kid goat to fool his father Isaac. Odysseus, another Bear's Son, covered himself with the skin of a sheep to outwit the giant Polyphemus. Rhys Carpenter shows that Odysseus had a long bear lineage.[47] Jack will continue to hide his true identity until he can avenge himself upon the usurper who harmed his parents.

Fourth Month—New Moon

So he walked along and he walked along and he walked along till he came to a great big tall house, and on the doorstep was a great big tall woman.

"Good morning, mum," says Jack, quite polite-like. "Could you be so kind as to give me some breakfast?" For he had n't had anything to eat, you know, the night before and was as hungry as a hunter.

"It's breakfast you want, is it?" says the great big tall woman, "it's breakfast you'll be if you don't move off from here. My man is an ogre and there's nothing he likes better than boys broiled on toast. You'd better be moving on or he'll soon be coming."

Charles Perrault was the first to use the word *ogre* in his fairy tales in 1697. It first appeared in English (spelled hogre) in a translation from French of *The Arabian Nights*. It comes from the Byzantine *Ogur* meaning "Hungarian," because Hungarians were mistakenly confused with Tartars and Huns.[48] Although the ogre was more like a giant bear than a Hungarian, Jack was more concerned about his stomach than anything else. Apparently eating in the other world was not a taboo for Jack. Perhaps that is because he was in the upper world rather than the lower world, where eating represented the lunar eclipse, which was the gateway to death. (See Chapter 13, "There Was a Man Lived in the Moon.")

"Oh! please mum, do give me something to eat, mum. I've had nothing to eat since yesterday morning, really and truly, mum," says Jack. "I may as well be broiled as die of hunger."

Well, the ogre's wife was not half so bad after all. So she took Jack into the kitchen, and gave him a junk of bread and cheese and a jug of milk. But Jack had n't half finished these when thump! thump! thump! the whole house began to tremble with the noise of some one coming.

Fourth Month—Full Moon
The Ogre Is a Bear

"Goodness gracious me! It's my old man," said the ogre's wife, "what on earth shall I do? Come along quick and jump in here." And she bundled Jack into the oven just as the ogre came in.

As in "Hansel and Gretel," the oven is an excellent metaphor for the lunar eclipse. The black iron oven with its black door is like the gray penumbra and black umbra of the earth closing its door on the moon. When the door is closed the moon turns red under the right atmospheric conditions, just as the iron of the oven turns red hot. (But we hope not while Jack is inside.)

He was a big one, to be sure. At his belt he had three calves strung up by the heels, and he unhooked them and threw them down on the table and said: "Here, wife, broil me a couple of these for breakfast. Ah! what's this I smell?

> *Fee-fi-fo-fum,*
> *I smell the blood of an Englishman,*
> *Be he alive, or be he dead*
> *I'll have his bones to grind my bread."*

"Nonsense, dear," said his wife, "you're dreaming. Or perhaps you smell the scraps of that little boy you liked so much for yesterday's dinner. Here, you go and have a wash and tidy up, and by the time you come back your breakfast 'll be ready for you."

The ogre exhibits all of the traits of a bear. He is large. (A grizzly bear can weigh fifteen hundred pounds.) He is a man-eater. He can stand upright. He is omnivorous. He has five fingers (claws) on each hand (paw). And, like the bear, as we shall see, the ogre has poor eyesight and a very keen sense of smell. He is also lazy and gluttonous. (In Geoffrey Chaucer's *Canterbury Tales*, Gluttony is carried by a bear in "The Parson's Tale.")[49] Of course, for the bear, gluttony is necessary in order to survive a long hibernation. Ogres also tend to be slow-witted, as a bear would be after coming out of a deep sleep; and although this version of Jack's story doesn't say so, we can presume that the ogre, like the bear, is hairy and unkempt.

Jack also had taken on bearlike qualities, such as laziness, gluttony, and foolishness. But, just as Jacob used the hide of a kid as a disguise, Jack used the traits of a bear as a disguise to hide his quickness and cleverness. The bear's son combines the characteristics of a bear with those of a human.

The three calves hanging on the ogre's belt are a sign that he, like the bear, is a ruler of the underworld, even if his home is in the sky. As we have seen, cows are symbols of the moon and the three denote the three days of the full moon in the underworld of the night sky. Having them broiled and eaten is another image of a lunar eclipse, when the full moon is eaten.

The Bags of Gold

So off the ogre went, and Jack was just going to jump out of the oven and run away when the woman told him not. "Wait till he's asleep," says she; "he always has a doze after breakfast."

Well, the ogre had his breakfast, and after that he goes to a big chest and takes out of it a couple of bags of gold, and down he sits and counts till at last his head began to nod and he began to snore till the whole house shook again.

Then Jack crept out on tiptoe from his oven, and as he was passing the ogre he took one of the bags of gold under his arm, and off he pelters till he came to the beanstalk, and then he threw down the bag of gold, which of course fell into his mother's garden, and then he climbed down and climbed down till at last he got home and told his mother and showed her the gold and said: "Well, mother, wasn't I right about the beans? They are really magical, you see."

Why does the ogre have so many gold coins? Granted he is a robber and he did steal Jack's father's money; but he, like the bear, is also the Lord of the Dead and takes the coins of the dead. Until recent times it was common to put coins in the eyes of the dead. In part this stems from an ancient custom of burying a person's wealth with his or her corpse. The Romans placed a coin under the tongue of each corpse and called it "Charon's obol." This referred to the boatman Charon, who ferried the dead across the River Styx.[50]

Like Charon, the ogre takes the coins from the dead and becomes rich. The coins are the gold of the sun going down into the winter sky and the silver of the full moon going down into the night sky, to be taken by the dark lunar eclipse. The tradition of the coins of the dead is found throughout the world. The Japanese, for a ferrying fee across the Sandzunogawa River, used to place six coins in the traveling purse of the dead. Now a picture of coins is frugally substituted. The six coins represented the six months of the sun's descent into winter.

In many versions of "Jack and the Beanstalk" the giant's money-bags contain both gold and silver.[51] This represents both the sun and the moon. In Europe, it is common to expose coins, especially silver, to the waxing moon in order to make them grow. It is also customary to turn coins over in one's pocket for the same purpose.[52] At Christmastime the Irish serve a surprise bread, known as barmbrack bread, with a coin hidden inside and wrapped in foil to look like silver.[53] The coin is reminiscent of the sun and moon in the underworld at the winter solstice.

Fifth Month—New Moon

Jack Returns

The end of the gold coins is the same as the new moon when there is no more moonlight:

> So they lived on the bag of gold for some time, but at last they came to the end of it, and Jack made up his mind to try his luck once more up at the top of the beanstalk. So one fine morning he rose up early, and got on to the beanstalk, and he climbed and he climbed and he climbed and he climbed and he climbed and he climbed till at last he came out on to the road again and up to the great big tall house he had been to before. There, sure enough, was the great big tall woman a-standing on the doorstep.
>
> "Good morning, mum," says Jack, as bold as brass, "could you be so good as to give me something to eat?"
>
> "Go away, my boy," said the big tall woman, "or else my man will eat you up for breakfast. But aren't you the youngster who came here once before? Do you know, that very day, my man missed one of his bags of gold."
>
> "That's strange, mum," said Jack, "I dare say I could tell you something about that, but I'm so hungry I can't speak till I've had something to eat."

Well, the big tall woman was so curious that she took him in and gave him something to eat. But he had scarcely begun munching it as slowly as he could when thump! thump! thump! they heard the giant's footstep, and his wife hid Jack away in the oven.

Fifth Month—Full Moon

The Golden Hen

All happened as it did before. In came the ogre as he did before, said: "Fee-fi-fo-fum," and had his breakfast of three broiled oxen. Then he said: "Wife, bring me the hen that lays the golden eggs." So she brought it, and the ogre said: "Lay," and it laid an egg all of gold. And then the ogre began to nod his head, and to snore till the house shook.

Then Jack crept out of the oven on tiptoe and caught hold of the golden hen, and was off before you could say "Jack Robinson." But this time the hen gave a cackle which woke the ogre, and just as Jack got out of the house he heard him calling: "Wife, wife, what have you done with my golden hen?"

And the wife said: "Why, my dear?"

But that was all Jack heard, for he rushed off to the beanstalk and climbed down like a house on fire. And when he got home he showed his mother the wonderful hen, and said "Lay" to it; and it laid a golden egg every time he said "Lay."

Again Jack hides in the oven, a symbol of the lunar eclipse. This time the ogre eats three oxen, indicating the three days of the full moon. The hen that lays golden eggs is also of lunar significance. Like the goose, the hen is the full moon and her eggs are the gibbous moons that precede her and follow her in the month. The footprint of the hen and other birds shows three toes pointing forward and one pointing back. This is like the trident of Poseidon (Neptune), the Greek god of the Ocean, of Lucifer, the ruler of the underworld in Christian tradition, and of Shiva, the Hindu god of death. The three prongs of the trident are the three days of the new moon and the full moon. Because of the shape of their prints, birds' feet are also metaphors for the female pudendum.[54]

In myth, the egg is related to both the sun and the moon. In Greece, Leto, the swan, hatched an egg, which gave birth to the sun

(Apollo) and the moon (Artemis). The Egyptian goose goddess, Hathor, hatched the golden egg of the sun.[55] According to the Finnish epic, *The Kalevala*, the sun is the yolk of the cosmic egg, and the moon is the white of the egg.[56] An Australian Aboriginal creation story says that the sun was created when an egg was cracked against a pile of branches in heaven and made fire.[57]

Sixth Month—New Moon

The Final Visit

Well, Jack was not content, and it wasn't very long before he determined to have another try at his luck up there at the top of the beanstalk. So one fine morning, he rose up early, and got on to the beanstalk, and he climbed and he climbed and he climbed and he climbed till he got to the top. But this time he knew better than to go straight to the ogre's house. And when he got near it, he waited behind a bush till he saw the ogre's wife come out with a pail to get some water, and then he crept into the house and got into the copper. He hadn't been there long when he heard thump! thump! thump! as before, and in come the ogre and his wife.

"Fee-fi-fo-fum, I smell the blood of an Englishman," cried out the ogre. "I smell him, wife, I smell him."

"Do you, my dearie?" says the ogre's wife. "Then, if it's that little rogue that stole your gold and the hen that laid the golden eggs he's sure to have got into the oven." And they both rushed to the oven. But Jack wasn't there, luckily, and the ogre's wife said: "There you are again with your fee-fi-fo-fum. Why of course it's the boy you caught last night that I've just broiled for your breakfast. How forgetful I am, and how careless you are not to know the difference between live and dead after all these years."

For the last time Jack comes to the door. In the original published version Jack audaciously asks a third time for food, while in this version he more practically sneaks into the house. This time a child is being served up, all the more reason to end this ogre's life.

Sixth Month—Full Moon

The Golden Harp

So the ogre sat down to the breakfast and ate it, but every now and then he would mutter: "Well, I could have sworn—" and he

'd get up and search the larder and the cupboards and everything,
only, luckily, he didn't think of the copper.

After breakfast was over, the ogre called out: "Wife, wife, bring
me my golden harp." So she brought it and put it on the table be-
fore him. Then he said: 'Sing!" and the golden harp sang most
beautifully. And it went on singing till the ogre fell asleep, and
commenced to snore like thunder.

The ogre snoring like thunder is an allusion to the bear as the lord
of thunder. The time when the bear comes out of hibernation is the
time when the air is warming, causing lightning and thunder.

Hiding under a copper lid is another metaphor for a lunar eclipse.
Total lunar eclipses can vary in color from orange to blood red to
copper to brown to black. Copper is the metal of Venus, another
feminine planet, often associated with the moon.

The harp itself is a symbol of the moon. There were seven strings
stretched across Orpheus's lyre.[58] Orpheus was the greatest musician
of all Greece. The seven strings are the seven days the moon takes to
descend from the horizon into the night sky and the seven days it
takes to ascend again. Music is naturally associated with birds, and
birds are creatures closely associated with the moon.

Don't Look Back

The story of Orpheus connects the harp or lyre with the underworld.
Orpheus so charmed the rulers of the lower regions with his playing
that they allowed him to take his lover, Eurydice, from the land of
death. However he failed to do so because he broke the gods' dictum
and looked back upon her as they traveled to the upper world. The
constellation of the Lyre was placed in the sky as a reminder of their
sad tale. Orpheus has often been depicted iconographically as a bear.
In a fifth-century picture in the Louvre Orpheus is a bear, and in a
painting in the palace of Onmeyade Orpheus is a bear seated on a
mountaintop charming an audience of animals.[59]

Orpheus is the moon, waxing each night as it goes deeper into the
night sky and waning each night as it rises back toward daylight
again. After the full moon, the bright half of the moon faces or looks
back in the direction from which it came the night before. (See
Figure 6, p. 29.) Similarly, after the new moon, each night the wax-

ing moon looks back to where the new moon was. By looking back, Orpheus loses what he wanted the most.

Likewise, Lot's wife turned to a pillar of salt because she looked back as they fled the burning of Sodom and Gomorrah (Gen. 19:26). The Hopi believe that if their salt gatherers look back at the lake where they obtained their salt, their souls will be trapped there and they will soon die.[60] Salt and the moon are related in that salt comes from the sea, and the sea's tides are controlled by the moon. Tossing a pinch of salt over one's shoulder for good luck is another form of the looking back taboo, in that one attempts to protect oneself against the spirits of the dead or evil spirits without looking at them.

The looking back taboo is also connected directly to the moon. We have seen it already in "There Was a Man and He Had Nought." It ends by saying, "He ran fourteen miles in fifteen days, / And never looked behind him." "There Was an Old Woman Lived Under a Hill" tells of her doing the same. Both of these rhymes describe the path of the phases of the moon and emphasize the importance of not looking back.

In Europe it is considered bad luck to glimpse the new moon over one's left shoulder.[61] In the Peruvian story "The Moon Rope," the mole is unable to climb to the moon because he keeps looking back.[62] In the Alutiiq story of "The Girl Who Marries the Moon," it is the girl from Kodiak Island who does not look when she is carried up to the sky who is chosen by the moon.[63]

In our story, the ogre is the Man in the Moon, and Jack runs away with his harp.

Then Jack lifted up the copper-lid very quietly and got down like a mouse and crept on hands and knees till he came to the table, when up he crawled, caught hold of the golden harp and dashed with it towards the door. But the harp called out quite loud: "Master! Master!" and the ogre woke up just in time to see Jack running off with his harp.

Seventh Month—New Moon

The harp is obviously still under the spell of the ogre, and only when the ogre is dead will the harp submit to a new master. Although the lyre is a lunar symbol, Hermes (Mercury) traded the lyre, which he invented, for Apollo's caduceus, thus giving the lyre to the sun. Jack, who is the sun ascending toward the summer solstice, steals the lyre from the moon.

Jack ran as fast as he could, and the ogre came rushing after, and would soon have caught him only Jack had a start and dodged him a bit and knew where he was going. When he got to the beanstalk the ogre was not more than twenty yards away when suddenly he saw Jack disappear like, and when he came to the end of the road he saw Jack underneath climbing down for dear life. Well, the ogre did n't like trusting himself to such a ladder, and he stood and waited, so Jack got another start. But just then the harp cried out: "Master! Master!" and the ogre swung himself down on to the beanstalk, which shook with his weight. Down climbs Jack, and after him climbed the ogre. By this time Jack had climbed down and climbed down and climbed down till he was very nearly home. So he called out: "Mother! Mother! bring me an axe, bring me an axe." And his mother came rushing out with the axe in her hand, but when she came to the beanstalk she stood stock still with fright for there she saw the ogre with his legs just through the clouds.

Seventh Month—Full Moon
Fall from Heaven

But Jack jumped down and got hold of the axe and gave a chop at the beanstalk which cut it half in two. The ogre felt the bean-stalk shake and quiver so he stopped to see what was the matter. Then Jack gave another chop with the axe, and the beanstalk was cut in two and began to topple over. Then the ogre fell down and broke his crown, and the beanstalk came toppling after.

Just as Lucifer fell from heaven and Hephaestus (Vulcan) fell from Mount Olympus, so the ogre fell from the sky. Digging a deep pit and placing sharp, upright stakes at the bottom and covering the top with branches and leaves was an ancient method of killing a bear. So too the leaves and fruit fall from the trees in the season of "fall," and the harvest is cut down. The Botocudo of South America believed that the moon sometimes fell from the sky.[64] The Snoqualmie of the Pacific Northwest tell how the moon fell to the earth when the rope, which he was climbing down to catch the thieves of fire, suddenly broke under his weight.[65] Each month the moon falls from the height of the sun at the new moon to the depths of the full moon in the night. Furthermore, the full moon, which was near the top of the sky near the winter solstice, is now relatively low on the horizon even at midnight near the summer solstice. It has fallen from its place of power in the winter sky. Jack, on the other hand, as the sun, is at the pinnacle of his success.

Then Jack showed his mother his golden harp, and what with showing that and selling the golden eggs Jack and his mother became very rich, and he married a great princess, and they lived happy ever after.

Jack has reached the seventh full moon, which is the summer solstice and the time for June weddings. In the original publication of the story, Jack's last visit was on "the longest day," emphasizing the victory of the sun over darkness. So a princess appears on the scene at the full moon, which is often a preferred time for weddings. For example, Scottish girls would schedule weddings only for the time of the full moon, believing it the most fortunate time for women.[66]

The Seven Days of the Week

It is worth comparing the seven episodes of the story to the seven planets and seven days of the week, but first we must note another change in the Joseph Jacobs version, which was gathered in Australia in 1860, from the 1807 version from which it came. In the original, the hen was taken first and next came the gold coins and finally the harp. The story was probably changed because the coins would run out, thus justifying another trip, whereas the golden eggs would never run out. Using the original order, which is found more frequently, the comparison is as follows:

Weekday	Planet	Episode
Sunday	Sun	Death of ogre
Monday	Moon	Harp
Tuesday	Mars	Coins
Wednesday	Mercury	Hen
Thursday	Jupiter	Story of father's death
Friday	Venus	Beanstalk
Saturday	Saturn	Cow and butcher

Saturn is a lord of death who presides over the Saturnalia in December at the death of the old year. As we have seen, the cow is sold to be butchered, and butchering usually occurred at the onset of winter. Venus is the goddess of vegetation and fertility, so it is very suitable for the bountiful beanstalk to be hers. Jupiter is the father of the gods, so Jack's father too is a great lord. Mercury has a winged hat and winged sandals and flies through the air between heaven and earth. The hen, as a bird, also fits, although domesticated hens do not usually fly. Mars is a looter of the dead and so coins are something that he would possess, just like Charon in the underworld. The moon, as we have seen, is associated with music. Finally, the sun conquers the ogre, the lord of darkness.

Fly Me to the Moon

Likewise, the seven moons fit with the sun's trip from winter to summer. In the first full moon was the butchering of the cow at midwinter, and in the seventh full moon was the victory of the sun at midsummer. That would place the fourth full moon in March at the spring equinox and connect it with the hen that laid golden eggs. Spring chickens are associated with Easter, which was originally celebrated at the spring equinox. Both chicks and eggs are integral parts of the celebration. But other winged creatures are also associated with spring. The goose and other migratory birds are seen flying north in the spring in the Northern Hemisphere. The Archangel Gabriel appeared to Mary at the Annunciation, which is celebrated on March 25. Angels also appeared at the tomb of Jesus on Easter Morning.

The fall equinox also has a preponderance of feather imagery. The goose, of course, flies south in the fall. Gabriel, six months before the Annunciation, on September 25, visited the elderly priest Zechariah and told him that his wife, Elizabeth, would have a child and they would name him John. On September 29 is the celebration of Michael the Archangel, who banished Lucifer into hell. In England and Canada today, goose is still eaten on Michaelmas Day, in memory of the angelic battle.

The winter solstice has its winged creatures as well, with the host of angels at Christmas and the Christmas turkey or goose. In a different version of "Jack and the Beanstalk," published in 1807, the same year as the other earliest version, Jack's mother finds a sixpence while sweeping the floor and sends Jack with it to buy a goose. He comes home with a bean instead.

Outside of the Christian tradition, Kukulcan (Quetzalcoatl) is a feathered serpent who brings civilization to humanity according to the Maya. At Chichen Itza at the spring and fall equinox, seven diamonds of light form his serpent body on the side of the stepped pyramid of the Castillo. The serpent represents the seven moons between the solstices and his feathers represent the flight from the lower to the upper world. The spring equinox was most likely when the lighted serpent was observed in the tenth century A.D., because there are few clouds in the spring whereas it is the rainy season in the fall. Also, the spring equinox is the time of the mating of snakes in Mexico.[67] This fits with the caduceus, which imitates the spiraling of the sun toward and away from the summer solstice.

Seraph, which originally was a "fiery serpent" or "lightning snake" in Hebrew, later became an angel. Just as Lucifer was both a winged spirit and a serpent, so *seraphim* were serpent-spirits.[68] Another winged serpent is the dragon. Dragons too were fiery. The oldest recorded dragon legend is that of Tiamat, the Babylonian monster of chaos. Marduk, the youngest of the gods, killed Tiamat and made half its body heaven and the other half earth. Babylonians celebrated this creation story each year at their spring New Year festival.[69]

Just as the winged Mercury flies midway between the upper and lower world, so the Egyptian god Toth and goddess Ma'at stand between heaven and earth with a scale and a feather. They weigh the deceased's heart, and if it is lighter than a feather then the person's soul may proceed to the upper world. A Mazovian legend tells of a pilgrim to the Holy Sepulchre who sees a ladder of birds' feathers. He climbs it for three months and reaches the Garden of Paradise.[70] Feathers at the equinox transport us from the lower world of the winter solstice to the upper world of midsummer.

The Cycle of the Year
In a description published in 1734 of a farcical play entitled "Enchantment Demonstrated in the Story of Jack Spriggins and the Enchanted Bean," Jack climbs the beanstalk until he reaches an inn where he meets a woman and twelve young men who call him their lord.[71] This is one more indication that this is a story about the cycle of the year—a story about the cycle of the sun and the moon from

midwinter to midsummer. Jack appears at the beginning of the story to be a Bear's Son and the moon's son, but he reveals himself also to be the sun, who avenges the life of his father and overcomes the moon in the form of the ogre. In the process he receives the secret of the number five, a secret that brings civilization to humanity by bringing order to the wanderings of the sun and the moon.

Chapter 12

Three Blind Mice:

Sacred Taboos I

Three blind mice, see how they run!
They all ran after the farmer's wife,
Who cut off their tails with a carving knife,
Did you ever see such a sight in your life,
As three blind mice?[1]

The Three New Moons

Because they are three and because they are blind the mice are like the three dark nights of the new moon. But their blindness has other associations with the new moon. Only during a new moon can the sun, the eye of heaven, be blinded in a solar eclipse. Furthermore, staring at a solar eclipse either before or after totality can cause blindness.

A mouse's tail can be imagined as curved, like the thin crescent moon that disappears at the new moon. The knife of the farmer's wife can also be seen as a crescent moon or as a crescent of the sun during a partial eclipse or just before or after a total eclipse.

Probably the best-known round in the world, a version of "Three Blind Mice" appeared in *Deuteromelia; or, The Seconde part of Musicks melodie* in 1609:

> Three blinde Mice, three blinde Mice,
> Dame Iulian, Dame Iulian,
> The Miller and his merry olde Wife,
> Shee scrapte her tripe licke thou the knife.[2]

In modern English, the last line reads, "She scraped her tripe, lick you the knife." Tripe is the edible (so they say) stomach of cud-chewing animals. This version, which surely would have been sung appreciatively by students used to dormitory food, does not appear to relate to the moon. In 1890, however, there is a record of a version going back three generations that does:

> Three blind mice, see how they run!
> A farmer married an ugly wife,
> And she cut her throat with a carving knife.
> Did you ever see such a fool in your life?
> Three blind mice.[3]

In this gruesome version we can see the farmer's ugly wife as the new moon because throughout the world the dark new moon is described as sooty and pockmarked.

Blinded by the Light

Blind characters in literature include Isaac, who was duped by Jacob; the Giant Polyphemus, who was blinded by Odysseus; Oedipus, who blinded himself; and Samson, who was blinded by the Philistines. Blindness is often connected with clairvoyance and wisdom.[4] The wisest of all Greeks, Tiresias, was said by some to have been blinded when he saw Athena, the goddess of wisdom, bathing. A more popular explanation was that he became blind as a result of interfering with two serpents mating.[5]

This explanation fits with the symbolism of the mating snakes being the path of the sun and moon through the year. By staring at the sun to learn the secrets of its wanderings, one can become blind. Some Hindu ascetics believed that they could obtain spiritual wisdom by staring into the sun until they were blind.[6] One reason for risking blindness was to learn more about eclipses. Although it is safe to look at the sun during the totality of an eclipse, looking directly at it before or afterward is dangerous. And yet this could have been a

Three Blind Mice

method for learning about Bailey's Beads and other secret phenomena that were considered valuable to ancient peoples.

One method for seeing these secrets without being completely blinded was to close or cover one eye while looking at the sun. The Norse god Odin gave up an eye in exchange for being able to see the invisible. (The invisible new moon in the daytime sky is visible during an eclipse of the sun.) In the Icelandic *Eddas*, Allfodr drinks from the spring of Mina in order to obtain wisdom but is allowed to do so only after he sacrifices an eye.[7]

The moon is associated with being one-legged and one-armed, and it is considered to be one-eyed. Among the Tewa of New Mexico, the moon was said to be one-eyed because the creator-spirits had determined that she and her husband, the sun, were too bright and that her husband would have to lose an eye so that people could sleep. She convinced them that she should lose her eye instead, and so today the moon does not shine as brightly as the sun.[8] Around the world the sun and moon are seen as the two eyes in the sky. If the moon were visible when it is new, the sun and new moon, which would appear to be the same size in the sky, would be close together, like on the human face. In some cultures, the moon is known as the left eye and the sun as the right eye. Among the Samoyeds of arctic Asia, the sun is known as the good eye and the moon, dark and invisible next to the sun, is known as the evil eye.[9]

Nibble, Nibble, Like a Mouse

The Algonquins of Canada tell the story of a man named Tcakabesh, who set a snare for a squirrel and caught the sun by mistake. All the animals tried to free the sun, but it was so hot they could not get near it. Finally, after many attempts, the mouse gnawed through the rope and freed the sun. In the effort the mouse singed the hair off his back, causing him to have short hair.

In Malaysia there is an old hunchback in the moon by a banyan tree. He is weaving a fishing line out of fibers from the tree, and when he finishes he will fish up everything from the world below. A rat nibbles his line in two each time before he finishes, thereby saving the world. Fortunately the man's cat does not catch the rat.[10]

The mouse and the rat in these stories are the new moon. Like the mouse, the new moon is able to get closest to the sun, as it does during a solar eclipse; and like the rat, the new moon nibbles at the path woven by the moon each month. The Sukuma of Tanzania have a tale about a spider, a fly, and a mouse who stole the sun and brought it to our world to give light. Mouse gnawed a hole in the sky and carried the sun back in a box.[11] Again the mouse would be the new moon, which would be able to steal the sun during the solar eclipse.

The Mouse and the Evil Eye
In the bear ceremony of the Mansi, after the bear dies, its spirit first becomes the size of a mouse and then grows into progressively larger animal sizes each night until it becomes the size of a bear spirit again.[12] This is like the waxing moon growing larger each night. The mouse, as one of the smallest mammals, represents the smallest crescent of the moon, as well as the soul. Many peoples believe it is dangerous to suddenly wake a sleeping person, because the soul may be out wandering in the form of a mouse, and the person will die if the soul does not return before the person is awakened. Mice and rats are portents of death, as in rats deserting a sinking ship.[13]

On the Fiji Islands, the moon wanted humans to disappear a little while and then come back to life, but the rat wanted humans to die like himself.[14] Aztec women saw the eclipse of the moon as an evil omen and feared that their unborn children would be turned to mice. They placed obsidian in their mouths or bosoms to avert this.[15] In Europe both the Devil and witches create mice, and both the Devil and witches turn into mice.

The Greeks thought that mice had the evil eye, and so they had coins struck with pictures of mice on them it order to ward against it.[16] Mice brought plague to the Philistines because they had stolen the Ark of the Covenant. When the Philistines finally gave the Ark back to the Israelites, they gave five golden mice along with it (1 Sam. 6:1–21).

Knives and Tails
The tail was believed to contain the strength of an animal, and therefore the Mongols used animal tails on their standards in battle. The Latin word for "tail" is *penis*. This double meaning is found in many Asian and North American myths.[17] It is also found in English slang.[18] The tail of an animal is the remnant that retains its potency for rebirth. Similarly the last waning crescent is the tail end of the moon, the vestige from which the moon will be reborn.

The farmer's wife and, in the earlier version, the miller's wife are both the wife of Father Time. The miller's wheel is the turning of time, and the farmer's furrows are the paths of the sun and the moon through the year. The farmer's wife is Cronus's (Saturn's) wife Rhea—"Mother Time, who wielded the castrating moon-sickle."[19] In China knives were emblems of the moon, both because they were curved and because they modeled the paring away of the waning moon.[20]

During a solar eclipse, the red-hot disc of the sun becomes a crescent—like a knife of red-hot iron. Bushman myth tells us that the moon was a man who made the sun angry. The sun started cutting away at him with its knifelike rays until he was almost gone. The moon pleaded for his life, and the sun relented, but every time the sun sees the full moon, it starts slicing away at him again.[21]

In many parts of the world knives ward off evil, probably because they are associated with iron. Iron is considered very powerful both for promoting good and for carrying out evil. Iron tools were not allowed in the construction of Greek temples. Their use was also prohibited in Solomon's Temple (1 Kings 6:7). Roman priests would not shave with an iron razor, and iron was not permitted to touch the king of Korea.

But iron was also a protection against evil. Women in India wear iron wedding bracelets to protect against evil spirits. Dragons fear iron in China. Iron is the most powerful charm against witchcraft and is used in Europe to ward off fairies. (In "Snow White" red-hot iron shoes were placed on the evil queen.)

Before the Iron Age, iron was found in its pure form only in meteorites. Babylonians called iron "heaven fire," and to Egyptians it was known as the "marvel from heaven."[22] One myth says that the moon, like iron, was forged by a smith.[23] The red moon in the shadow of the lunar eclipse would fit the metaphor of the iron in the smithy's furnace. Although the moon is often connected with the blacksmith, the sun is also seen as red-hot iron. Just as the sun is often seen as the combatant of the moon, so iron, particularly in the form of a knife, is sometimes seen as a threat to the moon.

The Moon Is the Evil Eye
Abyssinian ironworkers were outcasts and were thought to possess the evil eye. So far we have seen the evil eye associated with iron, mice,

and the moon. What is the evil eye? Some people supposedly have the power to cause harm, whether intended or not, to other people, animals, and things merely by looking at them. This belief is widespread in the Old World, particularly in Europe and the Mediterranean area. The eyes of old women and young brides were particularly dangerous. Children, young wives, horses, dogs, milk, and corn were especially susceptible to the evil eye. Protections against the evil eye include red-hot iron, salt, horns, the crescent shape, and horseshoes.[24] The custom of a bride wearing a veil stems from these beliefs.[25]

The hand is an especially effective protection against the evil eye. In the Arab world, the Hand of Fatima, the youngest daughter of Muhammad, is a very common sign used for this purpose. Also, to stretch out one's hand, palm outward toward the suspected evil eye, saying "five on you" will avert a curse. Sometimes another word is substituted for the word *five* in Arabic in order to avoid cursing or swearing in conversation.[26] In Sicily and southern Italy, the Black Hand was a symbol of evil. It was drawn on letters of extortion threatening well-to-do businessmen with violence if they did not pay money. This practice was exported to American cities at the beginning of the twentieth century and became known as the Black Hand.[27]

The Sacred Hand

Why was the hand both a protection against the evil eye and a curse? The hand is a symbol for the number five. Since Paleolithic times hand impressions on cavern walls have signified a sacred place. Even today the Christian benediction is given with the raised hand.[28] As we discovered in "Jack in the Beanstalk," the number five is the number of days of the winter solstice and of the summer solstice. Whoever understands this secret and its relationship to the cycles of the moon can predict the solstices and equinoxes precisely and thereby understand when the seasons change and control the social and sacred calendar. During and after the Ice Age, this secret, along with the secret of the eclipses, was one of the most important pieces of knowledge that humans possessed.

The creatures of the moon possessed five claws. The Chinese Imperial Dragon had five claws, and no artist could put five claws on any other dragon, upon threat of death. The bear, symbol to the moon, has five claws. The Devil, who dwells in the moon, also has five claws.[29]

The open hand is sometimes a sign of divinity and the sun. A tenth-century Irish cross shows the Right Hand of God above two coiled snakes. What better image could there be for the sun coiling toward the five days of the summer solstice? A very similar image was found in the New World, in Moundville, Alabama. An engraved stone disk dating between A.D. 1200 and 1600 shows an open hand with an eye on its palm. It is encircled by two rattlesnakes, which are twisted about each other. It is very similar to Asian depictions of a Bodhisattva showing a palm with the compassionate Eye of Mercy on it.[30] The eye is the sun, the hand is the five days of the solstice, and the rattlesnakes are the ascending and descending paths of the sun.

We began with the three blind mice, whose potency was cut off by the sickle of the waning moon; and we have ended with the sacred hand that conquers the evil eye.

The Flying Purple People Eater

Our myths, past and present, fit into constellations that reinforce one another. Even as we create new myths today, they often align themselves with the patterns of the past. For example, a song from my childhood tells of the "one-eyed, one-horned, flying purple people eater." How appropriate that a creature that is threatening to humans should have one eye and one horn, like so many lunar gods that date to the Ice Age. We still continue to be influenced by Paleolithic myths, sometimes subconsciously. It is humbling to become aware of just a part of the meaning of these distant myths.

Chapter 13

There Was a Man
Lived in the Moon:
Sacred Taboos II

There was a man lived in the moon, lived in
  the moon, lived in the moon,
There was a man lived in the moon,
And his name was Aiken Drum;
  And he played upon a ladle, a ladle, a ladle,
  And he played upon a ladle,
  And his name was Aiken Drum,

And his hat was made of good cream cheese,
  good cream cheese, good cream cheese,
And his hat was made of good cream cheese,
And his name was Aiken Drum.

And his coat was made of good roast beef,
  good roast beef, good roast beef,
And his coat was made of good roast beef,
And his name was Aiken Drum.

And his buttons were made of penny loaves,
  penny loaves, penny loaves,

And his buttons were made of penny loaves,
And his name was Aiken Drum.

His waistcoat was made of crust of pies,
    crust of pies, crust of pies,
His waistcoat was made of crust of pies,
And his name was Aiken Drum.

And his breeches were made of haggis bags,
    haggis bags, haggis bags,
And his breeches were made of haggis bags,
And his name was Aiken Drum.

There was a man in another town,
    another town, another town,
There was a man in another town,
And his name was Willy Wood;
    And he played upon a razor, a razor, a razor,
    And he played upon a razor,
    And his name was Willy Wood.

And he ate up all the good cream cheese,
    good cream cheese, good cream cheese,
And he ate up all the good cream cheese,
And his name was Willy Wood.

And he ate up all the good roast beef,
    good roast beef, good roast beef,
And he ate up all the good roast beef,
And his name was Willy Wood.

And he ate up all the penny loaves,
    penny loaves, penny loaves,
And he ate up all the penny loaves,
And his name was Willy Wood.

And he ate up all the good pie crust,
    good pie crust, good pie crust,

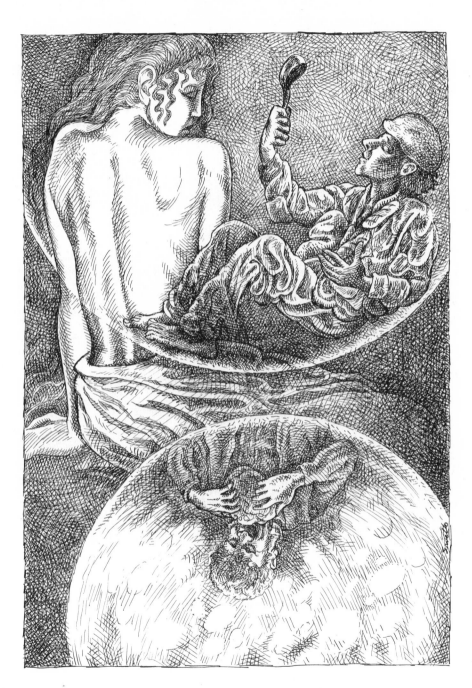

There Was a Man Lived in the Moon

And he ate up all the good pie crust,
And his name was Willy Wood.

But he choked upon the haggis bags,
    haggis bags, haggis bags,
But he choked upon the haggis bags,
And that ended Willy Wood.[1]

Moon Cakes

Poor Aiken Drum is like the Gingerbread Man. The waxing and waning of the moon take the form of food and clothes that are put on and then eaten away, leaving Aiken Drum rather undressed. In this light-hearted song the beginning verses each add an article of clothing to the moon as it grows each day from new moon to full moon. Then Willy Wood eats away at the clothes, until at the new moon he literally eats his last.

The association of the moon with food has a long history. At the harvest moon near the fall equinox the Chinese serve moon cakes that are six to twelve inches round. They have pictures of the moon goddess and the moon rabbit on them. The Israelite women made cakes for the Queen of Heaven, to the chagrin of Jeremiah (Jer. 7:18). The cakes were for Ishtar (Astarte, Aphrodite, Venus) and were in the shape of a star or a crescent. As we will see, Ishtar is related to the moon as the Queen of Heaven. In the nineteenth century in Lancashire, England, there was also a custom of making cakes for the Queen of Heaven. In ancient Rome hot cross buns were originally made in honor of the moon. At the festival of Pandia (the daughter of the moon), Greeks made and ate moon cakes.[3] Visitors to the underworld traditionally took cakes to mollify Cerberus, the infernal watchdog.[4]

Besides eating away the moon each month, the metaphor of eating could be extended to comparing teeth to the phases of the moon. This Mother Goose riddle is an example:

Thirty white horses
Upon a red hill,
Now they tramp,
Now they champ,
Now they stand still.

The horses are the teeth, and the red hill is the gums. The thirty teeth can be seen as the thirty days of the month and thirty phases of the moon, fifteen in the daytime sky and fifteen in the night sky. A young adult normally has twenty-eight teeth and the wisdom teeth add four, but because the wisdom teeth are unpredictable, thirty is an average.

Elixir of the Gods

In the Hindu tradition the moon is Soma, a plant from whose milky juice a divine sacrificial libation is derived. The sap is believed to have intoxicating or, more likely, hallucinogenic properties; but it is not known for certain which plant or plants may have been used. As a god, Soma was the lord of stars and planets, priests, plants, sacrifices, and devotions. He married the twenty-seven *naksatras*, the daughters of Daksa. Altogether they make up the phases of the moon. Because he could not treat them all with equal affection, he was afflicted with a wasting disease for half of each month.[5] In India it is believed that the waxing moon is replenishing the Soma drunk by the gods. The moon is "a cup, continually filled with and emptied of ambrosial fiery fluids."[6]

Dionysus, the Greek god of wine, is a lunar god, and several English rhymes assure us that "the man in the moon drinks claret."[7] In Mesoamerica, the moon was associated with intoxication and fermentation. The rabbit in the moon was related to *pulque*, a drink made with fermented agave sap.[8] Thus, the moon contains both the elixir of the gods and libation for humans.

The Bread and Water of Life

The Sumerians have a story about the bread of life and the water of life. As in most other cultures, there is a prohibition against humans eating or drinking while in the land of the dead, lest they not be able to return to earth again. By eating or drinking the moon of the night sky, which is the lunar eclipse, humans will come to reside in the land of death, which is the moon. The following story is a variation on this theme.

The Sumerian Adapa was the mortal son of Ea, the god of wisdom. Adapa, the first of the seven sages, brought language, bread, water, and fish to humans. However, he offended the gods by breaking the wing of the South Wind during a storm. Anu, the ruler of the gods, angrily sends for Adapa. Ea advises his son to dress in full mourning, in torn sackcloth and ashes, and to beg for forgiveness but not to eat bread or water or he will die. When the god Tammuz, who is guarding the gate of heaven, asks why Adapa is in mourning, Adapa, in order to get past Tammuz, responds that he is in mourning for him. Tammuz laughs and lets Adapa through. And Adapa makes his way to Anu, who forgives him. It turns out, however, that the bread and water that Anu offers and Adapa refuses are the bread and water of life, which would have made him eternal. Ea tricked his own son because he knew that mortals are creatures of time and only gods live forever.[9]

Heavenly Food and Food from Hell

The effect of eating in the story of Adam and Eve is the opposite of what it is in Adapa's story. By eating the forbidden fruit Adam and Eve gain the knowledge of good and evil, but they become mortals. Food that comes from the upper world contains life everlasting, whereas food that comes from the underworld contains death. The poisoned apple that Snow White ate, as well as Persephone's pomegranate and Adam and Eve's forbidden fruit, are descriptions of lunar eclipses, which occur in the night sky and thus in the underworld. In contrast, the story of Adapa tells of entering heaven. He first has to pass Tammuz, who is associated with the moon. Each year the Sumerians mourned for the return of Tammuz in the spring, so Ea's answer made him laugh. The sackcloth and ashes remind us of the sooty new moon. Adapa is dressed like the new moon during a solar eclipse.

The Food Taboo

The Serrano of California avoided eating during an eclipse in order to starve the spirits of the dead who were trying to eat the sun or the moon.[10] Other Native American customs during an eclipse included throwing out food and water and turning pots upside down.[11] In Europe one must not eat food in the land of fairies if one wants to return home. In North America, the Haida, Tsimshian, Kwakiutl, Pawnee, and Cherokee all believe that one must not eat while in another world. In Melanesia, New Caledonia, and New Zealand the same proscriptions prevail. One must not eat food in the land of the dead or in the land of the gods. Perhaps Adapa was prevented from becoming immortal so that he could return home.[12]

The moon is generous with its food. In India there is a tale about how the sun, the moon, and the wind went to a feast, and when they returned, the sun and the wind had no food for their mother, but the moon brought the best food for her. In reward their mother made the moon cool while the sun and wind are hot.[13] Another Hindu story tells of Rahu, a demon who tried to swallow soma, the elixir of immortality that comes from Soma, the moon. Rahu, in the midst of battle with the gods, began to swallow the soma, but he was spotted by the sun and the moon. They reported him to Vishnu, who cut off his head just as he was swallowing the liquid. His head became immortal, but his body died. So he wanders heaven attempting to swallow his betrayers, the sun and the moon. When he does manage to do so, they come out of his throat at the end of the eclipse.[14]

The food of the moon conveys both death and immortality. And because both death and immortality take humans away from their home in the everyday world, the taboo against eating in the other world often holds true for the upper world as well as the underworld.

Fertile, Feisty Inanna

A very ancient Sumerian myth that includes the food and water of life, as well as clothing and the moon, is the story of Inanna's descent into hell. Inanna was the feisty and fertile goddess of the planet Venus; and, like the Man in the Moon, she had her clothes removed piece by piece. She became the model for the great goddesses of the Middle East and Europe, including Ishtar, Isis, Aphrodite, and Venus.

Not satisfied with having sway in heaven and on earth, Inanna decides to abandon her seven celestial cities and to descend to the underworld, which is ruled by her sister, Ereshkigal. Hoping to outshine her sister, Inanna dons her best apparel, befitting her role as the planet Venus, the brightest object in the sky. Before she begins her visit, she prudently instructs her faithful advisor, Ninshubur, to wait three days for her and, if she doesn't return, to seek help from the gods. Then she demands entrance to the gates of hell, unintimidated by the monster with gaping jaws at the gates' threshold. The monster's teeth, like the fearsome teeth of Kali, the Hindu goddess of time and death, are the phases of the moon that encircle the world entrapping us in time and the cycle of life and death.

Inanna boldly announces to Neti, the gatekeeper of hell, that she has arrived for the funeral of the Bull of Heaven, the husband of Ereshkigal. Indifferent to Inanna's splendor, Neti makes her wait while he confers with Ereshkigal. He then mandates that Inanna remove an article of clothing at each of the seven gates of hell.

At the first gate the "crown of the plain" is taken from her head; at the second, her rod of lapis lazuli; at the third, her lapis lazuli choker; at the fourth, her jewel-studded necklace; at the fifth, her gold ring; at the sixth, her breastplate (for she is the goddess of war as well as of love); and, at the seventh, all her woman's clothing. Naked she appears before the seven judges of the underworld, who zap her with their evil eyes and turn her into a corpse, which hangs on a stake.

When, after three days, Inanna fails to return, Ninshubur does his duty and begs the gods for aid. Her father, Enlil, god of the air, and Nanna, the moon god, are not sympathetic, saying that she brought this on herself. But Enki, god of water, takes pity on her and creates two sexless creatures from the dirt underneath his fingernails. He sends them to Ereshkigal as mourners, and she releases the body to them. They then sprinkle Inanna with the water and food of life sixty times, which is the number of wholeness for Sumerians and is also the number of days and nights in a month.

Inanna revives, ascends through the gates of hell, retrieving her garments and accessories as she goes and taking many specters trapped in the underworld with her. Nonetheless, there is a cost for her release. She must find a substitute to replace her. As she wanders Sumer and spies her husband, Dumuzi (the Babylonian Tammuz), fat and happy at Uruk, she willingly delivers him to the wardens of hell.[15]

Naked Inanna, Venus, and the Moon

As in "There Was a Man Lived in the Moon," Inanna's exploits include the donning and removal of clothing and the importance of food. Anthony Aveni has an intriguing explanation of this myth based on the vagaries of the planet Venus, over which Inanna presides. The seven gates of hell are the seven wandering objects in the sky—the sun, the moon, and the five visible planets. If one watches Venus descend each night lower and lower in the sky, it appears paler and paler as it loses its original luster.

As for the three days hanging in hell—in February in Sumeria, the disappearance of Venus and its reappearance again could take as little as three days. It is also appropriate that the water god Enki should come to her rescue, because in the Tigris and Euphrates region water does not make its way down the mountains until March. So the three days of Venus's darkness in February is a harbinger of life-giving waters.[16]

There are other interpretations that can be added to Aveni's insightful critique. The other heavenly cycles that also influence this myth are the cycle of the sun through the year and the cycle of the moon through the month. Since Inanna is the goddess of love and fertility, her descent into Hades imitates the descent of the fertile earth toward the winter solstice and its resuscitation in the spring. More specifically she is the moon that stays out longer and longer in the night sky as the winter solstice approaches. There are usually either seven full moons or seven new moons between the summer solstice and the winter solstice, thus accounting for the seven gates of hell. Both she and her husband, Dumuzi, are like the seeds that must fall into the ground and die so that they may be born again. The water and food of life are the spring sunshine and spring waters that bring life to dry soil.

And finally, the third cycle of the skies that relates to the Man in the Moon is the cycle of the phases of the moon through the month. Inanna's name itself is similar to the name of Nanna, the moon god. Inanna, as the moon, begins at the horizon as the half moon at midnight, and each night she rises higher in the night sky (which means lower in the underworld) until on the seventh night she is the full moon at the height of the midnight sky. Each night she grows brighter because at each gate of hell she has another accouterment taken away, leaving her brilliant flesh as the full moon. The deadly stare of the evil eyes of her seven dark judges is the shadow of the earth during the lunar eclipse, which also passes through the seven levels to reach its victim and kill her just as the lunar eclipse kills the full moon. The stake on which she hangs is also the long dark shadow of the earth.

The three days are the three days that the full moon stays at the top of the night sky (bottom of the underworld) before it begins its return to the horizon and the earth. The full moon is the food and the thin crescent of the moon is the cup. At each gate Inanna reappoints herself with her gear, just as the moon grows a little darker each day till it arrives again as a half moon at the horizon.

Inanna then proceeds into the daytime sky with her dark specters, whom she freed from hell, until she becomes the new moon and then eclipses Dumuzi, who has taken the role of sun king. He is then kidnapped to take her part as the moon. It was traditional to mourn the death of Dumuzi or Tammuz each spring in the Middle East.

Are these all the sky cycles possible in this myth? Not necessarily. It can also illustrate the sun going into the underworld each night or the ages of the universe going through their cycles. There is no competition between these possible explanations but rather a harmony of all the cycles or—a music of the spheres.

The Star of Venus
From ancient times the pentagram or five-pointed star has been the symbol of the planet Venus and the goddesses that have represented it, including Ishtar, Astarte, Aphrodite, and Venus. Even today many countries whose cultures have had Arabic influence have a crescent moon and Venus as the five-pointed morning star on their flags. These countries include Algeria, Mauritania, Pakistan, Singapore, Tunisia, Turkey, and Uzbekistan.[17]

The pentagram is derived from the dates of the first appearances of Venus as the morning star. When these dates are marked on a circle of the months of the year, a five-pointed star can be traced within the circle connecting those dates. This is also true for other significant sightings of Venus, either as the morning star or as the evening star. For example, dates for the upper conjunctions of Venus, as determined by Martin Knapp, placed on an annual circle create a pentagram. (See Figure 9.)[18] "This 584-day cycle—call it the Venus year—meshes perfectly with the length of the year of our seasons—365 days—in the ratio of 5 to 8, like two gears of a celestial time piece."[19] In other words, every eight years the first appearance of Venus in the morning sky will occur on almost the same date.

Venus and the Moon
From Neolithic times in Old Europe, the Great Goddess was a Moon Goddess of life, death, and regeneration.[20] In the Near East the moon became supplanted as the Mother Goddess by the planet Venus. Inanna, Ishtar, and Astarte became the Queen of Heaven. They

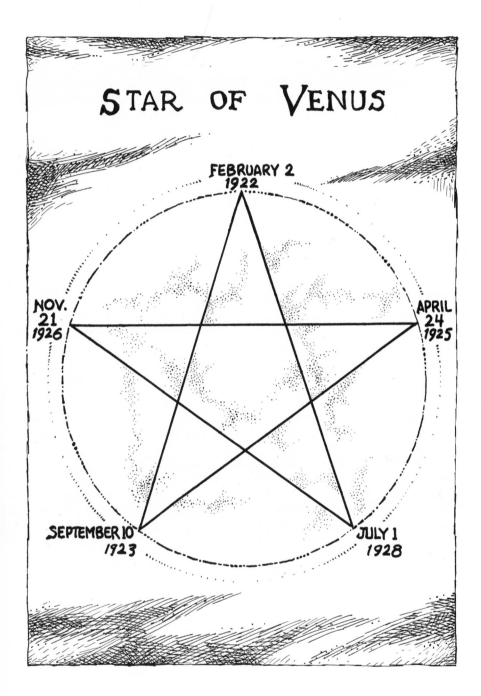

Figure 9. Adapted from The Mystery of Numbers by Annemarie
Schimmel, Oxford University Press, 1993.

retained many moonlike qualities, as we saw with Inanna, and the crescent moon was part of their adornments.

Why did Venus take center stage over the moon? The moon and Venus are very close to each other when the moon is new or close to new. At that time both the moon and Venus are near the sun and can be seen either near sunrise or near sunset. Venus is also associated with birth, like the moon, because it spends nine months as the morning star and nine months as the evening star. However, another reason that Venus supplanted the moon is that the number five, which had been associated with the moon, became associated with Venus and the pentagram, which has many examples in nature.

The apple blossom has five petals, and, if you cut an apple in two along its equator, each half will have inside a perfect pentacle formed by the core. (Try it and see.) As we have seen in "Snow White," the apple was associated with the moon, particularly with the lunar eclipse. But in Greek myth Paris awarded the golden apple to Aphrodite (Venus) for her beauty. As astronomy became more sophisticated, and the pentagram became linked with Venus, the number five no longer kept its association with the moon. The moon, which every seven moons was able to capture the secret of the five days of the solstice and bring it to earth for humans to use, no longer was needed for making the calculations after calendars were invented. We now continue our search for the number five in the moon by examining "Little Red Riding Hood" and "Cinderella," whose title characters are the moon's daughters.

Haggis Bag Is Lunar Eclipse

We began this discussion talking about clothing, food, and the moon. Our investigation may offer a second interpretation of "There Was a Man Lived in the Moon." The rhyme could begin at the full moon with Aiken Drum having no clothing on. As he adds each article of clothing/food, his body is covered up, thus making him a little darker each day. At the new moon he is completely covered; and Willy Wood, whose name associates him with the underworld (the dark woods), begins to eat away at the moon's clothes. As the clothes come off, Aiken Drum grows white and corpulent, until he becomes the full moon. But the haggis bags are Willy's undoing.

The haggis bag, a uniquely Scottish dish, is made of the "heart, liver and lungs of a sheep or calf, minced with onions and suet, seasoned and mixed with oatmeal, and boiled in the stomach of the animal which provided the heart, liver and lungs."[21] It does sound potentially lethal.

The haggis bag that Willy devoured to his own detriment was round and dark red—like the moon during a total lunar eclipse. So the dark shadow of the earth stretches down into the night sky—like the trunk of the tree of heaven—and blots out the moon—and, in this case, Willy Wood. Willy Wood died on this tree, this wood of the cross.

The first verse of this rhyme appeared in print in 1821 as a Scottish rhyme, but the name Aikendrum was known in Scotland as early as 1715. Many versions of the rhyme have been published, some using different names.[22]

The light lunacy of this song has inspired in us more than one interpretation. Whichever explanation you prefer, this verse has fun calling down the moon.

Chapter 14

Little Red Riding Hood

Nana

Like the other heroine tales in this book, this is a story about the moon and the lunar eclipse. The story begins with a young girl and her grandmother. In this translation of the Brothers Grimm version by Lucy Crane, the girl is called Little Red-cap. We, however, will be discussing her as Little Red Riding Hood.[1]

> There was once a sweet little maid, much beloved by everybody, but most of all by her grandmother, who never knew how to make enough of her. Once she sent her a little cap of red velvet, and as it was very becoming to her, and she never wore anything else, people called her Little Red-cap.

An affectionate name for grandmother in many families is Nana (or Nanna). The word derives from children's lip words and infants' imitative syllables, and variations of the word can be found in many languages. *Nanna* is the Greek word for "aunt," and *nana* is the word for "mother" in modern Persian and Serbo-Croatian. The Italian *nonna* means "grandmother," and it comes from the Late Latin *nonna* meaning "old woman" or "nun." The words *nun* and *nunnery* are related to *nonna*.[2] Nanny and Nan are nicknames for Anne. *Nanny* is an appropriate word for a female goat name because of the grandmotherly features of the old goat. And *nanny* is the word for a child's nurse because nannies carry out duties often performed by doting grandmothers and aunts.

In Latin *anus* (with a short *a*) means "old woman." *Ana* in Old High German means "grandmother," and similarly, *annis* in Greek is also "grandmother."[3] Saint Anne is the grandmother of Christ, and

Little Red Riding Hood

she is the patron of midwives and miners. Anne derives from the Hebrew Hannah meaning "grace." The names Jane, Jenny, Joanna, Jean, and Joan, as well as John, are related.

From Sumeria to Rome, Anna was the grandmother goddess long before the appearance of Saint Anne. In Rome she was celebrated as Anna Perenna, "Eternal Anna." She stood between the old year and the new as the Goddess of Time, with her two faces, Prorsa "looking forward" and Postverta "looking back." She later became Iana or Jana, the mate of Janus, the two-faced god of January.[4] Iana is a variant form of Diana, the name of the moon goddess.[5] It is appropriate that Grandmother Anna is also the moon, especially the new moon. Like Anna Perenna, the goddess of the New Year and new beginnings who looks both forward and back, the final thin crescent just before the new moon and the first crescent immediately after the new moon face in opposite directions.

In ancient Uruk, Nanna meant "Moon."[6] Nanna was also the epithet of Cybele, the Great Mother goddess of the Phrygians.[7] She was the lover of the dying Attis. Likewise, the Sumerian mother goddess Inanna or Nina was the consort of the dying Dumuzi, and Nanna was the wife of the Norse dying Balder. Anahita, the Iranian Great Mother goddess, is identified with Inanna, Ishtar, Cybele, Aphrodite, and Venus, as well as with the Canaanite war goddess Anath.[8]

The sign of Saint Anne is the pentagram or five-pointed star. This is the star that Venus traces out on the circle of the year over an eight-year period. (See Figure 9, p. 201.) The new moon and the thin crescent moons are close to Venus, which always orbits close to the sun. The full moon, however, is always far from Venus in its position opposite from the sun. Saint Anne is both the waning crescent and Venus, the evening star; her daughter Mary is both the waxing crescent and Venus, the morning star.

Nana Goat

The story of Little Red Riding Hood is very closely linked to the Grimms' tale "The Wolf and the Seven Kids." In that story a nanny goat leaves her seven kids at home, and, through a ruse, a wolf gets in and swallows six of the kids. The youngest escapes and tells his mother. They find the wolf asleep, cut open his belly, and retrieve the kids alive. They put stones in his stomach, and he drowns trying to get a drink. Alan Dundes points out the close relationship between the two stories and calls them cognates. The many French and Latin fables related to "The Wolf and the Seven Kids" cause Dundes to wonder whether the Latin *capella* meaning "she-goat" may have given rise to names such as Cappuccetto, which is an Italian name for Little Red Riding Hood.[9]

The goat has a long history as a victim of sacrifice and atonement. The Hebrew people of the Old Testament heaped their sins on the back of a goat and then ran the "scapegoat" out of town. In an Ides of March ritual in Rome, a man in a goatskin was led through the streets while being flogged. In ancient Athens the festival of Apaturia was devoted to Dionysus Melanaigis, or Dionysus "dressed in a black goatskin."[10] The origin of Greek tragedy is in Dionysian celebrations, and the word *tragedy* itself means "goat song." Even today in Scandinavia straw goats are made at Yuletide in place of the sacrificial animal. The sign of Capricorn, the goat, rules at Yuletide as well.

From China to Germany the goat is associated with lightning, probably because it is used to climbing in high places, where lightning strikes. The she-goat Amalthea suckled the lightning god Zeus. In the Middle Ages goats became connected to the Devil, who had goat's feet and horns. Hair shirts were woven from goat hair, and the goats in the New Testament were on the left hand at the Last Judgment. Goats were lascivious. The caper is a goat dance, and the word *capricious* suggests the devilishness of the goat.[11]

The spiral horns of the goat imitate the spiraling path of the moon. Whether the black goat as the new moon climbing high in the sky and stealing fire from the sun or the white goat as the full moon being sacrificed in the red fire of the lunar eclipse, the goat is associated with the moon.

Cake and Wine

One day her mother said to her, "Come, Little Red-cap, here are some cakes and a flask of wine for you to take to grandmother; she is weak and ill, and they will do her good. Make haste and start before it grows hot, and walk properly and nicely, and don't run, or you might fall and break the flask of wine, and there would be none left for grandmother. And when you go into her room, don't forget to say, Good morning, instead of staring about you."

Little Red Riding Hood's mother certainly gave plenty of instructions. The cake and wine she prepared are the food of life that come from the upper world and the sun. When the new moon is in the daytime sky it can take a piece of the life-giving sun during a solar eclipse. The sun is the cake, and the thin crescent closest to the new moon is the cup that holds the wine. Little Red Riding Hood, as the moon, travels down into the underworld, bringing the cake and wine to her ailing grandmother. The cake becomes the white full moon and the wine becomes the red of the lunar eclipse in the darkness of the night sky.

In "There Was a Man Lived in the Moon" we saw that the goddess Inanna was revived by being sprinkled sixty times with the water and food of life. We also saw that people around the world gave cakes to the Queen of Heaven. Little Red Riding Hood's grandmother is Inanna, whose name contains the names Anna and Nanna, and who receives the tribute of food as the Queen of Heaven.

The Moon's Circuit

"I will be sure to take care," said Little Red-cap to her mother, and gave her hand upon it. Now the grandmother lived away in the wood, half-an-hour's walk from the village; and when Little Red-cap had reached the wood, she met the wolf; but as she did not know what a bad sort of animal he was, she did not feel frightened.

For all the admonitions that the mother gives her daughter, she seems to forget to mention the wolf. Little Red Riding Hood lives in the village, which stands for civilization and sunlight, while her grandmother lives in the wood, which signifies the primitive and dark underworld. The grandmother lives half an hour from town, which means that the round trip is one hour. Just as the moon makes a half circle from new moon to full moon and a full circle back to the new moon again, so the trip to grandmother's and back is a full circle of an hour.

The Big, Bad Wolf

The wolf is an underworld figure throughout the world. In Scandinavia the god Tyr fettered the Fenris wolf, but at the end of the world it will break free of its chains. In American woodland mythology Wolf is the brother of Manabozho and is drowned, revived, and made ruler of the country of the dead.[12] In Greece, Hades was said to have worn a wolf skin.[13]

The wolf is also linked to fertility. The Romans celebrated the Lupercalia on February 15 in honor of the she-wolf Lupa who suckled the twins Romulus and Remus, who founded their city. Goats were sacrificed to Lupa. Youths dressed in wolf skins ritually purified the Palatine hills. In Turkey barren women still call upon the wolf for help. At the October festival in Kamchatka in eastern Asia, because of the wolf's association with fertility, a wolf is made out of straw and kept through the year so that young women can marry.[14]

The Catholic Church began celebrating Candlemas on February 2, partly to discourage Christians from celebrating the pagan festival of Lupercalia. Candlemas celebrates the Purification, the first time Mary was allowed out after the birth of Jesus. In Christian tradition a boy is churched or presented forty days after he is born. The feast is called Candlemas because it is a Feast of Lights, and candles are blessed that day. February 3 became the feast of Saint Blase, which is appropriate, because *blase* in Celtic means "wolf." Blase's miracles included forcing a wolf to disgorge a pig, which belonged to a poor woman, and removing a fishbone caught in a boy's throat. Because of these acts, the blessing of throats with crossed candles became a ritual on his day. Just as the pig emerged from the wolf, Persephone emerged from the cave of the underworld on Candlemas. Like the goat-god Faunus, who was flayed on the Lupercalia, Blase was flayed before he was martyred. The comb, which was used in his torture, has become his symbol.[15]

> *"Good day, Little Red-cap," said he.*
> *"Thank you kindly, Wolf," answered she.*
> *"Where are you going so early, Little Red-cap?"*
> *"To my grandmother's."*
> *"What are you carrying under your apron?"*
> *"Cakes and wine; we baked yesterday; and my grandmother is very weak and ill, so they will do her good, and strengthen her."*
> *"Where does your grandmother live, Little Red-cap?"*
> *"A quarter of an hour's walk from here; her house stands beneath the three oak trees, and you may know it by the hazel bushes," said Little Red-cap. The wolf thought to himself,*

"That tender young thing would be a delicious morsel, and would taste better than the old one; I must manage somehow to get both of them."

The Three Oaks

The three oaks in front of the grandmother's house are the three nights of the new or full moon, when a solar or lunar eclipse can occur. Together, a solar eclipse and a lunar eclipse fourteen days later make a shadowy world axis that cuts through the universe and unites the upper and lower worlds. In the circle of the sun through the year, midsummer is at the top of the oak and the Yule is at the bottom. The acorn is the tiny fruit that is planted in the underworld of midwinter and grows to the height of summer. In Shropshire the oak is said to bloom at midnight on Midsummer's Eve, but the blooms disappear by morning (just as the full moon blooms at midnight but leaves the sky in the morning). Grandmother's house is in the underworld, both at the darkness of midwinter and at the midnight of the full moon.

Rubor in Latin means both "oak" and "strength." Because of its great height the oak is the tree most often struck by lightning and is associated with the powerful lightning gods. For the Greeks and Celts, as well as the Yakuts of Siberia, the oak was the World Axis or World Tree.[16] Farmers in Northern Europe still plant oaks near their houses to act as lightning attractors in order to protect their buildings. Oak wood is associated with fires and is the wood used for the Yule log. In Wales rubbing oak wood in the palm of the left hand in silence on Midsummer's Day will prevent illnesses throughout the year. The oak tree was also the place of Druid sacrifices, and in Estonia the blood of sacrificed animals is poured on the roots of the oak.[17]

Besides being small, acorns have another important aspect. Most acorns have caps with small scales or spores spiraling around them. The spiral signifies the path of the sun and the moon. As we will see with the hazel, the spiral emphasizes the sacredness of the tree.

The Hazel Bushes

The hazel planted in front of the grandmother's house signifies that this is a story about death and rebirth—of the sun and the moon as well as of human beings. The hazel is the most magical of trees with much knowledge and fecundity. Hazel branches, being the favorite divining twigs for dowsers looking for water, were cut on Saint John's Eve (the summer solstice) in order to be powerful, and their power lasted for seven years.[18] In England nutting or gathering hazelnuts was an unrestrained form of courtship. In the early nineteenth century all the parishes of Surrey, England, had a ceremony of cracking nuts on Michaelmas (September 29) Eve.[19] In Hanover, Germany, crowds shouted "Nuts! Nuts!" at the groom, and three days after the wedding the bride handed out hazelnuts to symbolize that the marriage had been consummated. "To crack nuts" was a euphemism for sexual intercourse in Germany. In Ireland the hazel tree prevented barrenness, and in Normandy a cow was struck three times with a hazel switch to make it give milk.[20]

The hazel was also a sacred tree. The hazelnut is ovoid in shape, just like the path of the moon around the earth. The cracking of the hazelnut prefigures the fall of the Devil at Michaelmas. The solar and lunar eclipse cut through the center of the circle of the moon, like the cracking of a nut and like the breaking into the world of a human soul at conception and birth.

The Magic Spiral

The hazel tree reveals magic spirals. There are long pendulous male catkins that hang down in pairs from its branches. Looking closely, one sees scaly spores circling the catkin in a long spiral. The pair of catkins is a double helix, like the double spirals of the sun between the solstices. It is the caduceus, the symbol of wisdom.

In the Irish tale of the salmon in Connla's well, the salmon became wise by eating nuts from the nine hazel trees of wisdom. The hazel was the ninth tree in the ancient Irish tree calendar and symbolized the ninth month.[21] Finn McCool ate the salmon from the well and absorbed its wisdom. One day while sitting by a stream, Finn McCool saw shavings from a branch float by. Each whittling had nine curls in it. In his wisdom Finn knew that only the knife of Diarmuid could have done this. Finn was to have married Grainne, but the handsome Diarmuid had abducted her and had gone into hiding. Out of vengeance Finn caused a wild boar to attack and kill his enemy. Both the hazel trees and the shavings in this story signify the magic spirals of wisdom.

Initiation

The oak trees imply the sacredness of the grandmother's house, and the hazel connotes her wisdom. Some folklorists see "Little Red Riding Hood" as a description of a matriarchal initiation rite for pubescent girls. Yvonne Verdier expresses it simply: "The sojourn in the little house of the grandmother presents all the characteristics of an initiation. . . . Her entrance is death, her leaving is birth. . . . The little girl is instructed about her feminine future."[22]

Among the Ojibwa of North America, during menarche (the first menstrual flow) a girl smeared soot around her eyes and put on her oldest clothes. Her mother rushed her out of the village on an isolated path, and she was forbidden to touch or look at anything along the way. Her glance alone could cause paralysis or destroy the berry crop. She was left alone in a tiny hut in the forest, and her relatives called her *mukowe*—"she is a bear." Later she was visited by an elder woman, who was past menopause and therefore not susceptible to the girl's powers. They sewed, and the elder told stories and revealed the secrets of womanhood and told about men and childbearing. After the bleeding stopped the girl bathed herself in a stream and returned to the village. This often was the first time she was alone in her life.

Throughout North America menarche is a time of fasting and isolation. In the Winnebago tradition, the girl isolated herself and fasted until the bleeding stopped. In the Pacific Northwest the girl fasted for five days. Tribes tell of one girl who broke the taboo and ate. She turned into a bear and killed all the people of her village.[23] When a girl first menstruates among the White Mountain Apache, they hold a five-day ritual feast, which was instituted by White Painted Woman. Other common traits across the continent include not bathing during seclusion and not using one's fingers to scratch one's hair. A special stick was provided for the purpose instead.[24]

At Brauron in ancient Greece, as in North America, girls were initiated before they could be married. They went into seclusion at the sanctuary of Artemis, the moon goddess whose name is associated with the bear. The girls did not bath and were called *arktoi* or "she-bears." They even spoke roughly, like bears. According to legend, Apollo ordered a girl to be sacrificed to "the bear Artemis" for the killing of a bear in her temple. The girl's father dressed a goat to look like his daughter, and it was sacrificed instead. Goats were sacrificed to Artemis ever after, and the girls performed an imitative bear dance in orange yellow robes.[25]

Blood from the Sun

We have seen that sometimes the spots on the moon are explained as soot that the sun smeared on her brother, the moon, when he raped her in the dark. Some South American tribes say that it was menstrual blood that the sun smeared, rather than soot or ashes.[26] The Yuchi in the American Southeast believe that Sun created their people in the sky world from a drop of menstrual blood. The White Mountain Apache tell how Sun sent out a red beam into Changing Woman, as she lay in the ceremonial menstrual hut, and caused her to menstruate. In another story, Nanabozho, the stealer of fire, was said to have caused his grandmother to menstruate and decreed that henceforth all women would do so once each month.[27]

The sun is connected with menstruation because both are connected with the number five. The summer and winter solstices last for five days, and, as we have seen, the menstrual ritual lasted for five days. But why was it five days? That is the length of the average menstrual period.[28] Furthermore, ancient peoples saw the universe as a harmony between the heavens above and ourselves here below. Menstruation was linked with the dark period of the moon, the time when the new moon is in the day sky, closest to the sun. Just as the new moon steals fire from the sun during an eclipse, so women steal the power of the sun and the fire of new life during menstruation.

The red blood contains the red of the sun here on earth. That new life reveals itself in the placental blood at childbirth and is symbolized in the red of the lunar eclipse. It is interesting that on the west coast of India, one tribe provides seclusion for the mother in childbirth by requiring all the other inhabitants of a house to find shelter elsewhere for five days. The reason for this, besides giving privacy, is to protect the family from the powerful forces that are manifested in the parturient fluids at childbirth. Around the world there are taboos associated with women's activities both during menstruation and during the period of childbirth. In many cases there is a cleansing ceremony to remove the taboo.[29]

During menarche the Ojibwa girl's hands can devastate what they touch, and just walking in her footsteps can cause harm. In Europe, the basilisk was a legendary reptile that was born of menstrual blood and killed at a glance.[30] The Ojibwa girl also possesses the evil eye, which we have already seen to be connected with the hand and the number five. (See Chapter 12, "Three Blind Mice.") Why is it that girls were not allowed to scratch their hair? One reason may be that they had turned into bears and so their fingers were sharp claws with which they could harm themselves. Another is that their fingers contained the powerful number five and therefore their touch could harm themselves as well as others. The bear may be associated with menstruation because of the old belief that bears are drawn by the scent of menstrual blood. The U.S. Forest Service and U.S. Park Service actually issue warnings that women should not camp in grizzly country while they are menstruating.[31] Also, because it grows large, hibernates underground, and grows thin again, the bear is associated with the moon. Moreover, the bear is said to steal fire and eclipse the sun. Therefore he also steals the sacred number five.

Tempting Flowers
The wolf tempts our heroine:
> *Then he walked by Little Red-cap a little while, and said,*
> *"Little Red-cap, just look at the pretty flowers that are growing all round you, and I don't think you are listening to the song of the birds; you are posting along just as if you were going to school, and it is so delightful out here in the wood."*
> *Little Red-cap glanced round her, and when she saw the sunbeams darting here and there through the trees, and lovely flowers everywhere, she thought to herself,*
> *"If I were to take a fresh nosegay to my grandmother she would be very pleased, and it is so early in the day that I shall reach her in plenty of time;" and so she ran about in the wood, looking for flowers. And as she picked one she saw a still prettier one a little farther off, and so she went farther and farther into the wood.*

Just as Persephone was lured by the beautiful narcissus blooms and roamed away from the safety of her companions, so Little Red Riding Hood strayed from the instructions of her mother and fell prey to the wolf. When humans enter into Fairyland, which is in the underworld, there are two things they must avoid doing if they wish to return to the everyday world. One is eating and the other is picking the flowers.[32] Unfortunately, Little Red Riding Hood did not know she was entering the underworld. As the moon takes time to travel from the new moon to the full moon in the night sky, so our heroine takes time in getting to her grandmother's house.

The Oats Goat

But the wolf went straight to the grandmother's house and knocked at the door.

"Who is there?" cried the grandmother.

"Little Red-cap," he answered, "and I have brought you some cake and wine. Please open the door."

"Lift the latch," cried the grandmother; "I am too feeble to get up."

So the wolf lifted the latch, and the door flew open, and he fell on the grandmother and ate her up without saying one word. Then he drew on her clothes, put on her cap, lay down in her bed, and drew the curtains.

The grandmother is old Mother Time at the winter solstice. Like Rhea, the wife of Cronus (Saturn), or Mrs. Santa Claus in our culture, the grandmother is also the Oats Goat, which is associated with the harvest and the end of the year. The Oats Goat is the spirit of the growing oats in Eastern Europe, often represented as a puppet with goat horns made from the last sheaf. In Northern Germany harvesters rushed to keep ahead of the Oats Goat spirit, and in Grenoble, France, a goat was covered with flowers and ribbons and set free in the fields. At the end of reaping it was killed and roasted and eaten at the harvest supper. The goatskin was made into a cloak that was worn during threshing or when a member of the family was ill from backache caused by mowing the oats. In Bohemia a mummer called the Oats Goat dressed in straw and goat horns and went from home to home at Shrovetide (Mardi Gras) dancing with the women. This is similar to the *Fastnachtsbar* or Shrovetide Bear, and in some parts of Lithuania the goat and bear appeared together.[33]

The grandmother is the sacrificial goat of winter. The wolf not only consumes the sacrifice but puts on her clothes (the goatskin) as well. The grandmother is weak and feeble because she is the end of the harvest—the small remnant of the year, that which is swallowed up by the darkness of the winter solstice. The wolf is the Lord of Darkness—the darkness of the winter solstice, the new moon, and the shadows of the eclipses. By taking the place of the grandmother, the wolf reveals the dark and frightening side of Mother Time. The large mouth and long teeth of the wolf/grandmother resemble the features of the Hindu goddess Kali, whose name means "time."[34]

The Full Moon

Little Red-cap was all this time running about among the flowers, and when she had gathered as many as she could hold, she remembered her grandmother, and set off to go to her. She was surprised to find the door standing open, and when she came inside she felt very strange, and thought to herself,

"Oh dear, how uncomfortable I feel, and I was so glad this morning to go to my grandmother!"

And when she said, "Good morning," there was no answer. Then she went up to the bed and drew back the curtains; there lay the grandmother with her cap pulled over her eyes, so that she looked very odd.

Little Red Riding Hood gathering flowers is like the moon waxing brighter each night as it spirals downward into the night sky. When she can hold no more flowers—when she is the full moon and can hold no more sunlight—she remembers her grandmother at the bottom of the underworld. Finding the door ajar, Little Red Riding Hood goes in and pulls back the curtains. This is a description of the umbra beginning to overshadow the moon at the lunar eclipse. Gradually the shadow grows larger, and Little Red Riding Hood grows more uncomfortable.

The Total Eclipse

"O grandmother, what large ears you have got!"

"The better to hear with."

"O grandmother, what great eyes you have got!"

"The better to see with."

"O grandmother, what large hands you have got!"

"The better to take hold of you with."

"But, grandmother, what a terrible large mouth you have got!"

"The better to devour you!" And no sooner had the wolf said it than he make one bound from the bed, and swallowed up poor Little Red-cap.

At totality the moon often turns a dark red during an eclipse. This is the red cap or hood that covers the heroine. The wolf is the Lord of Darkness who engulfs her and appears to take her life. In the Roman Catholic tradition, red is also the color of the vestments worn by priests on the feasts of martyrs, symbolizing their blood. Little Red Riding Hood, like her grandmother, is the victim—the scapegoat—who dies to atone for our sins and to appease the ever-hungry Lord of the Underworld.

The red cap or hood was a relatively recent addition to the story, first appearing in Charles Perrault's version in 1695. It was not to be found in the French oral tale from which it derived.[35] Despite this, Barbara Walker links Little Red Riding Hood to ancient tradition and especially to the lunar eclipse. In Britain a prophetess or priestess wore "a red woven hood"; and in India the goddess Kali wore a red garment and, as the red lunar eclipse, foretold disaster and evoked fear. Even without the red cap or hood, the color red is inevitably connected with this story because of the gory eating habits of the wolf.

Other cultures associate the red moon with blood. Romanian priests stated that the red of the eclipsed moon was due to her wolves attacking her and her blood pouring out. They said it was a reminder to humans to repent their sins.[36] According to the Norse *Eddas*, the moon is reddened with blood.[37] Two wolves chase the sun and the moon. Skoll pursues the sun, and Hati Hrodvitnisson follows the moon. Every so often they succeed in catching their prey and there is an eclipse. But they release them again, and life goes on. At the Twilight of the Gods, the sun and moon will be swallowed for good, and the world will end.[38]

Moon Dogs

It is not only wolves that redden the moon with her blood. A Native American myth explains the lunar eclipse as huge dogs tearing at the moon and causing her to bleed.[39] In China, Hou Ye, the heavenly archer, shot an arrow to drive away the Celestial Dog that swallows the moon.[40] The Burmese tell the story of "Master Putrid," a dog who chases the moon because it stole a magic pestle from his master. Sometimes the dog apprehends the moon, causing an eclipse, but then he disgorges it and the chase resumes.[41]

All kinds of canines are associated with the moon. In Peru there is a fox in the moon.[42] The Pima in North America say the sun and moon are the parents of Coyote.[43] Coyote is often the stealer of light.[44] The Creek say there is a man and a dog in the moon.[45] The Pawnee say a wolf guards the moon.[46]

Why are the dog, wolf, coyote, and others lunar animals? One explanation is that they are scavengers and therefore close to death and to the moon. Another possible reason is that canines, perhaps because on the plains they had to turn around several times to mat down the long grass, turn around several times before they lie down. Whatever the reason, ancient observers may have seen the behavior as an imitation of the moon's circling seven times to reach its apex. The Anasazi in the American Southwest depicted in caves twin spirals coiling around seven times.[47] The Buddha circled the Bodhi tree seven times before sitting beneath it to receive enlightenment.[48] So, too, the wolf behaves like the moon.

Springing to Life

Then the wolf, having satisfied his hunger, lay down again in the bed, went to sleep, and began to snore loudly. The huntsman heard him as he was passing by the house, and thought,

"How the old woman snores—I had better see if there is anything the matter with her."

The he went into the room, and walked up to the bed, and saw the wolf lying there.

"At last I find you, you old sinner!" said he; "I have been looking for you a long time." And he made up his mind that the wolf had swallowed the grandmother whole, and that she might yet be saved. So he did not fire, but took a pair of shears and began to slit up the wolf's body. When he made a few snips Little Red-cap appeared, and after a few more snips she jumped out and cried, "Oh dear, how frightened I have been! It is so dark inside the wolf." And then out came the old grandmother, still living and breathing. But Little Red-cap went and quickly fetched some large stones, with which she filled the wolf's body, so that when he waked up, and was going to rush away, the stones were so heavy that he sank down and fell dead.

They were all three very pleased. The huntsman took off the wolf's skin, and carried it home. The grandmother ate the cakes, and drank the wine, and held up her head again, and Little Red-cap said to herself that she would never more stray about in the wood alone, but would mind what her mother told her.

It is suitable that the wolf should snore loudly, like thunder. Thunder comes in the spring before the flowers bloom and vegetation emerges from the earth. The lightning that accompanies thunder is also connected to the lightning-attracting oak trees that stood outside grandmother's house and to goats, which are sacrificed to the wolf. The snoring foretells the coming forth of Little Red Riding Hood and her grandmother. They remind us of Persephone and Demeter, just as the wolf reminds us of Hades, who wore a wolf skin, and of the bear, who hibernates till spring.

The story of Saint Margaret resembles to our tale. Saint Margaret was the daughter of a pagan priest, but she refused her rich suitor, who was the governor of Antioch, and chose Christianity and virginity instead. After excruciating torture, she was swallowed by the Devil, who took the form of a dragon. Using her cross to cut him open, she burst forth unharmed. Margaret was the patron of childbearing women.[49]

The Cross of Life
Saint Margaret used the cross to defend herself against the Devil. The crossed candles of Saint Blase are a protection at the time of Candlemas, when Mary emerges from the seclusion of childbirth and is purified and when Persephone emerges from the earth. Persephone's epiphany was celebrated on January 6 in Alexandria, before the time of the Christian Epiphany, which is celebrated on the same date. At the Koreion (Kore is another name for Persephone), followers brought up from underground a statue of the goddess wearing only five cruciform seals—on her forehead, hands, and knees.[50] In recent times in Africa, Hottentot women kept crosses above them for protection during confinement. They most likely saw the crosses as moon symbols. The cross was associated with Astarte and Aphrodite, goddesses of life and love. The symbol for the planet Venus is a circle with a cross hanging beneath it.[51] The Madonna is often depicted

with the Christ Child, who is holding an orb—a sphere with a cross on top—a symbol of kingly power.

Christian missionaries were amazed to find mother goddesses with crosses in distant places such as the Americas and Asia. In China the Queen of Heaven was pictured with a child in her arms holding a cross.[52] The Aztec goddess of the rains carried a cross, which was probably associated with the sun or the wind. The Athapascans in North America used crosses in their sacrifices to the new moon.[53] In ancient Peru crosses were used as symbols of the sun.[54]

Down to Earth

Little Red Riding Hood fills the wolf with stones, and he falls to the earth and dies. The planetary symbol for the earth is a cross within a circle. The cross divides the circle into quarters, like the four quarters of the circle of the moon that have their center in the earth, and the four quarters of the circle of the year that also have their center in the earth. The crossroads, at the center, is the place where good and evil spirits dwell. Suicides and criminals are buried there and Hecate can be found there.[55]

The outcome of the Greek story of Cronus (Saturn), the father of the gods who swallowed his children whole, has similarities to our story. Like Little Red Riding Hood filling the wolf with stones, Rhea, Cronus's wife, gave her husband a stone wrapped in a blanket to swallow in place of her sixth child, Zeus. When Zeus was grown, with the help of his grandmother, Gaea (Ge), the earth, he forced his father to disgorge the stone and his five children.[56] The five children who were swallowed are the five days of the winter solstice when the sun "stands still" in the dark winter sky. (See Chapter 11, "Jack and the Beanstalk.")

The earth helped Zeus against his father, just as the earth helps Little Red Riding Hood against the wolf. Whether the wolf is the darkness of night, of winter, or of the lunar eclipse, he is brought down to earth by his bellyful of stones. The opening of the wolf's stomach is a form of birth for Little Red Riding Hood and her grandmother. Childbirth is a time when the lifeblood of the sun, which is revealed in the five days of menstruation, is captured and brought to earth. The winter solstice is the five days when the lifeblood of the sun is brought to earth and revealed in the full moon high in the night sky. The lunar eclipse is the time when the lifeblood of the sun is captured and brought to earth in the blood-red moon.

Perrault's Version

One of the primary metaphors for Little Red Riding Hood is the eclipse of the moon. The rebirth of the heroine at the end of the story is the reemergence of the full moon after the darkness of the eclipse. In the tragic version of Perrault, the story ends with Red Riding Hood being eaten up for good. And yet, this tale also includes metaphors for the moon. For instance, it tells us that when the wolf eats the grandmother, he had not eaten in three days. This is the three days of the new and full moon. Furthermore, when Little Red Riding Hood arrives at the house, she undresses and climbs into bed with her "grandmother."[57] The undressing sequence is the moon waxing toward its fullness becoming ever brighter with each article of clothing that she removes. When all her clothes are removed she is the full moon, bright like Artemis (Diana), the moon goddess at her bath in the deep woods. The full moon has climbed to the height of the night sky, just as Red Riding Hood has climbed into bed with the wolf.

There are sexual overtones, particularly in the Perrault version, in the heroine's undressing and getting into bed with the wolf. The wolf or dog is often the mythic ancestor of specific tribes. In contrast to the attitudes expressed in "Little Red Riding Hood," Native Americans have great respect for the gentleness of the wolf toward its young and its willingness to sacrifice itself for its family. The Dyaks of Borneo believe that a woman married a dog in order to found the human race.[58] One of the most widespread of Native American tales is that of "Dog Husband," about a woman who marries a man who is a dog by day and a man by night.[59] Ancient respect for wolves and other canines contrasts with our current story, which juxtaposes themes of sex and death, showing the close relationship in our psyches of the conception of life and the end of life.

The French Little Red Riding Hood

The French oral tradition behind "Little Red Riding Hood" was less delicate than the story as we know it. The tradition tells of a girl who met a wolf while she was carrying a hot loaf of bread and a bottle of milk to her grandmother. The girl takes the path of needles while the wolf takes the path of pins. The wolf kills the grandmother and puts her flesh in the cupboard and a bottle of her blood on the shelf. The heroine arrives, gives the bread and milk to the "grandmother," and eats the meat and wine (flesh and blood) that is offered her. She then proceeds to take off each article of clothing one at a time, and the wolf instructs her to throw each into the fire. The girl gets into bed; and, as she realizes that her grandmother is really a wolf who is about to eat her, she says she has to answer the call of nature and asks to be excused. The wolf tells her to do it in the bed but finally agrees to tie a woolen string to her foot and allow her outside. She ties the rope around a plum tree and hurries home. The wolf discovers that she has escaped and rushes to her house a moment too late to catch her.[60]

The bread and milk are the light of the full moon, which will restore the grandmother, who is the new moon. Perhaps the needles and pins relate to the fact that both can be magnetized and floated on water to tell which way is north. Both are made of iron, which suggests the sun and the moon. The heroine gives the cake and milk to the supposed grandmother, just as Psyche had given a piece of cake to the dog Cerberus when she visited the underworld.[61] The girl eating her grandmother's flesh and blood is the light of the full moon consuming the darkness of the new moon and also hearkens to prehistoric human sacrifices at the winter solstice. The burning of the clothes one article at a time is the darkness of the moon being slowly removed and being burned in the bonfire of the full moon and the red flames of the lunar eclipse. The woolen rope is the woven path of the moon, the plum tree is the red fruit of the lunar eclipse in the night sky, and the black tree trunk is the shadow of the earth. It is interesting that the plum blossom has five petals, which symbolize the five days of the winter and summer solstices. It is a sacred tree that saves the little girl. Her house is the new moon, where she is able to close the door against the wolf.

The Asian Little Red Riding Hood

Besides an Italian version in which the grandmother's flesh is eaten by the girl, there are very popular Chinese, Korean, and Japanese versions of the Little Red Riding Hood tale that are very similar. They involve an ogress, who is usually a wolf or a tiger. In the Chinese versions she pretends to be the grandmother or grandaunt of children whose mother is not home. The ogress eats all the siblings except for one who is allowed outside on a rope, as in the French version. Ultimately the ogress is killed by the child. The Japanese versions are similar and in some the wolf is cut open in the end and the mother who was eaten is let free.[62]

Among the Min-nan people of Taipei, Taiwan, there were usually two children in the story. In the night the tiger eats one child, and the surviving child asks what the grandaunt is chewing. The tiger responds that it is a peanut and gives one to the child. In reality it is a finger of the dead sibling. The child climbs a tree and, when found, asks for a pot of boiling liquid. The child then pours it on the tiger, killing it.[63]

In the Korean story "The Sun Boy and the Moon Girl," a tiger eats the mother of a boy and girl and then takes the mother's place. The children escape up a tree, but the tiger sees their reflection in a well. It thinks the children are in the well but discovers them in the tree when it hears them laughing. They trick the tiger into putting sesame oil on its paws so it cannot climb. After removing the oil, the tiger tries again, but a rope drops from heaven and the children climb up to safety. A second rope descends and the tiger climbs up it, but it is made of rotten straw and the tiger plunges to its death. In heaven, the girl becomes the sun, the boy becomes the moon, and their mother becomes the stars.[64] The well is the lunar eclipse and the rope is the solar eclipse. The tiger, as usual, is the Lord of Darkness.

This celestial ending is found in both Korean and Japanese versions of the tale. Wolfram Eberhard theorizes that the Chinese versions may also have had a solar and lunar meaning in the past. In one Japanese and two Korean versions the tiger falls to the earth and its blood colors the millet red.[65] This is the tiger falling into the full moon at the bottom of the underworld, causing the red of the lunar eclipse.

Who's Afraid of the Big, Bad Wolf?

In "The Three Little Pigs," which is very similar to "Little Red Riding Hood," the wolf attempts to swallow the pigs, like the sacrificial boar.[66] Other folktales about the wolf are also similar to "The Three Little Pigs." In these versions the wolf usually falls to his death because of his gluttony. We saw that the story of Diarmuid includes a boar and sacred hazel trees. The story of Attis includes a boar and a sacred pine tree. Attis, the lover of Cybele, was gored to death by a wild boar. In another version of the story Attis unmanned himself and died under a pine tree.[67] The pinecone, like the hazel catkin and the acorn cap, has scales that spiral around the outside of the cone. The sacred spiral makes the pine a sacred tree. In Hawaii the boar is also sacred, but rather than being associated with the pine or the hazel, which are not indigenous, it is served with the fruit with spiraling scales—the pineapple. Both the pine tree and the pig are connected with the winter solstice—the pine with the Christmas tree and the pig with the New Year meal.

The Chinese story "Lon Po Po" tells of three children who outwit the hungry wolf.[68] The fall of the wolf from the top of the house or the top of a tree is the fall of the shadow of the solar and lunar eclipse, throwing the wolf down from heaven into hell. In Western fairy tales it is more difficult to discern the solar and lunar aspects of these stories, but it becomes much more evident in some of the Asian versions. One thing that is true in both the Western and Eastern stories is that the antagonist is very often a werewolf or were-tiger, with the ability to change from human to animal form. Were-animals are lunar animals and their shape shifting imitates the shape shifting of the moon through the month.[69]

The wolf is a much-maligned character, and "Little Red Riding Hood" is one of many stories that have perpetuated the image of the wolf as evil. Documented cases of humans being attacked by wolves are rare. Wolves are very dedicated to their families and are kind to one another.[70] However, because of their ferocity they have come to represent darkness and death. In our story, the wolf is overcome, and our heroine is reborn like the moon.

If the saying is true that "you are what you eat," then the wolf is both the grandmother and Little Red Riding Hood. All three are united insofar as both females take on qualities of the wolf before being reborn.[71] They take on the loyalty and nurturing character of the wolf as well as its dark savagery. They are no longer afraid of the big, bad wolf, having come to understand him by becoming a part of him.

Chapter 15

The Grimms' Cinderella

"Cinderella" is the most studied and written-about folktale in the world. And yet nowhere is Cinderella revealed for what she is—the moon, especially the full moon during the lunar eclipse. Snow White and Little Red Riding Hood are the full moon during the red lunar eclipse; Cinderella is the full moon during the black lunar eclipse. Atmospheric conditions on earth cause the light refracted on the moon during an eclipse to appear as a range of colors, of which red is the most outstanding. When little or no light is refracted the shadow on the moon is black.

Most of the stories that are reprinted in this book are Lucy Crane's translations of the Grimms' tales. For "Cinderella," too, Crane's version is the best, though Crane uses the heroine's less familiar German name of Aschenputtel. Not only is this tale full of fascinating details, but the young girl has much more initiative and vitality than the girl in Perrault's story, which was made famous by Walt Disney.

First Month
Full Moon—Death of the Mother

There was once a rich man whose wife lay sick, and when she felt her end drawing near she called to her only daughter to come near her bed, and said,

"Dear child, be pious and good, and God will always take care of you, and I will look down upon you from heaven, and will be with you."

And then she closed her eyes and expired. The maiden went every day to her mother's grave and wept, and was always pious and good. When the winter came the snow covered the grave with a white covering, and when the sun came in the early spring and melted it away, the man took to himself another wife.

Like Snow White's mother, Cinderella's mother dies at the beginning of the story, and the story begins with the onset of winter. Cinderella's mother goes into the underworld of death just as the full moon goes into the underworld of the night sky each month.

Cinderella's tears are like rain, which is said to come from the moon. In an Algerian tale the spots on the moon are the tearstains of an orphan child.[1] As rain washes salt into the oceans, so Cinderella's tears wash salt into the earth on her mother's grave. As we shall see, this salt of the earth represents both death and new life.

The father remarries quickly, a common occurrence at a time when women frequently died young. Unfortunately, the second marriage was not always beneficial for the first wife's children.

New Moon—The Stepmother and Stepsisters

The new wife brought two daughters home with her, and they were beautiful and fair in appearance, but at heart were black and ugly. And then began very evil times for the poor step-daughter.

The stepmother in the center and her two daughters, one on either side, are the traditional three days of the new moon. The stepmother as the new moon at the height of the daytime sky and at the height of power within the household is pure blackness and quintessential evil. Since the new moon in actuality does not last quite three days, the two daughters both reveal the slightest crescents as they move toward and away from the new moon. This makes them beautiful, even though they are still the black new moon. In addition, the last and first crescents just before and after the new moon are very close to the sun, and therefore to Venus, the goddess of beauty, in the morning and evening sky. In their place of power and beauty, these women looked with disdain upon Cinderella, who was the full moon, far from the sun and far from her former power.

Second Month
Full Moon—The Kitchen Fire

"Is the stupid creature to sit in the same room with us?" said they; "those who eat food must earn it. Out upon her for a kitchen-maid!"

The Grimms' Cinderella

They took away her pretty dresses, and put on her an old gray kirtle, and gave her wooden shoes to wear.

"Just look now at the proud princess, how she is decked out!" cried they laughing, and then they sent her into the kitchen. There she was obliged to do heavy work from morning to night, get up early in the morning, draw water, make the fires, cook, and wash. Besides that, the sisters did their utmost to torment her,—mocking her, and strewing peas and lentils among the ashes, and setting her to pick them up. In the evenings, when she was quite tired out with her hard day's work, she had no bed to lie on, but was obliged to rest on the hearth among the cinders. And as she always looked dusty and dirty, they named her Aschenputtel.

As we have seen in "Little Polly Flinders," in many cultures ashes have been connected with the darkness of the moon. For example, Aztec women feared the moon during the lunar eclipse and saw it as a face growing black and sooty.[2] People of Ghana blow ashes to the new moon and say, "I saw you before you saw me" so the moon will not sap their strength as it grows.[3] The Inuit say that the moon is a woman who was burned black on one side by her brother the sun, who chases her but never catches her.[4] Other stories from around the world tell of the moon being covered with mud and other black substances. From the Solomon Islands comes a tale about a boy who tries to fish for the moon. When he fails, the people of Simba Island throw black, sticky mud at the moon so that it will not shine as brightly on other islands as it does on them. The black mud becomes the spots on the moon.[5]

As we saw in "Rumpelstiltskin," the moon is associated with endless, repetitive toil. In an Uigar version of "Cinderella" from Sinkiang in western China, the heroine must spin a huge amount of cotton.[6] For Cinderella, her incessant drudgery includes picking up peas and lentils. Peas and lentils in the ashes are the markings on the moon, and the fine dresses that are taken away from her are the brightness of the full moon. The redness of the kitchen fire is the redness that accompanies the lunar eclipse.

New Moon—The Hazel Twig

It happened one day that the father went to the fair, and he asked his two step-daughters what he should bring back for them.

"Fine clothes!" said one.

"Pearls and jewels!" said the other.

"But what will you have, Aschenputtel?" said he.

"The first twig, father, that strikes against your hat on the way home; that is what I should like you to bring me."

So he bought for the two step-daughters fine clothes, pearls, and jewels, and on his way back, as he rode through a green lane, a hazel-twig struck against his hat; and he broke it off and carried it home with him. And when he reached home he gave to the step-daughters what they had wished for, and to Aschenputtel he gave the hazel-twig.

At first appearance, Cinderella's request is very modest. As we saw in "Little Red Riding Hood," the hazelnut tree is related to the moon and the solar and lunar eclipse, as well as to the winter and summer solstices. It is an especially powerful tree that has control over serpents and their wisdom, particularly because of its double-helix catkins. Cinderella's father's trip to the town and to the fair is a journey to the daytime sky and to the land of the sun. One sister wants dresses, which are the glory of the sun itself, while the other wants jewels, which are like the Bailey Beads necklace just before and after a total solar eclipse. (See Chapter 5, "Rumpelstiltskin.") In contrast, Cinderella is not concerned with appearances and wants the power of the shadow of the eclipse itself. Just as her mother was the moon, so her father is the sun. The falling hat is a metaphor for the sun losing its head, that is, a total solar eclipse.

Third Month
Full Moon—The White Bird in a Tree

She thanked him, and went to her mother's grave, and planted this twig there, weeping so bitterly that the tears fell upon it and watered it, and it flourished and became a fine tree. Aschenputtel went to see it three times a day, and wept and prayed, and each time a white bird rose up from the tree, and if she uttered any wish the bird brought her whatever she had wished for.

The hazel tree now becomes replanted as the shadow of the earth during a lunar eclipse. Through the door of the eclipse Cinderella is able to commune with her mother in the underworld and reach up to the sun in the highest heaven. The white bird acts as a messenger.

The white bird is neither the full moon nor the new moon but rather the half moon, which can be seen at the first and third quarters of the month. The half moon looks like the open wings of a dove, which is a messenger found in both the Old and the New Testament. Like the half moon, which spends half its time in the daytime sky and half its time in the night sky, the dove is a messenger between the upper and lower worlds.

Another biblical messenger with wings is the angel. Traditionally, three times each day while the bells of the local church tolled, pious Catholics recited the Angelus: "The Angel of the Lord declared to Mary. And she conceived of the Holy Spirit. The Word was made flesh. And dwelt among us."[7] In paintings of this event, the Annunciation, the Holy Spirit is often shown as a dove. The angel and the dove are the intermediaries between the divine world and the physical world. As we noted in "Jack in the Beanstalk," the Annunciation is celebrated on March 25, which is halfway between the winter and summer solstices. Likewise, the other angelic visit of Gabriel in the New Testament, announcing the conception of John the Baptist, occurs on September 25, again halfway between the solstices. The white dove is an intermediary between this imperfect world and an ideal world above.

New Moon—Three Bowls of Lentils

Now it came to pass that the king ordained a festival that should last for three days, and to which all the beautiful young women of that country were bidden, so that the king's son might choose a bride from among them. When the two step-daughters heard that they too were bidden to appear, they felt very pleased, and they called Aschenputtel, and said,

"Comb our hair, brush our shoes, and make our buckles fast, we are going to the wedding feast at the king's castle."

Aschenputtel, when she heard this, could not help crying, for she too would have liked to go to the dance, and she begged her step-mother to allow her.

"What, you Aschenputtel!" said she, "in all your dust and dirt, you want to go to the festival! you that have no dress and no shoes! you want to dance!"

But as she persisted in asking, at last the step-mother said,

"I have strewed a dish-full of lentils in the ashes, and if you can pick them all up again in two hours you may go with us."

Then the maiden went to the back-door that led into the garden, and called out,

> *"O gentle doves, O turtle-doves,*
> *And all the birds that be,*
> *The lentils that in ashes lie*
> *Come and pick up for me!*
> *The good must be put in the dish,*
> *The bad you may eat if you wish."*

Then there came to the kitchen-window two white doves, and after them some turtle-doves, and at last a crowd of all the birds under heaven, chirping and fluttering, and they alighted among the ashes; and the doves nodded with their heads, and began to pick, peck, pick, peck, and then all the others began to pick, peck, pick, peck, and put all the good grains into the dish. Before an hour was over all was done, and they flew away. Then the maiden brought the dish to her step-mother, feeling joyful, and thinking that now she should go to the feast; but the step-mother said,

"No, Aschenputtel, you have no proper clothes, and you do not know how to dance, and you would be laughed at!"

And when Aschenputtel cried for disappointment, she added,

"If you can pick two dishes full of lentils out of the ashes, nice and clean, you shall go with us," thinking to herself, *"for that is not possible."* When she had strewed two dishes full of lentils among the ashes the maiden went through the back-door into the garden, and cried,

> *"O gentle doves, O turtle-doves,*
> *And all the birds that be,*
> *The lentils that in ashes lie*
> *Come and pick up for me!*
> *The good must be put in the dish,*
> *The bad you may eat if you wish."*

So there came to the kitchen-window two white doves, and then some turtle-doves, and at last a crowd of all the other birds under heaven, chirping and fluttering, and they alighted among the ashes, and the doves nodded with their heads and began to pick, peck, pick, peck, and then all the others began to pick, peck, pick, peck, *and put all the good grains into the dish. And before half-an-hour was over it was all done, and they flew away. Then the maiden took the dishes to the step-mother, feeling joyful, and thinking that now she should go with them to the feast; but she said "All this is of no good to you; you cannot come with us, for you have no proper clothes, and cannot dance; you would put us to shame."*

Then she turned her back on poor Aschenputtel, and made haste to set out with her two proud daughters.

The three dishes of ash-covered lentils are the three pockmarked new moons, symbols of the three spiteful women, who were on their way to the king's palace in the sun. The lentils strewn in the ashes are the dark days of the winter solstice, when seeds are buried in the earth, waiting to burst forth and bear fruit. Like the beans in "Jack in the Beanstalk," the lentils represent fertility and potential life. Cinderella, like the seeds in the ground and the lentils in the ashes, is covered with dirt and soot, eager to change from Nothingness into Being.

Fourth Month
Full Moon—The Dress of Gold and Silver

And as there was no one left in the house, Aschenputtel went to her mother's grave, under the hazel bush, and cried,

"Little tree, little tree, shake over me,
That silver and gold may come down and cover me."

Then the bird threw down a dress of gold and silver, and a pair of slippers embroidered with silk and silver. And in all haste she put on the dress and went to the festival.

The spiraling path of the moon through the month shuttles back and forth around the tree weaving a dress of silver and gold. There are many stories relating the moon to spinning and weaving. The Hawaiians tell the story of Hina, who pounds tapas, a fibrous bark, into fine clothing. One day she becomes tired of her husband constantly making her do more work, so she prays to be given a rest. The rainbow hears her and takes her up to the sun, but it is too hot and she is burned. The next day the rainbow takes her to the moon. Her husband sees her escaping and grabs her by the foot. He breaks her foot, but she escapes. Today she can be seen in the markings on the moon, with her lame foot, either with her calabash (gourd shell) or with her mallet, pounding out the tapas into cloth. The cirrus clouds around the moon are her fine cloths.[8]

In an Italian version of "Cinderella," known as "La Sendraoeula," the girl's sisters describe the mysterious princess at the ball as "all dressed like the moon."[9] As the full moon, in her new gown, Cinderella heads off to the palace in the daytime sky.

New Moon—The First Day

But her step-mother and sisters did not know her, and thought she must be a foreign princess, she looked so beautiful in her golden dress. Of Aschenputtel they never thought at all, and supposed that she was sitting at home, and picking the lentils out of the ashes. The King's son came to meet her, and took her by the hand and danced with her, and he refused to stand up with any one else, so that he might not be obliged to let go her hand; and when any one came to claim it he answered,

"She is my partner."

Unlike the ball in Perrault's "Cinderella," the festival in this version takes place during the day, which is fitting because the palace of the king is the land of the sun, which is the daytime sky. Cinderella's grimy clothes are a disguise, hiding the brilliance of her true self, which is revealed by her radiant dress. She represents us all, who travel incognito in everyday flesh and blood, hiding the magnificence of our souls.

Cinderella leaves her place in the kitchen far from the sun at the lunar eclipse and transits through the month to become the crescent moon that is able to hold hands with the sun (the prince) because they are so close to each other in the sky.

Fifth Month
Full Moon—The Pigeon House

And when the evening came she wanted to go home, but the prince said he would go with her to take care of her, for he wanted to see where the beautiful maiden lived. But she escaped him, and jumped up into the pigeon-house. Then the prince waited until the father came, and told him the strange maiden had jumped into the pigeon-house. The father thought to himself,

"It cannot surely be Aschenputtel," and called for axes and hatchets, and had the pigeon-house cut down, but there was no one in it. And when they entered the house there sat Aschenputtel in her dirty clothes among the cinders, and a little oil-lamp burnt dimly in the chimney; for Aschenputtel had been very quick, and had jumped out of the pigeon-house again, and had run to the hazel bush; and there she had taken off her beautiful dress and had laid it on the grave, and the bird had carried it away again, and then she had put on her little gray kirtle again, and had sat down in the kitchen among the cinders.

The next day, when the festival began anew, and the parents and step-sisters had gone to it, Aschenputtel went to the hazel bush, and cried,

> *"Little tree, little tree, shake over me,*
> *That silver and gold may come down and cover me."*

Then the bird cast down a still more splendid dress than on the day before. And when she appeared in it among the guests every one was astonished at her beauty.

Back at her father's house, she hides inside the pigeon house, just as the full moon hides within the shadow of the lunar eclipse. The cutting down of the house is the disappearance of the eclipse.

Like other birds, the pigeon is a messenger between the upper and lower worlds. Entering the pigeon-house at evening represents being halfway between the world of day and the world of night. Specifically, the pigeon symbolizes love, which is demonstrated by the male, which incubates the eggs. In Algeria it was believed that the sounds of pigeons were the voices of the dead. In ancient China, the hawk of winter was transformed into the pigeon of summer after the spring equinox, again at the halfway point.[10]

Cinderella is back in the night sky as the lunar eclipse. Cinderella is the keeper of the hearth and the hearth fire. Around the world household gods protect the hearth and home. The Latin word for hearth is *focus,* a word we use in English. The fireplace is the focal point of the home. *Focus* also meant an "altar-fire" and a "funeral pyre."[11] Roman household spirits were known as *lares* and were treated with great respect. Each family had its own specific *lares,* who were originally spirits of the dead. At one time they were worshipped at the household grave of the departed, but the ceremonies were later moved to the hearth and the home. Fairies are also sometimes thought to once have been spirits of the dead or ancestral gods. There are specific fairies known as household familiars, who attach themselves to a household and are called dwarfs, kobolds, brownies, or billies. They sleep on the hearth, enter and leave by the chimney, sweep the floor, wash the dishes, and lay the fire.[12]

The little oil lamp burning dimly in the chimney is also an image of the lunar eclipse. The red fire of the lamp is the dull red of the moon during total eclipse. The chimney is the shadow of the earth, which causes the eclipse. The oil lamp is reminiscent of sanctuary lamps in Catholic churches, which signify the divine presence. In Rome the Vestal Virgins kept a perpetual fire in the temple of Vesta (the Greek Hestia), the goddess of the hearth.[13] The fire represented the hearth fire for all of Rome and the *lares* of the state.

New Moon—The Second Day

The prince had been waiting until she came, and he took her hand and danced with her alone. And when any one else came to invite her he said,

"She is my partner."

So again Cinderella climbs into the day sky and becomes the crescent moon near the sun.

Sixth Month

Full Moon—The Pear Tree

And when the evening came she wanted to go home, and the prince followed her, for he wanted to see to what house she belonged; but she broke away from him, and ran into the garden at the back of the house. There stood a fine large tree, bearing splendid pears; she leapt as lightly as a squirrel among the branches, and the prince did not know what had become of her. So he waited until the father came, and then he told him that the strange maiden had rushed from him, and that he thought she had gone up into the pear-tree. The father thought to himself,

"It cannot surely be Aschenputtel," and called for an axe, and felled the tree, but there was no one in it. And when they went into the kitchen there sat Aschenputtel among the cinders, as usual, for she had got down the other side of the tree, and had taken back her

beautiful clothes to the bird on the hazel bush, and had put on her old gray kirtle again.

   On the third day, when the parents and the step-children had set off, Aschenputtel went again to her mother's grave, and said to the tree,

   "*Little tree, little tree, shake over me,*
   That silver and gold may come down and cover me."

   Then the bird cast down a dress, the like of which had never been seen for splendour and brilliancy, and slippers that were of gold.

This time at close of day she hides in the branches of a pear tree. In China the white pear blossom is a symbol of mourning and of the fleeting nature of life, because it is so short-lived and because the wind so easily scatters it.[14] In Ireland bringing a pear blossom into the house portends a death in the family.[15]

The Yuletide "partridge in a pear tree" echoes a Greek myth about Perdix, whose name means "partridge." Daedalus, Perdix's uncle, threw him from the peak of Athena's temple in a fit of anger, but the goddess intervened and turned Perdix into a partridge. Another name for Athena, the goddess of wisdom, was *Once* or "Pear Tree."[16] The yellow globular fruit reminds us of the full moon in the underworld and of the world of the flesh. The pear can also be golden red. In that case, the chopping down of the pear tree signifies the removal of the shadow of the lunar eclipse, which was Cinderella's hiding place.

In a Korean version of "Cinderella," the heroine is named Pear Blossom.[17] Why is the pear so important that it appears in the German and Korean versions? The answer may be in the number five. Like the apple blossom, the pear blossom has five petals. Furthermore, when a pear is cut in two across its equator, the core makes a five-pointed star. How appropriate that the goddess of wisdom should be named for a fruit tree that contains the number five—the number of days of both the summer and the winter solstice period. How suitable that the partridge in the pear tree is a symbol of the winter solstice and of rebirth. And how suitable, too, that Cinderella, whose wisdom is already symbolized in the hazel bush, should also know the wisdom of the number five.

For the third and last time Cinderella invokes the power of the lunar eclipse, which is appropriate because the lunar eclipse can occur only during the three days of the full moon. This time her slippers are made of gold rather than silver. Gold is more valuable than silver; and, as we shall see, these are no ordinary slippers. Of all the differences between Perrault's and the Grimms' versions of "Cinderella," the most noticeable is that the slippers in one are of glass and in the other are of gold. An interesting theory that has developed around the glass slippers suggests that in Perrault's original French version, the slippers were made of fur, but that in translation, the Old French word *vair* was mistranslated as *verre*, meaning "glass." This theory was introduced into the *Encyclopedia Britannica*; but there was no evidence that the mistranslation ever occurred or that there is a need for such an explanation, since the French, Scottish, and Irish oral stories from which Perrault could have drawn use glass slippers. But the theory has become so ingrained in popular belief that it is impossible to eradicate.[18]

New Moon—The Third Day

And when she appeared in this dress at the feast nobody knew what to say for wonderment. The prince danced with her alone, and if any one else asked her he answered,

"She is my partner."

And when it was evening Aschenputtel wanted to go home, and the prince was about to go with her, when she ran past him so quickly that he could not follow her. But he had laid a plan, and had caused all the steps to be spread with pitch, so that as she rushed down them the left shoe of the maiden remained sticking in it. The prince picked it up, and saw that it was of gold, and very small and slender.

This time the prince fooled the beautiful maiden. Interpreting this psychologically, we can see the stairs as Jacob's ladder of psychological growth and self-awakening.[19] The fleeing back down the stairs from the fifth level of change and growth past the fourth level of Nothingness and the subconscious (black pitch) results in leaving part of her psyche back at the higher level. Using a metaphor from Thomas Aquinas, she must therefore "limp" home on one shoe because she has been crippled, having one foot in heaven and one on earth. Using a theme from the land of fairies, to rescue someone from a fairy ring, one must put one foot into the ring while keeping the other out. Then the lost person becomes visible and can be pulled out.[20]

Cinderella lost her left shoe. In "Diddle, Diddle, Dumpling" we saw an example of a one-shoed hero, and in "Goosey, Goosey Gander" we saw that being left sided is connected with the moon. When one observes the moon at the same time each night, it moves retrograde or in the opposite direction from the sun, which moves from left to right. Therefore moving toward the left or counterclockwise became associated with the moon, with women, and subsequently with witches' dances and with evil.[21]

Pitch is used in reference to the moon. For instance, the Estonian story "Painting the Moon" tells of the Devil having his assistant climb a ladder to the moon in order to cover it with pitch. The assistant dropped a bucket of pitch on the Devil by accident, then, as he was darkening the moon, Old Father saw him and stopped him before the moon was completely covered. The assistant can still be seen in the moon with his pitch bucket and brush.[22] Brer Rabbit's encounter with the tar baby is another story about the new moon being blackened. The rabbit is a universal sign for the moon. It is covered with tar when it gets into a fight with the silent tar baby. Joel Chandler Harris popularized this and other "Uncle Remus" tales, which were brought to the American South by slaves from Africa.[23]

The description of the gold slipper as "small and slender" is a description of the crescent moon just before it disappears into the new moon. If the new moon is facing us, the last crescent is on its left and is therefore the "left shoe." The black pitch is the new moon, which Cinderella steps into with her left shoe. After the new moon the first crescent is her right shoe, which she takes with her out of the daytime sky.

Seventh Month
Full Moon—The Shoe Test

The next morning he went to the father and told him that none should be his bride save the one whose foot the golden shoe should fit. Then the two sisters were very glad, because they had pretty feet. The eldest went to her room to try on the shoe, and her mother stood by. But she could not get her great toe into it, for the shoe was too small; then her mother handed her a knife, and said,

"Cut the toe off, for when you are queen you will never have to go on foot." So the girl cut her toe off, squeezed her foot into the shoe, concealed the pain, and went down to the prince. Then he took her with him on his horse as his bride, and rode off. They had to pass by the grave, and there sat the two pigeons on the hazel bush, and cried,

> *"There they go, there they go!*
> *There is blood on her shoe;*
> *The shoe is too small,*
> *—Not the right bride at all!"*

Then the prince looked at her shoe, and saw the blood flowing. And he turned his horse round and took the false bride home again, saying she was not the right one, and that the other sister must try on the shoe. So she went into her room to do so, and got her toes comfortably in, but her heel was too large. Then her mother handed her the knife, saying, "Cut a piece off your heel; when you are queen you will never have to go on foot."

So the girl cut a piece off her heel, and thrust her foot into the shoe, concealed the pain, and went down to the prince, who took his bride before him on his horse and rode off. When they passed by the hazel bush the two pigeons sat there and cried,

> *"There they go, there they go!*
> *There is blood on her shoe;*
> *The shoe is too small,*
> *—Not the right bride at all!"*

Then the prince looked at her foot, and saw how the blood was flowing from the shoe, and staining the white stocking. And he turned his horse round and brought the false bride home again.

"This is not the right one," said he, "have you no other daughter?"

"No," said the man, "only my dead wife left behind her a little stunted Aschenputtel; it is impossible that she can be the bride."

But the King's son ordered her to be sent for, but the mother said,

"Oh no! She is much too dirty, I could not let her be seen."

But he would have her fetched, and so Aschenputtel had to appear.

First she washed her face and hands quite clean, and went in and curtseyed to the prince, who held out to her the golden shoe.

Then she sat down on a stool, drew her foot out of the heavy wooden shoe, and slipped it into the golden one, which fitted it perfectly. And when she stood up, and the prince looked in her face, he knew again the beautiful maiden that had danced with him, and he cried,

  "This is the right bride!"

The step-mother and the two sisters were thunderstruck, and grew pale with anger; but he put Aschenputtel before him on his horse and rode off. And as they passed the hazel bush, the two white pigeons cried,

> *"There they go, there they go!*
> *No blood on her shoe;*
> *The shoe's not too small,*
> *The right bride is she after all."*

And when they had thus cried, they came flying after and perched on Aschenputtel's shoulders, one on the right, the other on the left, and so remained.

The two pigeons are the gatekeepers between the upper and lower worlds. Like the half moons at the first and third quarters of the lunar cycle, they keep watch along the path between the day and night sky. Their outspread wings look like the half moon; and like the feather that the Egyptian gods Ma'at and Toth used to measure the hearts of the deceased, these feathered creatures pass judgment on those attempting to ascend to the land of the sun. (See Chapter 11, "Jack in the Beanstalk.")

The horse is another symbol of the transition between the upper and lower worlds. The horseshoe is a talisman against evil and was traditionally placed on chimneys and on the doors of houses, stables, and churches in North America and Europe. Its crescent shape called up the power of the new moon, and its iron repelled the Devil, witches, and fairies.[24] Its crescent shape also calls up the crescent of the sun just before and after the total solar eclipse. Like the blacksmith, who in the form of the new moon stole the fire of the sun and who pounds the red-hot iron into horseshoes, Cinderella resides by her underground fire blackened by soot and ashes. Ultimately her crescent shoe identifies her as belonging to the upper world as well.

Because of its thundering hooves, the horse has long been associated with thunder and lightning, which also travel back and forth from heaven to earth. The winged white horse Pegasus was said to carry the thunder and lightning of Zeus.[25] The dual nature of horses was conveyed by the Hindu twin "horse boys," the Asvins, and by the Greek twins Castor and Pollux, who were talented horsemen. The British legendary kings Hengist and Horsa literally mean "stallion" and "mare."[26] The association of horses with travel to the other world is evident in the medieval custom of calling a funeral bier "Saint Michael's horse."[27] The feast of Saint Michael being halfway between the solstices denotes the transitional nature of the horse.

The wounding of the foot and the trail of blood are both suggestive of the story of the Bear's Son. In the European version of the tale, the young man sets out from his home and does battle with a supernatural being (dwarf, giant, ogre, demon, or the like), wounding him. The Bear's Son follows the trail of blood into the underworld, kills the monster, and rescues a princess or finds treasure. The story of Beowulf's wounding of Grendel and following its trail of blood uses the same Bear's Son theme.[28] In "Cinderella," the greedy sisters oblige the prince by wounding themselves. Their subsequent lameness is a sign that they are daughters of the moon.

This wounding scenario fits the solar eclipse theme. The mother and daughters are the three days of the new moon. When they eclipse the sun they are wounded in the battle. The knife of the solar crescent just before and after totality cuts them, and their blood is the shadow of the moon, which races across the landscape after the eclipse. The toe and heel are the lunar crescents before (toe) and after (heel) the new moon.

Although not usually considered part of the Cinderella cycle, because it is a legend rather than a folktale and because it does not contain enough of the elements of the Cinderella story, there is a shoe-test tale that comes from ancient Egypt.[29] A Greek slave girl named Rhodopis receives a pair of rose-red golden slippers from her admiring master, and the other slave girls are jealous of her. One day an eagle grabs one of her slippers from the riverbank and flies high overhead. The eagle drops it into the lap of the pharaoh, and at first he thinks it is "a piece of the sun" until he sees the eagle wheeling above. He vows that he will marry the owner of the slipper, and he searches all over until he finds Rhodopis and places the slipper on her foot. In the first century B.C. the Roman historian Strabo told this story about the Egyptian pharaoh Amasis (Dynasty XXVI, 570–526 B.C.) and his queen, Rhodopis.[30]

The eagle is a widespread symbol for the sun.[31] The rose-red gold slipper that looks like a piece of the sun is the red-hot crescent of the sun just before or after a solar eclipse. This also fits with Cinderella's slipper being the crescent moon, because the moon carries the light of the sun, in the shape of a crescent from the day sky to the night sky. The slipper appears later in the month as the red crescent of the moon immediately before or after a lunar eclipse.

New Moon—The Wedding

And when her wedding with the prince was appointed to be held the false sisters came, hoping to curry favour, and to take part in the festivities. So as the bridal procession went to the church, the eldest walked on the right side and the younger on the left, and the pigeons picked out an eye of each of them. And as they returned the elder was on the left side and the younger on the right, and the pigeons picked out the other eye of each of them. And so they were condemned to go blind for the rest of their days because of their wickedness and falsehood.

The seventh new moon after the winter solstice is the summer solstice, which is in June, the month of weddings. It is also the time when punishment is meted out to the stepsisters. First each sister is made one-eyed, like the one-eyed moon of the Tewa in the American Southwest. Then they are totally blinded just as Odysseus blinded one-eyed Polyphemus. As we have seen, blindness is a result of watching the solar eclipse for too long with the unaided eye. The blotting out of the sun is also a metaphor for the blinding of the eye of the sky. (See Chapter 12, "Three Blind Mice.") The pigeons, as the judges of souls, carried out the punishment. Now the women are lame and blind. They must walk with the aid of a crutch or cane, which means they are "three-legged." Three is the number of the new moon. They are the waning and new moon of death, while Cinderella is the waxing and full moon of life.

From Solstice to Solstice

Here is Cinderella's journey from midwinter to midsummer, starting from the bottom left:

Month	Full Moon	New Moon
June	Shoe test	Wedding
May	Pear tree	Third day
April	Pigeon house	Second day
March	Dress of gold and silver	First day
February	White bird in tree	Three bowls of lentils
January	Kitchen fire	Hazel twig
December	Death of mother	Stepmother and sisters

The death of Cinderella's mother is the death of the old year. The stepmother is Mother Time, and she and her two daughters are the three Fates. They symbolize the old year and the cutting off of the thread of life. The kitchen fire and the hazel twig are signs of fertility and domesticity. The dove in the tree is a sign of hope as well as an intermediary with the upper world, just as the dove that Noah sent out from the ark returned with an olive branch as a sign of hope and of high ground. The three bowls of lentils represent the work that Cinderella accepted as her duty. The picking out of the lentils from the ashes portrays the mind making distinctions (like a bean counter). The dress of gold and silver marks the transition from the lower to the upper world. The pigeon house is after the spring equinox, fitting the pigeons' role as guardians of the upper world. The pitch stands for the Nothingness that must be surpassed. Finally, the fitting of the slipper is the level of Becoming, while marriage to the prince is the union with Being.

The seven stages of the story also align with the seven days of the week and the seven planets, working backward from Saturn and Saturday. The stepmother is Rhea, the wife of Cronus (Saturn). The hazel branch is the fertility of Venus, and the bowls of lentils are the duty and mindfulness of Jupiter, and the pigeons are the wings of Mercury. The pear symbolizes Mars, mourning, the underworld, and Nothingness, like the apple in "Snow White." The golden slipper is the moon and Becoming, and the marriage is the sun and Being. Cinderella has completed her journey.

Chapter 16

Other Cinderellas

Perrault's version of Cinderella, which has become the standard, with the help of Walt Disney, has many aspects that are not found in most other versions of the story. These include the fairy godmother, the pumpkin coach, the mouse-horses, the rat-coachmen, and the lizard-footmen. The witching hour of midnight is also a Perrault invention.[1] The 1812 version of the Grimms' "Cinderella" has many similarities to Perrault's version, including the midnight deadline. The version we analyzed is the final one, published in 1857.[2] It has much of the folkloric tradition left out by Perrault, such as the help of the dead mother, which is an important part of versions of the tale from other countries.

Old-World Cinderellas

Cap o' Rushes

At the beginning of the Grimms' version of "Cinderella" the father asks the girls what they want, and Cinderella's request is very modest, while her sisters' are very grand. This is very much like Shakespeare's *King Lear*, in which Cordelia, unlike her two sisters who heap praise upon their father when he asks how much they love him, merely says, "I love my majesty /According to my bond; nor more nor less." (1.1.94–95.) Both Cordelia and Cinderella, besides having had two sisters as rivals, were unostentatious in their speech to their fathers. Alan Dundes calls the two heroines "kissing cousins." He notes that the Lear plot is the "love like salt" folktale plot as well as the folktale plot of the mad father who tries to marry his own daughter, as found in "The Dress of Gold, of Silver, and of Stars" and other folktales that are very closely linked to the Cinderella cycle.[3]

The English folktale "Cap o' Rushes" is a good example of the "love like salt" tale type. A king asks his three daughters how much they love him, and the two elder are expansive in their answer, while Cap o' Rushes merely says "I love you as our need is, which is even as fresh meat loves salt." Enraged, the king says that she does not love him and casts her out. She makes a coat and hood for herself out of rushes and seeks work in the palace of the king, where she becomes a kitchen maid. A ball is held at the palace, and a fairy provides a silver dress for her to wear. She impresses the prince with her beauty but escapes before he can follow her. The next evening she attends the ball in a gold dress, and on the third evening her dress is made of the feathers of all the birds of the air. This time the prince slips a gold ring into her hand before she escapes.

After this the prince falls ill from missing the princess and is near death. Cap o' Rushes begs to make a soup for him. She places the ring in the soup, and the prince discovers it when he empties the bowl. He leaps from his bed and demands to see whoever made the soup. Cap o' Rushes is sent to him, and she removes her hood and coat before him, revealing her dress of feathers. They plan to marry, and Cap o' Rushes's father is invited to the wedding. When she discovers this, she orders that not one grain of salt be added to the meal. All the guests reject the tasteless food, but Cap o' Rushes's father cries and says that it reminds him of the daughter he sent away, who he now realizes loved him most of all. She embraces him, and he rejoices that she is still alive.[4]

Where Cinderella is covered with ashes, the heroine of this story is covered with rushes. In other versions of this tale type she is covered with an ashy pelt, a cat skin, a deerskin, a donkey skin, a hiding box, a mossy coat, a leather suit, a rabbit skin, a tattered coat, pieces of fur, and a wooden cloak. Giambattista Basile relates a version of the tale entitled "The She-bear" in the *Pentamerone* (Day 2, Tale 6), published between 1634 and 1636. In it the heroine turns into a she-bear by putting a magic piece of wood in her mouth in order to escape her father, who wants to marry her. A prince falls in love with her, but she continues to hide herself in the form of a bear, until one day he kisses her before she can put the piece of wood in her mouth. He marries her, and her father accepts the situation.[5] The dark coverings and the metamorphosis into a bear all represent the moon being covered by the shadow of the earth at the lunar eclipse. It also is an analogy for the descent into the darkness of winter.

The story of Cap o' Rushes also introduces the gold ring as a sign of love. As in "Rumpelstiltskin," the gold ring is the annular eclipse of the sun, which occurs during the new moon. The prince discovers the ring in the empty bowl, which is the waning crescent moon just before the new moon.

The love-like-salt theme of the story draws upon the ancient symbolism of salt. Salt is associated with the moon. According to the Apache, the moon suitably is called Changing Woman. Among the Navaho, Salt Woman is a variant of Changing Woman. In the American Southwest ceremonies were celebrated both at the departure and return of men who journeyed to procure salt.[6] As we saw in "Jack in the Beanstalk," the gathering of salt was a dangerous occupation, and if a man would look back at the lake where the salt was gathered, his soul would be captured and he would soon die.

Although salt is linked to death, it is also linked to life. Salt is mentioned in the Roman Catholic baptism ceremony, where it symbolizes the seasoning of spiritual nourishment. In the Old Testament all sacrifices were to include salt, which symbolized the Israelites' covenant with God (2 Chron. 13:5 and Lev. 2:13). In Japan salt is used to purify and protect. It is poured over the graves of the dead, on the rims of wells, and at the entrances of homes.[7] In Europe, it can be used as a protection against fairies.[8]

Salt makes land barren, but it preserves meat and keeps it fresh. In the Old Testament babies were rubbed with salt (Ezek. 16:4), and even in modern times corpses have been covered with salt so that their spirits do not wander the earth.[9] The belief that putting salt on a bird's tail will prevent it from flying may derive from the belief that birds contain the souls of the dead.

As ashes are the remnant of the old fire, so salt is the remnant of the old rain and the old tears, but as ashes are the seed of the new fire, so salt is the seed of new rain and new life. Both ashes and salt stand for the death and rebirth of the moon each month. Just as the bear is related to the moon, so it is also connected to salt. In the World Renewal Ceremony, which is a New Year bear ritual of the Munsee-Mahican Delaware, unsalted bear meat is eaten on the first five days of the festival, after which time the mood of the ceremonies lightens.[10]

Just like the unsalted meat at the wedding of Cap o' Rushes, the meal causes sadness. The slayers of the bear are mourning the death of their victim and salting its flesh with their tears.

Mary

One description of the Virgin Mary is *Mater Dolorosa* or "Grieving Mother." As Cinderella wept over her mother's grave, so Mary wept over the body of Jesus. Although the origin of Mary's name is uncertain, since the early days of the Christian Church it has been associated with the name Mara, which in Hebrew means "bitter" (Ruth 1:20). Another Mary, Mary Magdalen, is often associated with the woman who washed Jesus' feet with her bitter tears of repentance and dried them with her hair. She also anointed and kissed his feet (Luke 7:44–46). Myrrh, a sweet-smelling bitter-tasting ointment, which is used for anointing kings as well as the dead, comes from the myrtle tree. Etymologically myrrh comes from the Hebrew word *mor*, which implies bitterness.[11] At the Passover Seder the *maror* is the bitter herb, which is soaked in saltwater in memory of the tears the Israelites shed in Egypt.

A name for Mary among the early Christians was *Stella Maris* or "Star of the Sea." The word *star* is often connected with the morning and evening star, the brightest star in the sky, the planet Venus. Venus is often a mourning goddess, who laments the death of her lover, the slain moon god. Examples include Ishtar and Tammuz, Venus and Adonis, Inanna and Dumuzi, and Isis and Osiris. The dying god imitates the thin crescent moon, which leaves Venus and the day sky each month to descend into the underworld of the night sky as the full moon. Another goddess of the planet Venus is the Hindu Tara. The goddess Tara ("Star"), like Persephone, was abducted. The moon god Soma carried her off causing a war between Soma and her husband Brhaspati (Jupiter).[12] While in captivity, Tara conceived a son, Budha (Mercury). Tara, like the Middle Eastern goddesses, was a Great Goddess, and her name is linked etymologically to our words *star, stellar,* and *astronomy,* as are Astarte, Ishtar, and Ostara (Eostre, goddess of Easter).[13]

Tara was a manifestation of Durga, the devouring mother goddess who lived on human sacrifice, even into the nineteenth century. Other forms of Durga include Mari and Kali. In India Mari was the goddess of death and pestilence (from the Sanskrit *mara* meaning "death"). Kali (*kala* means "time") is the terrifying wife of Shiva, the god of destruction. She is pictured as a hideous, emaciated, naked black goddess with pointed fangs carrying a noose, a skull-capped scepter, a severed head, and a sword. Her necklace is adorned with human skulls. She haunts crematoria and burial grounds. Besides being death and time, she is stripped of all illusions and distinctions and is Nothingness, which is the dynamic potential from which all manifestation comes.[14]

Mary is *Stella*, the bright and beautiful wishing star Venus, and *Maris*, the bitter sea, filled with all the tears poured out for the dead. She is the *Pieta* so beautifully sculpted by Michelangelo. As Venus lamented the loss of her lover, and Cinderella lamented the loss of her mother, so Mary wept for her son. Traditionally, being covered with ashes is a sign of mourning. As Cinderella was pictured as blackened with ashes and black Kali danced among the ashes of the dead, so Mary often was painted or sculpted as black as well.

There are over four hundred images of the black Madonna and child venerated in churches throughout Europe, North Africa, and Latin America today. The peak of the cult of the Black Virgin was in the twelfth century, when the Crusades and the Cathar (Albigensian) heresy brought Eastern influences into Europe. Among other tenants, the heresy taught the primacy of the human spirit over the material world and gave women equal status with men. At the same time as troubadour poets were putting Love on a pedestal, the Church was increasing veneration of the Blessed Virgin, including the Black Madonna. The veneration is also linked to Sara, the black Egyptian servant who is said to have accompanied Mary Magdalen, Mary Salome, Mary the mother of James, Martha, Lazarus, and others when they sailed from Israel. They are said to have landed on the southern coast of France fourteen years after the ascension of Christ at what came to be known as Les Saintes Maries de la Mer. The Gypsies gave Sara the highest regard and linked her veneration with that of the Black Madonna. Both Sara and the Madonna are reminiscent of another woman who traveled by sea and was often depicted as black—the goddess Isis, the wife and sister of the slain Osiris.

All of these women were associated with mourning and weeping. There were three Marys who wept beneath the cross of Christ. In over fifty sites throughout Europe, the black Madonna has been associated with Mary Magdalen and in some cases with Mary the Egyptian, both of whom were penitents.[15]

The Queen of Sheba

An intriguing woman who lends insight into "Cinderella" is the Queen of Sheba. She was a queen, probably from Arabia, who had much knowledge and visited King Solomon to test his wisdom. His great understanding "took her breath away." They exchanged lavish gifts, and he gave to her "every desire that she expressed" (1 Kings 10:1–13). An Ethiopian tradition says that this included an heir who later became their king.[16] Traditionally the Queen of Sheba is identified with the woman in the love poem *The Song of Solomon* who declares, "I am black and beautiful" (Song of Sol. 1:5). In the New Testament she is called the Queen of the South (Matt. 12:42), and in Christian iconography she is pictured as being black.

The Queen of Sheba's story became intertwined with the history of the cross used to crucify Christ and was popularized in the thirteenth-century *Golden Legend* by Jacobus de Voragine. In the beginning, Seth, Adam's son, plucks a branch from the tree in the Garden of Eden and plants it in the mouth of his dead father (like Cinderella, who plants a hazel branch on the grave of her mother). The branch grows from the Old Adam and is a precursor of the Second Adam. King Solomon orders the tree cut down and used in the construction of the temple, but the wood refuses to comply with the workman's tools and so they toss it into the stream Kidron nearby, where it becomes a footbridge.

The Queen of Sheba, when she visits Solomon, begins to cross the bridge, but being a wise woman she foresees that this wood will be the instrument of the salvation of the world, and so she chooses not to desecrate it with her pagan feet and wades the stream instead. Solomon has the wood from the bridge lodged deep beneath the pool at Bethesda in Jerusalem, where it stays, causing many miracles, until at the time of the Crucifixion it floats up to become the Cross.

In the Muslim version of the story, as found in the Koran, Solomon has a magic pavement placed across his courtyard that looks like a stream but is actually a mirror. When the queen arrives she bares her legs to walk across it. The explanation for Solomon's behavior is found in legends that say that the queen had the hooves or hairy legs of an ass. Solomon uses his knowledge of magic to cure her ailment, and she is forever grateful. This story made its way into Western Europe, but her deformity changed to being web-footed, splayfooted, or bird-footed, or to having limbs of a reptile, dragon, or griffin. In the Cathedral of Otranto in Puglia, Italy, is a mosaic created in 1165, which includes the Queen of the South. It shows her holding one shoe in her right hand and revealing her left foot, which has no divisions between the toes, as the other figures do.

A twelfth-century legend of the cross describes the queen as goose-footed. One explanation for the transition from the Muslim ass-footed queen to the European goose-footed one may be a mistaken transition of letters by a scribe. "Goose-footed" in Latin is *pes anserinus*, while "ass-footed" is *pes asininus*. There are numerous instances in which the Queen of Sheba is depicted in Western literature and art with a single goose's foot. This is very similar to Goose-footed Bertha in France and to Berchta in Germany, as we have seen in "Goosey, Goosey Gander." Like the limping queen, the Devil is also often described as limping, especially on the left foot.[17]

Cinderella's Cross

As Eve plucked the fruit from the tree in the garden, beginning the cycle of life and death, so Mary, the Second Eve, who brought new life to the world, wept beneath that same tree, transformed into a cross. Cinderella watered the hazel tree with her tears and hid in the pear tree to avoid detection. Ashes, like those on Aschenputtel, are the remnants of a tree. On Ash Wednesday ashes are placed on the foreheads of Roman Catholics in the form of a cross. In an Austrian version of the Cinderella story entitled "Broomthrow, Brushthrow, Combthrow," a mother and daughter both have golden crosses on their foreheads. When the mother suddenly dies, her husband the king tells his daughter that if he does not find another woman with a golden cross on her forehead, he will marry her. She leaves and becomes a kitchen maid and the story continues much like the story of Cap o' Rushes. The title comes from the names of the places that she says she is from when the prince asks her at each ball. She makes up places by naming the items the prince had thrown at her that day in her capacity as kitchen maid.[18]

Making the sign of the cross is one of the oldest and most deeply engrained customs in the world. If the African Fulani accidentally spill milk, they dip their fingers in the milk and make the sign of the cross with it on their bodies.[19] Crossing fingers brings good luck, and the teller of a lie crosses fingers for protection from the Devil. Crossing one's heart means to swear an oath. A cross, especially one made of iron, protects against fairies.[20] The cross also repels vampires. The Epiphany King and Queen drew crosses on the ceiling with white chalk to drive out evil spirits.[21] New World natives called the cross the Tree of Life, sometimes picturing it with foliage, as in the Palenque cross.[22]

We normally associate the cross with the number four. In fact, the Arabic numeral 4 is simply a cursive form of the cross. But the cross has earlier associations with the number five. Before the end of the last Ice Age, the five points of the cross included the point at the center. For example, the Wu Yo or five sacred mountains located in the north, south, east, west, and center of China delineate a cross.[23] In Teotihuacan in ancient Mexico, Quetzalcoatl, the "plumed serpent" god, brought about the world of the fifth sun, which is the present world. His symbol is the cross with five points, known as the quincunx.[24] In ancient India the five points of the cross are protective against evil. There are still popular European customs that hearken back to the significance of the number five in early matriarchal society. An example is the superstition that if five breadcrumbs are thrown on a table and a cross can be formed by moving one crumb, then a question asked during the toss will be answered in the affirmative.[25]

The tree in the Garden of Eden also contained the number five, if we consider it to be an apple tree with its five-petal blossoms. For Cinderella, the pear tree held the number five. It was in the Garden of Eden that time and space began for humans, and it is with the discovery of how to measure the five days of the winter and summer solstice that humans began to understand time and space. It meant that the equinoxes and the months and the seasons could be measured; and, since the sun rises exactly in the east and sets exactly in the west at the equinox, space could also be measured thanks to knowing the secret of the five days.

The black Queen of Sheba knew the number five in the Holy Cross. Persephone wore a black dress as the queen of the underworld. Her statue, as it emerged from the earth, wore five crosses, one on its forehead and one on each hand and knee. Cinderella, blackened with ashes, revealed the number five in her pear tree and in the five toes of her bare foot. The women's blackness represents the underworld. Their possession of the number five indicates that they have stolen the secret from the sun of the summer solstice and brought it down to earth and into the winter sky where it is planted at the winter solstice so the New Year can be reborn.

Cinderella's Foot

The Queen of Sheba with her goose's foot is related to Mother Goose, Goose-footed Bertha, Berchta, and Holde in Europe; the mother goddess Tomam in Siberia; and the Old Woman Who Never Dies in North America. (See Chapter 6, "Goosey, Goosey Gander.") As the Queen of the South she is the Queen of the Dead, and the spirits of the dead travel to her in the form of birds migrating south in the winter. Cinderella, Snow White, Persephone, Eve, Little Red Riding Hood, the Queen of Sheba, and the Black Virgin are all Queens of the Dead and goddesses of last year's harvest. At the same time they are Queens of the Living and goddesses of the new grain.

Cinderella, Eve, the Queen of Sheba, and the Blessed Virgin have another way in which they reveal their secret knowledge—through their sacred foot. In Genesis God put enmity between the woman and the snake. He says that the children of Eve will strike at the serpent's head and the serpent will strike at their heels. Mary, as the Second Eve, is often pictured with one bare foot revealed, stepping on the head of a snake. Just as geese and birds in general are enemies of the serpent, the Queen of Sheba demonstrates her dislike of snakes by her goose's foot. The snake is the path of the sun and moon winding from winter to summer solstice and then back to winter again, whereas the foot is the five days of the solstice, which is able to tame the snaking path into a year that can be controlled.

The snake is not only the enemy of woman. He is often her mate as well. According to an ancient Persian myth the first woman began to menstruate immediately after being seduced by a serpent. Similarly, a rabbinical teaching says that menstruation began when Eve was seduced by the snake in the garden. The Chiriguano of South America chase out all the snakes after a girl experiences menarche, believing a snake was responsible. Very many tribes ascribe to this belief.[26] It is natural to associate the snake with menstruation, since each month the moon snakes toward the new moon, which is associated with the menstrual period, and since each year the sun snakes toward the summer solstice, which lasts for five days—the same as a woman's period. Because the new moon is at its highest point in the sky near the summer solstice, it, too, is connected with the menstrual period. And since cycles in nature are usually complementary, it would be natural to assume that a woman's fertile period also is five days—corresponding to the five-day winter solstice. In actuality, the fertile period averages between five and six days in length.[27] Appropriately, the snake is also connected with fertility and pregnancy around the world.

The foot and the hand have been regarded as sacred since primordial times. Hands next to crosses can be found on European cave paintings that are over ten thousand years old. Feet next to crosses and snakes are marked on gallery graves in France dating from 3000 B.C. and earlier. The cross in the form of a swastika is found on the footprints of the Buddha in India.[28] The moon has taken the number five and brought it to earth, just as the crescent moon brings sunlight to the earth. In Greece, the smith Hephaestus made golden soles for the gods to wear so that they could walk on land, sea, and air.[29] Like the golden soles, various versions of the English and Welsh tale "The Buried Moon" describe the first crescent of the moon as the white feet of the new moon peeking out beneath her dark cloak as she comes to earth.[30]

Saint Bridget

In Ireland, Bridget leaves her footprints in the ashes of the hearth when she visits a home.[31] Flowers and shamrocks were said to spring from her footsteps.[32] When she dips her foot into the water on her feast day, the first good weather comes.[33] Many traditions of Saint Bridget (Brigit, Brigid, Bride) were transferred from the traditions surrounding the Celtic goddess Brigit (Brig, Brigantia, Brigindo).[34] Brigit was the goddess of fire and the hearth and was the patron of smiths. Saint Bridget was also a patron of smiths. When she took her vows, a pillar of fire stood above her head.[35] Nuns at Kildare kept her fire burning without interruption for over a thousand years.[36] On her feast day a candle is kept burning in each home throughout the night, awaiting her arrival.[37] Her name is invoked when the glowing peat in the hearth is covered with ashes, and she is asked to keep the seed of the fire alive through the night.[38]

Saint Bridget, who died in the sixth century, was a contemporary of Saint Patrick. Although her father was a chieftain, her mother was a slave, and because of the jealousy of her father's wife, Bridget was treated as a slave and a servant girl.[39] However, she rose to become Ireland's first abbess, wielding much power.[40] When she was a young woman, not wanting to be married, she begged God to take away her beauty. He obliged her, but when she took the veil as the bride of Christ, all her deformities disappeared.[41] She was much like Cinderella. She was a servant in her father's house, disliked by the woman of the house, and she hid her beauty only to have it revealed again. Her eternal flame is like the oil lamp by the hearth where Cinderella sat. In Scotland Brigit's symbol was the white swan—the "ugly duckling" that ultimately displays its magnificence.[42]

Bridget and Berchta
The swan and the goose are sometimes interchangeable in fairy tales and folklore.[43] Saint Bridget and the goddess Brigit are similarly interchangeable with the goose-footed Berchta and Holde. They all are patrons of the hearth. They protect the cattle and the crops and oversee the spinning. Saint Bridget is a shepherdess, as is Holde.[44] Food is set out for Saint Bridget on her feast day, as it is for Berchta on Twelfth Night. The barmbrack fruit bread with the silver coin hidden in it on Saint Bridget's Eve is like the Twelfth Night cake on the eve of Berchta's special day.[45] Bridget also watches over the cradle, as does Berchta.

However, Berchta and Holde were known for their ugliness, while Saint Bridget was known for her beauty. Yet Saint Bridget was ugly for a while, and the goddess Brigit was described as having a face that was ugly and black on one side and beautiful and white on the other (a description of the half moon).[46] Also, Berchta and Holde were both sometimes a beautiful white lady who bathed in a lake.[47] This is also a reference to the moon. Artemis (Diana), the moon, was known for bathing in her sacred pool. Saint Bridget was said to dress in white, and on her feast day the maiden representing her wore a white dress.[48] The goddess Brigit was known as the moon. Saint Bridget was called the "Queen of Heaven," an epithet of the moon, and in Ireland she was given the highest reverence next to Mary.

Another connection between Berchta and Saint Bridget are the dancers that go from house to house jumping up and down. In

Germany they are called "Berchten" and are elaborately costumed. On Twelfth Night farmers feed them to ensure the fertility of their crops. The dancers are divided into the beautiful and the ugly Berchten, representing good and evil spirits of the dead.[49] On Saint Bridget's eve boys dressed as girls escort a girl or a doll representing the saint. Going from house to house carrying her cross and girdle, they are offered refreshments.[50]

A similar festivity in northern England is Plow Monday, which was celebrated on the Monday following Twelfth Night. A man dressed up as a grotesque old woman named "Bessie," "Betsy," or "Besom Bet" goes from house to house with his fellows all dressed in white and adorned with flowers and ribbons. They drag a white plow and beg for "plow money" or sweets.[51] They also sweep out evil spirits with their brooms.[52] Berchta too was concerned with sweeping on Twelfth Night. (For more on sweeping, see Chapter 9, "There Was a Man and He Had Nought.")

Other Saint Bridget Traditions

The goddess Brigit is called the "Three Mothers" and the "Three Blessed Ladies of Britain."[53] This links her to the Greek Moirae or Fates—the three women who spin, measure, and cut off the thread of human life. Saint Bridget was also a spinner and made the first cloth woven in Ireland. Furthermore, she was devoted to the three Marys, who lamented at the foot of the cross. The goddess Brigit searched out and found her dead son Ruadan on the battlefield and keened for him. She began the custom of keening or sorrowful wailing for the dead in Ireland.[54] Both Brigit and Cinderella cried for the dead. Wailing is associated with the moon because of the very widespread custom of loudly lamenting the disappearance of the moon and the sun during an eclipse. The moon is also the land of the dead around the world.

Another epithet of Saint Bridget is "Queen of the South." Like the Queen of Sheba, Saint Bridget is a prophetess. As the Queen of the South she receives the souls of the dead on the wings of migrating birds. It was said she was able to cause the wild ducks to come to her when she called.[55] On her feast day the birds first appear, and Irish country folk close the north door of the house and open the south door to let her in.[56] In Glastonbury, England, many were cured at a special opening on the south wall of her church.[57]

Saint Bridget has much in common with Cap o' Rushes. In Ireland a girl wearing a crown of rushes and carrying Saint Bridget's cross leads a procession on Saint Bridget's Day.[58] Her crosses were made of rushes and placed over doorways for luck.[59] A person would place a rush, called "Bridget's ribbon," around the head to protect against headaches.[60] On the Isle of Man on Saint Bridget's Eve, it was customary to stand with a bundle of green rushes at the threshold of the house and invite the saint to stay the night. The rushes were then strewn on the floor as a mat for her rest.[61] Salt was an important aspect of the Cap o' Rushes story. Rushes grow in the salt marshes. In one story, when a merchant refused her salt, Saint Bridget turned the salt into stone.[62] "Cap o' Rushes" has some motifs in common with versions of the "Swan Maiden." The heroine has a dress made of feathers, and she gives a ring to the man she loves.[63] Brigit's emblem was a swan. As Cap o' Rushes cloak protected her, so Saint Bridget's mantle protected those who prayed to her.[64] Both Saint Bridget and Cap o' Rushes are treated poorly by their fathers, both serve as kitchen maids, and both disguise their beauty until they can marry the men of their choice.

Saint Bridget also has allusions to Persephone. Saint Bridget tamed a wild boar, and the pig was sacred to Persephone.[65] Her feast day is on February 1, the first day of spring in Ireland. The next day is Candlemas, when Persephone emerges from beneath the earth. Bridget's girdle is a rope made of straw, about four to six feet in diameter. People pass through it on her feast day to safeguard against ailments.[66] The ritual may be a metaphor for the new vegetation emerging from the earth. A traditional verse says:

> This is the day of Bride
> The Queen will come from the mound;
> This is the day of Bride
> The serpent will come from the hole.[67]

The number five is also connected to Bridget. She once fed five pieces of bacon to a hungry hound when she was entertaining a noble guest. However, when it came time to eat, no bacon was missing.[68] In another tale, she gives away apples that were given to her. When the donor took the apples back, saying they were for her and her sisters, not for the poor, Saint Bridget cursed the person's orchards and they never produced apples again.[69] In County Armagh apple griddlecakes are made for the eve of the saint's day.[70] The apple contains the number five, and so does the saint's cross. The number five can be found on the saint's footprint, and it can be found on the footprints of birds as well. The swan, duck, and other birds have three toes pointing forward and one toe pointing back. Like the cross, this makes four outer points and a fifth point is made at the center, where the four toes diverge. This would explain the significance of the goose's foot of Queen Bertha, Berchta, and the Queen of Sheba.

As a final note about Saint Bridget, she had a particular affinity for cows and fishes. She was the patron of dairymaids and had a miraculous cow that was white with red ears. She lived solely on the milk of the cow. She was also a cowherd, and even though she gave away most of the milk and butter to the poor, the little that was left could fill the largest vessels her master gave to her. Once when she had already milked the cows twice in one day, she milked them a third time and filled the Lake of Milk. The saint also had marvelous influence over water, making it swell and shrink at her request. Sea creatures honored her more than they did the other saints. At her sacred well near the sea, there was a fish that appeared once every seven years. Anyone who saw that fish was cured of every ill.[71] As we shall see, the cow and the fish are significant to Cinderella stories in both Europe and Asia.

A Chinese Cinderella

There are versions of "Cinderella" throughout the inhabited world. The oldest printed version of the story was published in China about A.D. 850–860. In that story the heroine is downtrodden by her stepmother after her mother and father die. The girl cares for a small red and gold fish that grows to ten feet long and lives in their pool. The stepmother discovers the fish, kills it, eats it, and throws the bones on the dunghill. The girl retrieves the bones and prays to them, and they grant her every wish. She receives a dress made of kingfisher feathers and wears it to the cave-festival. Her stepsister recognizes her, and as she hurries away, she loses her shoe. It comes into the hands of a powerful lord, who finally finds the owner of the shoe and marries her. The stepmother and stepsister are subsequently killed by flying stones.[72]

The flying stones make an interesting ending. As we have seen, the moon is known to throw stones. Although this is the earliest printed version of the Cinderella story, Anna Birgitta Rooth identifies the "One-eye, Two-eyes, and Three-eyes" story as the earliest variation of "Cinderella," originating in the Balkans some two thousand years ago.[73] The following is a Russian variation of that tale.

A Russian Cinderella

In the Russian tale, "Burenushka, the Little Red Cow," Maria, the heroine, lives with her stepmother and her two stepsisters, of whom one has two eyes and the other has three eyes. Maria is sent out each day with a crust of bread to pasture Burenushka, a cow, which her mother had given her. In the field Maria bows to the cow and it gives her a beautiful gown and fine food to eat. Maria returns in the evening without eating the crust of bread. The stepmother sends Two-eyes to spy on Maria, but Maria waits till her stepsister is asleep before asking the cow for food and clothes. The next day the stepmother sends Three-eyes on the same mission. This time Maria forgets about the third eye, and the stepsister sees the cow give the gifts. The stepmother makes Maria's father slaughter the cow for food, and Maria begs him for a bit of the entrails. She takes them and places them on a gatepost and a berry bush grows from them. Prince Ivan hears of Maria and comes to the house and puts a bowl on the table, saying that whichever girl fills the bowl with berries will be his wife. The two stepsisters try to pick the berries, but the birds in the bush will not let them near. However, the birds help Maria fill the bowl when it is her turn.

After Maria is married and has a child, the stepmother turns Maria into a goose and substitutes Two-eyes as Ivan's wife. The child's caretaker takes the baby to the fields and calls to the geese for the baby's mother. The geese reveal where she is, and the mother flies down, takes off her goose skin and nurses the boy. This happens a second day and the mother says that the next day she must fly beyond the mountains. But her husband burns her feather gown and destroys all the other forms she takes until he has her back. The false wife is killed and Maria lives happily with her family.[74]

This story ends with the "Swan Maiden" motif, which can be found throughout the Old World, as well as in both North and South America. Cinderella as turkey or goose girl who is revealed for who she is by the birds is a variant of the tale found in different parts of the world.[75] In a Persian version of Cinderella, Fatima visits the underground home of an ugly old crone and does chores for her. The crone rewards her with a shining moon on her forehead and star on her chin. The crone is similar to Holde or Mother Holle in Germany and to the frightening Baba Yaga in Russia. The tree that grows from the grave takes many forms, which include an apple tree and a rose tree.[76] The apple as we know contains a star, and the green calyx at the base of a rose blossom has five leaves, which form a five-pointed star.

The Sacred Remains

In an Armenian version of the "Cinderella" story, the heroine's two sisters kill their mother and eat her. The heroine refuses to eat her mother and takes the bones and buries them. She receives every gift she requests from her mother's grave, including beautiful dresses, which she wears to church. The king sees her and pursues her, they are married, and the girl forgives her sisters.[77]

Whether the remains are of a fish, a cow, or a mother, the care of the remains of the sacrificed victim is central to the Cinderella story. The theme derives from a tradition that goes back to Ice Age beliefs and is best portrayed in the bear ceremonies of the Old and the New World. A common trait of bear ceremonies is the burial of the bear's skull and bones so that they may secure a new life for the animal. Rituals of atonement and prayers for new life for the bear are said over the remains. The care with which the Saami (Lapp) treat the bones of the bear has been compared to the ban in the Old Testament against crushing the bones of the paschal lamb.

In a gesture reminiscent of the blood of the lamb on the doorposts and lintels of the Israelites' houses (Exod. 12:7), during the bear ceremony, Saami women sprinkle their husbands with bloodlike alder bark juice as they enter the holy back door of the women's tent.[78] In the African story "Princess of the Full Moon," the ugly hunchback shepherd is sprayed with the blood of a seven-headed snake and becomes the "Prince of the Noonday Sun" and marries the princess.[79]

The bear, the mother, the cow, and the fish are all symbols of the moon. The bones, ashes, blood, or other remains of the moon are the new moon or the eclipsed moon, and out of them the moon is reborn. The Guarani of South America tell the story very clearly. An ogre eats the moon, which was in the form of a fish. The sun takes the fish bones and resuscitates them.[80] In a Cinderella story from Eastern Kwangtung in China, the empress bursts forth from the rags of an ugly, naughty orphan girl. Two roosters that signify the phoenix herald her.[81] The phoenix bursts from the ashes as the moon bursts from the shadow of an eclipse.

New-World Cinderellas
How Old Is Cinderella?

The ritualistic care of the remains of the sacrificial victim gives evidence that Cinderella has its origins in the late Ice Age or earlier. This is in direct contradiction to the accepted view held by many leading folklorists. They consider Cinderella to be a tale that developed in Europe and Asia over the past two thousand years. Yet, the relationship between Cinderella and the hearth goddess Brigit is older than that. Under her various names, Brigit can be found across Europe. The Celtic culture in 500 B.C. stretched across Europe from the British Isles to Asia Minor and from Spain to Hungary. This non-Mediterranean society originated in France and Germany around 750 B.C.[82] The goddess Brigit is older still. Her relationship with birds, cattle, and fish reveal her as the mother goddess of Old Europe, dating back more than ten thousand years. Marija Gimbutas details the history of her symbols and her lunar aspects in *The Language of the Goddess*.

Many folklorists hold that all Native American versions of "Cinderella" derive from recent Eurasian contact. But, because of the matriarchal nature of the story, folklorist Jack Zipes states that Cinderella originates near the end of the Ice Age.[83] Our findings agree with this conclusion and open up the possibility that the Native American Cinderellas are equally ancient in origin.

Those who assert the recent Eurasian origin of the New World stories must present compelling evidence for their argument, taking into account three reasons for believing otherwise: The Native American stories do not show the same structure as their Eurasian counterparts. The New World versions are totally assimilated into their local cultures and do not appear to be laminated onto local traditions. And at least in one instance a Native American story directly states the lunar origins of Cinderella, unlike Old World variants.

Sootface

The Ojibwa story of "Sootface" tells of a girl whose two sisters cover her with ashes. Her hair and skin are burnt from the fire, and her clothes are full of patches. A mighty warrior from across the lake wishes to marry. He has the ability to make himself invisible, and so he says that he will marry whoever could tell his sister of what his invisible bow and bowstring are made. All the women of the village, including Sootface's sisters, are unable to answer his question. Sootface washes her face and makes a dress out of birch bark and a necklace out of wildflowers. When the warrior approaches, the other women can see only his white moccasins, but Sootface can see all of him and tells his sister that his bow is the rainbow and his bowstring is "white fire, like the Milky Way, the Path of Souls." The warrior's sister makes Sootface beautiful and gives her a beautiful buckskin dress. Sootface wins the warrior's heart, and he names her "Dawn-Light," and they are married.[84]

The warrior is a metaphor for the moon. The new moon is invisible in the daytime sky. The two white moccasins are the thin crescent moons just before and after the new moon. The rainbow is a bridge or pathway to the sky. Like the moon it is associated with rain. The Milky Way is the path that souls take to go to the land of the dead. It is also the path that migrating birds take in the spring and the fall. The moon is the land of the dead and the place where birds fly in the winter. "Dawn-Light" is the appropriate name for Sootface, because in dawn light the new moon, which is invisible during the day, becomes visible on the horizon. The birch-bark dress is like the cloak of rushes. The birch, like the hazel, has catkins with scalelike spores that spiral around their outside. This is a sign of a sacred tree. Her burnt skin is like the pockmarked face of some Chinese versions of Cinderella.[85] In the Saami bear ceremony wives threw ashes and hot embers at their husbands. Ojibwa girls put soot on their faces and wore old clothes during their initiation rites. Although there may have been some European influence, this Ojibwa tale shows subtleties not found in its Old World counterparts.

Turkey Girl

"Turkey Girl" is a Zuni Cinderella story about a poor girl who is left to care for the turkeys. Because she treats them kindly, the turkeys reward her by giving her a beautiful mantle and silver jewelry to wear to the dance celebration in the village. They warn her, however, that she must return before sunset or face the consequences. She forgets the turkeys' warning and stays too late. Her garments return to rags and she lives out her days in poverty.[86] Mary Austin strongly believes that the story was not an adaptation of Cinderella, while the famous folklorist Stith Thompson is confident that it was, despite its sad ending.[87] It contains "Goose Girl" and "Cinderella" themes that are found in Europe. Its sad ending is like some "Swan Maiden" stories in the Old and the New World. It is possible that this is a European import or a Zuni tale influenced by European stories.

Moon and Otter and Frog
The Modoc originally lived near the Klamath Lakes on the border between California and Oregon. Their Cinderella story reveals the true origin of Cinderella and has no need of European sources to explain it. It is based on a widely held Native American belief that a frog can be seen in the moon.

In the earliest times Moon was lonely and when the grizzly bear clouds begin eating away at him he comes down to earth to visit his friend otter. Moon decides to seek a wife so that he will not be lonely in the sky. Otter introduces him to ten pretty green frog sisters and one ugly sister. The ten pretty frogs dress their best and bake cakes to give to the moon. The ugly frog in her tattered blanket does her hair with mud and sticks and puts green leaves on her feet. She uses a big branch for a canoe and a stick for a paddle. When the Moon sees her, wildflowers burst into bloom on the shore each time she puts her stick into the water, and little rainbows appear around her in the water. Moon says, "Whenever she places the branch in the water, things come to life," and he chooses her as his bride.

At the wedding the jealous sisters run the ugly frog through the gauntlet. She has put wildflowers in her hair, but when she reaches Moon she is crying and bleeding and muddy. He sprinkles cornmeal on her to heal her and gives her a beautiful blanket and a silver comb. After they marry he takes her up to the sky. One day the grizzly bear clouds start chewing at Moon, and he begins to disappear. Otter weeps and the frog sways as she sings sacred songs. Gradually Moon begins to appear again. Today Moon is chewed each month, but Frog brings him back to life. She can be seen in the moon with her blanket and silver comb.[88]

This story has much in common with Sootface and with Saint Bridget that it does not have in common with the Eurasian Cinderella cycle. In all three cases the heroine is made beautiful only after she is chosen in marriage, whereas Cinderella, Cap o' Rushes, and others are made beautiful before they are chosen. Both Frog and Sootface use wildflowers to dress themselves up. Both stories involve seeing rainbows and other magic objects that are not visible to everyone. Both stories have an intercessor who makes the introduction for the heroine. These are indications that the Ojibwa and Modoc stories are closer to each other than they are to the Eurasian Cinderella.

They are also closer to Saint Bridget, the descendant of a Paleolithic mother goddess. Like the ugly frog, when Saint Bridget puts her foot (or finger) into the water, spring arrives. Wildflowers spring from her footprints. Both Saint Bridget and Frog are actually ugly, whereas Cinderella is made to appear ugly by being covered with ashes. Saint Bridget's doll had a seashell pinned to the front of it, and the silver comb of Frog had shrimp and scallops engraved on it. These are signs of the watery moon and the spiral path of the moon. Also, just as Saint Bridget is linked to the matriarchal number five, so the ten sisters signify the five days of the winter solstice plus the five days of the summer solstice.

Primordial Cinderella

The lamentation for the disappearance of the moon and the rejoicing at its reappearance are key to understanding the origins of "Cinderella." We have taken a long journey to see that the Cinderella story stretches far back in time. There are many variations of the story, including some in which the Cinderella character is a male, such as the Tsimshian boy from the Northwest Coast known as Amala, which means "smoke hole." But we have come far enough to connect Cinderella's story to Siberian wayfarers who crossed the Bering land bridge over ten thousand years ago, at a time when the moon goddess was held in esteem. Reading "Cinderella" today, we can be in touch with our ancestors of long ago.

Chapter 17

Conclusion

As Above, So Below

The simple saying attributed to Hermes Trismegistos, "As above, so below," sums up in four words the faith of ancient peoples.[1] Folk belief says:

1. Nature imitates the sun, moon, and stars.
2. By understanding nature, one can understand the sun, moon, and stars; by understanding the sun, moon, and stars, one can understand nature.
3. The everyday world imitates the eternal world.
4. By understanding the everyday world one can understand the eternal world; by understanding the eternal world, one can understand the everyday world.

These concepts never appear in isolation. First, the sun, moon, and stars become gods, angels, saints, fairies, and other spirits, making things more complicated. Second, myths serve multiple social and psychological functions. But as we have seen, it is possible to break through our myths to the simple principles that can be found within them. Wilhelm Mannhardt (1831–80) was an ardent student of folkloric mythology. He said, "I am convinced that a part of the earliest myths owed their origin to a poetry of nature which is not immediately comprehensible to us any more but needs to be explained by analogies [to contemporary primitives]."[2] The purpose of this book is to better understand the analogies that were used around the world but that have become inaccessible to us today. By understanding this poetry, we can better understand the myths that drive our lives and use those myths to be more in touch with our selves and our universe.

We have found that our most popular fairy tales and nursery rhymes are based on ancient myths about the sun, the moon, solar and lunar eclipses, and the summer and winter solstices. We have peeled away myths about the seven planets in Eastern and Western thought to reach the beliefs that were commonly held before the end of the last Ice Age. The number seven signifies the seven new or full moons between the solstices, the seven days that the moon ascends from the horizon to the top of the sky, and the seven full moons between lunar eclipses.

In "Jack and the Beanstalk" we learned that the five magic beans stand for the five days of the winter solstice. The sun appears to stand still for five days at both the winter and summer solstices. In order to predict a solstice, first a person must note the phase of the moon the day after the five standing-still days. Then, when that phase occurs for the seventh time, it will be the first standing-still day of the next solstice. This secret allowed Ice Age peoples to accurately predict the equinoxes (at the fourth appearance of the same phase of the moon), the seasons, and festival days. Thus the numbers five and seven became sacred gifts from heaven that structured their lives and their religion. Also, although many social and economic factors influenced the place of women in society, their association with the moon and with the five-day period helped to elevate the status of women in religion and culture.

The cycles of the sun and moon became the cycles of life and death. The new moon is highest in the daytime sky during or near the summer solstice, and the full moon is highest in the nighttime sky during or near the winter solstice. The various cycles of the sun and moon do not normally all line up together, but if they did, metaphorically it should be like this: During a solar eclipse the black new moon at the summer solstice steals the fiery red lifeblood of the sun from the upper world and brings it to the lower world. And during a lunar eclipse the white full moon at the winter solstice steals the fiery red lifeblood of the sun in the lower world and brings it to the upper world.

Fairy Fates

The word fairy comes from the Latin *fatum* and means "what has been spoken" or "fate." The Fates included the Scandinavian Norns, the Anglo-Saxon Wyrds, the Roman Fata or Parcae, and the Greek Moirae. The Greek Erinyes were also Fates known as the Furies. They were associated with Demeter in the form of a horse. It is interesting that the Greek Keres, another form of Fates and spirits of the dead, have a name similar to Demeter's Roman name, Ceres. Fairy godmothers and spinners in fairy tales represent the Fates. We have seen how Mother Goose, Rumpelstiltskin, Berchta, Holde, the Queen of Sheba, and others also fulfill that role. Even animals can be associated with the Fates. For example, wolves are known as the "hounds of the Norns."³

But the fairies and the Fates are not just the dark deliverers of death. They are also the givers of life. The Fates include not only Demeter but also Persephone. Snow White, Eve, Jack, Little Red Riding Hood, Cinderella, and Saint Bridget are all examples of the life-giving aspect of the Fates and fairies. Ultimately the moon was seen as the dispenser of fate. We have been able to trace our favorite fairy tales to Ice Age stories about the moon as both the stealer and provider of life.

At the Crossroads

In 1998 Easter occurred on April 12, the day after the full moon. During the week before Easter, I could see the rabbit in the gibbous moon in the evening as geese and other birds were returning from their winter home. I realized it was the Easter Rabbit painted on the Easter egg in the sky. Early Christians celebrated Christ's Crucifixion at the spring equinox. When the full moon occurs at the equinox, a perfect cross is formed in the sky. When the sun is setting precisely in the west, the full moon is rising precisely in the east, and vice versa. Also, the day of the equinox is the only time when the full moon at the top of the night sky is at exactly the same height as the sun is at the top of the day sky. The sun and moon divide the day into four equal quarters.

I also realized that the circle of the moon through the month is not a circle. It is egg-shaped. In the winter the small end of the egg is pointed toward the full moon, which is high in the midnight sky. In the summer the small end of the egg is pointed toward the new moon, which is high in the midday sky. And at the equinoxes, the egg is lying on its side, with the big and small ends pointing toward the half moons on the horizon in the midday and midnight skies. Lines drawn between the new and full moon and between the half moons form a cross upon the egg.

In Albrecht Dürer's woodcuts of scenes of the Crucifixion, the sun and the full moon are on opposite sides of the cross. This represents "the moon rising full on its fifteenth night, confronting with equal radiance the sun setting at that moment on the opposite horizon: the moon not quenched in solar light, but, fully illuminated, self-equaling."[4] In pre-Christian times the cross was associated with Astarte, Aphrodite (Venus), and Artemis (Diana, the moon).[5] In ancient Mexico the cross was depicted with seven flowers, associating it with the sun and the moon. In other instances there were six flowers with the sunbird in the middle, like the migrating bird of spring and fall in the middle between the solstices.[6] From Paleolithic times the cross, which represents the number five, has been a sacred and powerful sign.

The cross at the equinoxes, halfway between summer and winter, and at sunrise and sunset, halfway between day and night, represents the human condition. We turn between life and death, between sky and earth, between the eternal and the everyday, between past and future, between parent and child, between man and woman, between good and evil and between the finite and the infinite. We have had the opportunity to see through the eyes of our ancestors and to understand the balance in nature and the universe as told through our myths. It is humbling to contemplate the millennia over which stories have been handed down to us. We can only hope that this wisdom will continue to be handed on for millennia to come.

Notes

Chapter 1: Introduction

[1] Barbara G. Walker, *The Woman's Encyclopedia of Myths and Secrets* (New York: Harper & Row, 1983), 1069.

[2] Timothy Harley, *Moon Lore* (London: Swann Sonnenschein, Le Bas and Lowrey, 1885), 130, 219.

[3] Joseph Campbell, *The Hero with a Thousand Faces*, Bollingen Series 17 (1949; Princeton, N.J.: Princeton University Press, 1968), 17–19.

[4] Walker, *The Woman's Encyclopedia of Myths*, 267.

[5] Hamilton Wright, Helen Wright, and Samuel Rapport, eds., *To the Moon!* (New York: Meredith Press, 1968), 17.

[6] Chris Scarre, *Smithsonian Timelines of the Ancient World* (New York: Dorling Kindersly, 1993), 50–69.

[7] Jack Zipes, *Breaking the Magic Spell: Radical Theories of Folk and Fairy Tales* (Austin: University of Texas Press, 1979), 5–6.

[8] Ibid., 47.

[9] Ibid., 172.

[10] Neil Philip, *The Cinderella Story* (New York: Penguin Books, 1989), 7.

[11] Richard M. Dorson, "The Eclipse of Solar Mythology," *Journal of American Folklore* 68 (1955): 393–416.

[12] Jan de Vries, "Theories Concerning 'Nature Myths,'" in *Sacred Narrative: Readings in the Theory of Myth*, ed. Alan Dundes (Berkeley and Los Angeles: University of California Press, 1984), 30.

[13] E. C. Krupp, "Celestial Analogy and Cyclical Renewal: Configurational Approaches to Culture Through Analogy" (paper presented to the American Anthropological Association, Washington, D.C., November 19, 1993), 6. Paper kindly provided to me by the author, who is director of the Griffith Observatory, Los Angeles, Calif.

[14] Alta Jablow and Carl Withers, *The Man in the Moon: Sky Tales from Many Lands* (New York: Holt, Rinehart and Winston, 1969), 115.

[15] Zipes, *Breaking the Magic Spell*, 11.

[16] Mircea Eliade, *Patterns in Comparative Religion*, trans. Rosemary Sheed (New York: Meridian Books, 1958), 155, 180.

Chapter 2: The Discovery

[1] Joseph Campbell, *The Inner Reaches of Outer Space: Metaphor as Myth and as Religion* (New York: Harper & Row, 1986), 63–68.

[2] Ernest Klein, *A Comprehensive Etymological Dictionary of the English Language: Dealing with the Origin of Words and Their Sense Development Thus Illustrating the History of Civilization and Culture* (New York: Elsevier, 1966), 75–78.

[3] Campbell, *The Inner Reaches of Outer Space*, 62.

[4] *Spenser: Poetical Works,* ed. J. C. Smith and E. de Selincourt (New York: Oxford University Press, 1912), 395–406.

[5] Campbell, *The Inner Reaches of Outer Space*, 80–104.

[6] Eviatar Zerubavel, *The Seven Day Circle: The History and Meaning of the Week* (New York: The Free Press, Macmillan, 1985), 14–15.

[7] Ibid.

[8] David Fideler, *Jesus Christ, Sun of God: Ancient Cosmology and Early Christian Symbolism* (Wheaton, Ill.: Quest Books, The Theosophical Publishing House, 1993), 245.

[9] Zerubavel, *The Seven Day Circle*, 16–19.

[10] Ibid., 19–26.

[11] *Funk and Wagnalls New Encyclopedia*, 1987 ed., s.v. "Mithraism."

[12] Eliade, *Patterns in Comparative Religion*, 104–5.

[13] S. J. Tester, *A History of Western Astrology* (Wolfeboro, N.H.: Boydell Press, 1987), 104–5.

[14] Tester, *A History of Western Astrology*, 119.

[15] Ibid., 118–19.

[16] Ibid., 86.

[17] Valerie J. Roebuck, *The Circle of Stars: An Introduction to Indian Astrology* (Rockport, Mass.: Element Books Limited, 1992), 40.

[18] *Siva Samhita* (2,4) in *The Oxford Dictionary of World Religions*, s.v. "Cakra."

[19] Margaret Stutley and James Stutley, *Harper's Dictionary of Hinduism: Its Mythology, Folklore, Philosophy, Literature, and History* (San Francisco: Harper & Row, 1977), 106, 236, 280.

[20] Geoffrey Ashe, *Dawn Behind the Dawn: A Search for the Earthly Paradise* (New York: Henry Holt and Company, 1992), 1–225.

[21] Richard Heinberg, *Celebrate the Solstice: Honoring the Earth's Seasonal Rhythms Through Festival and Ceremony* (Wheaton, Ill.: Quest Books, The Theosophical Publishing House, 1993), 55–57.

[22] Ibid., 59–62.

[23] William H. Calvin, *How the Shaman Stole the Moon: In Search of Ancient Prophet-Scientists from Stonehenge to the Grand Canyon* (New York: Bantam Books, 1991), 31–2.

[24] E. C. Krupp, *Beyond the Blue Horizon: Myths and Legends of the Sun, Moon, Stars, and Planets* (New York: Oxford University Press, 1991), 162.

[25] New Revised Standard Version (NRSV hereafter).

[26] Campbell, *The Inner Reaches of Outer Space*, 72.

[27] Eliade, *Patterns in Comparative Religion*, 154.

[28] Ibid., 170.

[29] Joseph Campbell, assisted by M. J. Abadie, *The Mythic Image* (Princeton, N.J.: Princeton University Press, 1974), 288.

[30] Campbell, *The Inner Reaches of Outer Space*, 88–89.

[31] Krupp, *Beyond the Blue Horizon*, 163.

[32] Harley, *Moon Lore*, 154–55.

[33] Krupp, *Beyond the Blue Horizon*, 162–63.

[34] Carolyn McVickar Edwards, *Sun Stories: Tales from Around the World to Illuminate the Days and Nights of Our Lives* (New York: HarperSanFrancisco, 1995), 8–12.

[35] Krupp, *Beyond the Blue Horizon*, 96–99.

[36] Eliade, *Patterns in Comparative Religion*, 168–69.

[37] Jean Chevalier and Alain Gheerbrant, *A Dictionary of Symbols*, trans. John Buchanan-Brown (New York: Penguin Books, 1994), 673.

[38] Eliade, *Patterns in Comparative Religion*, 101.

[39] Richard Erdoes and Alfonso Ortiz, eds., *American Indian Myths and Legends* (New York: Pantheon, 1984), 168–69

[40] Krupp, *Beyond the Blue Horizon*, 167–68.

[41] Stutley and Stutley, *Harper's Dictionary of Hinduism*, 167–84.

[42] Klein, *Etymological Dictionary*, 982–1009.

[43] J. V. Stewart, *Astrology: What's Really in the Stars?* (Amherst, N.Y.: Prometheus Books, 1996), 28.

[44] Eliade, *Patterns in Comparative Religion*, 155–56.

[45] Harley, *Moon Lore*, 155.

[46] Jean Rhys Bram, "Moon," in *The Encyclopedia of Religion*, ed. Mircea Eliade, 10:89.

[47] Harley, *Moon Lore*, 168.

[48] Krupp, *Beyond the Blue Horizon*, 168.

[49] Harley, *Moon Lore*, 155.

[50] Ibid., 168–69.

[51] Krupp, *Beyond the Blue Horizon*, 165–66.

[52] Ibid., 163, 165.

[53] Harley, *Moon Lore*, 197.

[54] Krupp, *Beyond the Blue Horizon*, 165.

[55] Eliade, *Patterns in Comparative Religion*, 163.

[56] Jablow and Withers, *The Man in the Moon*, 22.

[57] Harley, *Moon Lore*, 49–50.

[58] Ibid.

[59] Bram, "Moon," 89.

[60] Eliade, *Patterns in Comparative Religion*, 171–74.

[61] Percy Tezise and Dick Roughsey, *Gidja the Moon* (Milwaukee, Wisc.: Gareth Stevens, 1984).

[62] Ed Young, *Moon Mother: A Native American Creation Tale* (New York: HarperCollins, Willa Perlman Books, 1993).

[63] Calvin, *How the Shaman Stole the Moon*, 7–8.

[64] Eliade, *Patterns in Comparative Religion*, 181.

[65] Walker, *The Woman's Encyclopedia of Myths*, 358.

[66] Ibid., 218.

[67] E. O. James, *Seasonal Feasts and Festivals* (New York: Barnes & Noble University Paperback, 1963), 83–84.

[68] Krupp, *Beyond the Blue Horizon*, 163.

[69] Marija Gimbutas, *The Language of the Goddess* (New York: HarperCollins, 1991), 319.

[70] David Rockwell, *Giving Voice to the Bear: North American Indian Rituals, Myths, and Images of the Bear* (Niwot, Colo.: Roberts Rinehart, 1991), 167, 174.

[71] Walker, *The Woman's Encyclopedia of Myths*, 358, 449.

[72] Campbell, *The Inner Reaches of Outer Space*, 103–4.

[73] Jablow and Withers, *The Man in the Moon*, 41–3.

[74] Rockwell, *Giving Voice to the Bear*, 166–67.

[75] Harley, *Moon Lore*, 156.

[76] Walker, *The Woman's Encyclopedia of Myths*, 359.

Chapter 3: Snow White and the Seven Dwarfs

[1] "Snow-white," in *Household Stories from the Collection of the Brothers Grimm*, trans. Lucy Crane; illus. Walter Crane (New York: McGraw Hill, 1966), 212–21. This is a reprint of the work first published by Macmillan & Co. in 1866. This version has been reprinted in full.

[2] Stutley and Stutley, *Harper's Dictionary of Hinduism*, 245.

[3] Harley, *Moon Lore*, 145–46.

[4] Maria Leach and Jerome Fried, eds., *Funk and Wagnalls Standard Dictionary of Folklore, Mythology, and Legend* (New York: HarperSanFrancisco, 1972), s.v. "colors."

[5] Ibid., s.v. "New Year."

[6] Ibid., s.v. "solstice dances."

[7] John Warren Stewig, *The Moon's Choice*, illus. Jan Palmer (New York: Simon and Schuster, 1993).

[8] Bram, "Moon," 88.

[9] Judy Gail and Linda A. Houlding, *Day of the Moon Shadow: Tales with Ancient Answers to Scientific Questions*, illus. Kimberly Louise Shaw (Englewood, Colo.: Libraries Unlimited, 1995), 100.

[10] Harley, *Moon Lore*, 217.

[11] Walker, *The Woman's Encyclopedia of Myths*, 661.

[12] Gimbutas, *The Language of the Goddess*, 195–97.

[13] Campbell, *The Mythic Image*, 459–65.

[14] Ibid., 465–66.

[15] James George Frazer, *The Golden Bough: A Study in Magic and Religion*, 1-vol. abridged ed. (New York: Macmillan, 1922, Macmillan Paperbacks Edition, 1963), 434, 551.

[16] Tun Li-ch'en, *Annual Customs and Festivals in Peking as Recorded in the Yen-ching Sui-shih-chi*, trans. Derk Bodde, 2nd ed. (Hong Kong: Hong Kong University Press, 1965), 87.

[17] *Standard Dictionary of Folklore*, s.v. "New Year."

[18] Campbell, *The Mythic Image*, 466.

[19] Walker, *The Woman's Encyclopedia of Myths*, 112–13.

[20] Campbell, *The Mythic Image*, 452.

[21] From R. Harper, ed., *Assyrian and Babylonian Literature: Selected Translations* (D. Appleton, 1901) as quoted in Stewart, *Astrology*, 28.

[22] Klein, *Etymological Dictionary*, 985.

[23] Thomas Moore, *The Planets Within: The Astrological Psychology of Marsilio Ficino* (Hudson, N.Y.: Lindisfarne Press, 1982), 140–41.

[24] Eliade, *Patterns in Comparative Religion*, 180–81.

[25] Moore, *The Planets Within*, 127–36.

[26] Ibid., 160.

[27] Frederic Guirma, *Princess of the Full Moon,* trans. John Garrett (New York: Macmillan, 1970).

[28] Bram, "Moon," 88.

[29] Elizabeth Wayland Barber, *Women's Work: The First Twenty-Thousand Years: Women, Cloth, and Society in Early Times* (New York: W. W. Norton, 1994), 142.

[30] Stewig, *The Moon's Choice*.

[31] Gimbutas, *The Language of the Goddess*, 300–301.

[32] Stewig, *The Moon's Choice*.

[33] Alfred Slote, *The Moon in Fact and Fantasy,* illus. John Kaufmann (New York: World Publishing, 1967), 18.

[34] Harley, *Moon Lore*, 155.

[35] Eliade, *Patterns in Comparative Religion*, 154.

[36] Stewig, *The Moon's Choice*.

[37] Barbara G. Walker, *The Woman's Dictionary of Symbols and Sacred Objects* (New York: HarperSanFrancisco, 1988), 399.

[38] Gimbutas, *The Language of the Goddess*, 190.

[39] Jablow and Withers, *The Man in the Moon*, 15–17.

[40] Chevalier and Gheerbrant, *A Dictionary of Symbols,* 138.

[41] William Shakespeare, *A Midsummer-Night's Dream* 5.1.261–3.

[42] Marcea Eliade, *Shamanism: Archaic Techniques of Ecstasy,* trans. Willard R. Trask, Bollingen Series 76 (Princeton, N.J.: Princeton University Press, 1964), 470–74.

[43] Walker, *The Woman's Encyclopedia of Myths*, 944–45.

[44] Ibid.

[45] Jablow and Withers, *The Man in the Moon*, 7–9.

[46] Joseph Campbell, *The Power of Myth with Bill Moyers,* ed. Betty Sue Flowers (New York: Doubleday, 1988), 110–11.

[47] Harley, *Moon Lore*, 194.

[48] Chevalier and Gheerbrant, *A Dictionary of Symbols*, 670.

[49] Bram, "Moon," 90.

[50] Walker, *The Woman's Encyclopedia of Myths*, 661.

[51] Carolyn Myss, *Why People Don't Heal and How They Can* (New York: Harmony Books, 1997), 249–51.

[52] Gimbutas, *The Language of the Goddess*, 300–301.

Chapter 4: Snow White, Persephone, and Eve

[1] "The Juniper Tree," Tale #47 in *The Complete Fairy Tales of the Brothers Grimm*, trans. Jack Zipes (New York: Bantam Books, 1992), 170–79.

[2] *Standard Dictionary of Folklore*, s.v. "Deirdre."

[3] Walker, *Woman's Encyclopedia of Myths*, 358–59.

[4] Kay Stone, "Three Transformations of Snow White," in *The Brothers Grimm and Folktale*, ed. James M. McGlathery (Urbana: University of Illinois Press, 1988), 57–58.

[5] Iona Opie and Peter Opie, *The Classic Fairy Tales* (New York: Oxford University Press, 1980), 227–28.

[6] Steven Swann Jones, "The Construction of the Folktale: 'Snow White'" (Ph.D. diss., University of California, Davis, 1979).

[7] Kay E. Vandergrift, "Snow White Text: Snow White Alternative Texts," [created January 6, 1997]; available at http://www.scils.rutgers.edu/special/kay/snowwhite.html.

[8] Ibid.

[9] Jones, "Construction of the Folktale," 78–134.

[10] Roy Vickery, comp., *A Dictionary of Plant-Lore* (New York: Oxford University Press, 1995), 251.

[11] Walker, *Woman's Dictionary of Symbols*, 449.

[12] *Standard Dictionary of Folklore*, s.v. "Dionysus."

[13] *Funk and Wagnalls New Encyclopedia*, s.v. "myrtle."

[14] Vandergrift, "Snow White Text."

[15] Jones, "Construction of the Folktale," 78–134.

[16] William A. Gutsch, Jr., *1001 Things Everyone Should Know About the Universe* (New York: Doubleday, 1998), 84.

[17] E. C. Krupp, "Moon Maids," *Griffith Observer* 52 (December 1988): 3–4.

[18] Jones, "Construction of the Folktale," 78–134.

[19] Ibid., 137.

[20] Ibid., 78–134.

[21] Edward Tripp, *Crowell's Handbook of Classical Mythology* (New York: Thomas Y. Crowell, 1970), 194–97.

[22] Campbell, *The Mythic Image*, 468.

[23] Tripp, *Crowell's Handbook of Classical Mythology*, 194–97.

[24] *Encyclopedia Britannica*, 1910 ed., as quoted in Lawrence Durdin-Robertson, *The Year of the Goddess: A Perpetual Calendar of Festivals* (Wellingborough, Northamptonshire: The Aquarian Press, 1990), 125.

[25] Edward A. Beach, "The Ecole Initiative: The Eleusinian Mysteries," [copyright 1995]; available at http://www3.erols.com/nbeach/eleusis.html.

[26] *Standard Dictionary of Folklore*, s.v. "beans," "Demeter."

[27] Walker, *Woman's Encyclopedia of Myths*, 218–20.

[28] Frazer, *The Golden Bough*, 544.

[29] Bram, "Moon," 89.

[30] Ibid.

[31] Eliade, *Patterns in Comparative Religion*, 168.

[32] Walker, *Woman's Dictionary of Symbols*, 493.

[33] *NRSV.*

[34] Chevalier and Gheerbrant, *A Dictionary of Symbols*, 766–67.

[35] Robert Graves, *The White Goddess: A Historical Grammar of Poetic Myth* (New York: Farrar, Straus and Giroux, 1948), 410.

[36] Harley, *Moon Lore*, 121.

[37] Rockwell, *Giving Voice to Bear*, 121.

[38] Bram, "Moon," 86–87.

[39] Paul Shepard and Barry Sanders, *The Sacred Paw: The Bear in Nature, Myth, and Literature* (New York: Arkana, Viking Penguin, 1985), 127–28; Joanna Cole, comp., *Best-Loved Folktales of the World* (New York: Anchor Books, Doubleday, 1982), 287–95; and Tale #101 in *Complete Fairy Tales of the Brothers Grimm*, 370–73.

[40] Durdin-Robertson, *The Year of the Goddess*, 39.

[41] David Rockwell, *Giving Voice to Bear*, 190.

[42] Ibid.

[43] Ibid., 198.

[44] Marija Gimbutas, *The Goddesses and Gods of Old Europe: 6500–3500 B.C. Myths and Cult Images* (Berkeley and Los Angeles: University of California Press, 1974; new and updated edition in paperback, 1982), 190–95.

[45] Eliade, *Patterns in Comparative Religion*, 157.

[46] Laura Simms, *Moon and Otter and Frog*, illus. Clifford Brucelea (New York: Hyperion Books for Children, 1995).

[47] Erdoes and Ortiz, *American Indian Myths*, 143–45; Jablow and Withers, *Man in the Moon*, 39.

[48] Harley, *Moon Lore*, 169.

[49] *Standard Dictionary of Folklore*, s.v. "groundhog."

[50] Shepard and Sanders, *The Sacred Paw*, 132, 136.

[51] Annemarie Schimmel, *The Mystery of Numbers* (New York: Oxford University Press, 1993), 254.

[52] *Standard Dictionary of Folklore*, s.v. "groundhog."

[53] Frazer, *The Golden Bough*, 417–19.

[54] Ibid., 432, 486.

[55] Shepard and Sanders, *The Sacred Paw*, 88.

[56] David Rockwell, *Giving Voice to Bear*, 132–33, 192.

[57] Eliade, *Patterns in Comparative Religion*, 174–75.

[58] Vandergrift, "Snow White Text."

[59] Walker, *Woman's Encyclopedia of Myths*, 220.

[60] Frazer, *The Golden Bough*, 417–19.

[61] Notes in *The New Oxford Annotated Bible with Apocryphal/Deuterocanonical Books: New Revised Standard Version*, ed. Bruce M. Metzger and Roland E. Murphy (New York: Oxford University Press, 1994), 4, 6OT.

[62] *New Saint Joseph Sunday Missal Complete Edition: The Complete Masses for Sundays, Holy Days and the Easter Triduum* (New York: Catholic Book Publishing, 1986), 238.

[63] Carl-Martin Edsman, "Bears," trans. Verne Moberg, in *Encyclopedia of Religion*, ed. Mircea Eliade, 2:87.

[64] Eliade, *Patterns in Comparative Religion*, 168–69.

[65] Krupp, "Moon Maids," 7.

[66] E32, D437.1, and D437.2 in Stith Thompson, *Motif-index of Folk-literature: A Classification of Narrative Elements in Folktales, Ballads, Myths, Fables, Mediaeval Romances, Exempla, Fabliaux, Jest-books, and Local Legends* (Bloomington: Indiana University Press, 1966).

[67] Chevalier and Gheerbrant, *Dictionary of Symbols*, 766–77.

[68] Ibid.

[69] NRSV.

[70] *Standard Dictionary of Folklore*, s.v. "pomegranate."

[71] Ibid., s.v. "forbidden fruit."

[72] Natalia Belting, *The Moon Is a Crystal Ball: Unfamiliar Legends of the Stars* (New York: Bobbs-Merrill, 1952), 80–87.

[73] Krupp, "Moon Maids," 4.

[74] E90.1, A714.2 in Thompson, *Motif-index of Folk-literature*.

[75] Eliade, *Patterns in Comparative Religion*, 174–5.

[76] Bram, "Moon," 89.

[77] Gen. 3:14, NRSV.

[78] Gen. 3:15, in Stephen Mitchell, *Genesis: A New Translation of the Classic Biblical Stories* (New York: HarperCollins, 1996) 7–8. The only difference in this translation from the New Standard Revised Version is the use of "they" instead of "he" in reference to Eve's offspring, making the passage easier to understand.

[79] Walker, *Woman's Encyclopedia of Myths*, 288

[80] Ibid., 904–5.

[81] Chevalier and Gheerbrant, *Dictionary of Symbols*, 671.

[82] Erdoes and Ortiz, *American Indian Myths*, 168–69.

[83] William Sleator, *The Angry Moon*, illus. Blair Lent (Boston: Atlantic Monthly Press, Little, Brown, 1970).

[84] NRSV.

[85] Charles F. Lummis, *The Man Who Married the Moon and Other Pueblo Indian Folk-stories* (New York: The Century Co., 1894; reprinted by AMS Press, New York, 1976), 53–70.

Chapter 5: Rumpelstiltskin

[1] *Standard Dictionary of Folklore*, s.v. "Rumpelstiltskin."

[2] The version of "Rumpelstiltskin" reprinted here in full is from *Household Stories from the Collection of the Brothers Grimm*, 228–31.

[3] Giorgio de Santillana and Hertha von Dechend, *Hamlet's Mill: An Essay on Myth and the Frame of Time* (Boston: Gambit, 1969).

[4] Barber, *Women's Work*, 34–39.

[5] Ibid., 207, 210–11.

[6] Ibid., 246.

[7] Ibid., 38, 247.

[8] Maria Tatar, *The Hard Facts of the Grimm's Fairy Tales* (Princeton, N.J.: Princeton University Press, 1987), 132.

[9] Eliade, *Patterns in Comparative Religion*, 180–81.

[10] Chevalier and Gheerbrant, *A Dictionary of Symbols*, 671.

[11] Walker, *Woman's Dictionary of Symbols*, 419–20.

[12] Chevalier and Gheerbrant, *A Dictionary of Symbols*, 904–5.

[13] Erdoes and Ortiz, *American Indian Myths*, 168–69

[14] Edwards, *Sun Stories*, 24–28.

[15] Jablow and Withers, *The Man in the Moon*, 18.

[16] Eliade, *Patterns in Comparative Religion*, 148.

[17] Philip S Harrington, *Eclipse! The What, Where, When, Why, and How Guide to Watching Solar and Lunar Eclipses* (New York: John Wiley & Sons, 1997), 44–45.

[18] H1151.15, F357, N698, F102.3, H1023.21 in Thompson, *Motif-index of Folk-literature*.

[19] Roebuck, *The Circle of Stars*, 87.

[20] Harrington, *Eclipse!* 46.

[21] K401.2.2, A652.1.1 in Thompson, *Motif-index of Folk-literature*.

[22] Edith Hamilton, *Mythology* (New York: A Mentor Book, Penguin Books, 1942), 254–67.

[23] *Standard Dictionary of Folklore*, s.v. "Harmonia's necklace."

[24] Edwards, *Sun Stories*, 78–82.

[25] *Funk and Wagnalls New Encyclopedia* (1986), s.v. "eclipse."

[26] Chevalier and Gheerbrant, *Dictionary of Symbols*, 805.

[27] N352, H1199.9.1, B548.2.1, N211.1, N865.1, H1132.1.1, and D1662.1.1 in Thompson, *Motif-index of Folk-literature*.

[28] Harrington, *Eclipse!* 45–47.

[29] Chevalier and Gheerbrant, *Dictionary of Symbols*, 808.

[30] *Funk and Wagnalls New Encyclopedia*, s.v. "eclipse."

[31] Rockwell, *Giving Voice to the Bear*, 137–40.

[32] Stutley and Stutley, *Harper's Dictionary of Hinduism*, 201–3.

[33] Klein, *Etymological Dictionary*, 1026.

[34] Stutley and Stutley, *Harper's Dictionary of Hinduism*, 201–3.

[35] *Standard Dictionary of Folklore*, s.v. "name tabu."

[36] Ibid.

[37] Stutley and Stutley, *Harper's Dictionary of Hinduism*, 203.

[38] *Standard Dictionary of Folklore*, s.v. "names."

[39] Carl Hentze, *Mythes et symboles lunaires: Chine ancienne, civilisations anciennes de l'Asie, peuple limitrophes du Pacifique* (Anvers: Editions "de Sikkel," 1932), 153.

[40] Walker, *Woman's Encyclopedia of Myth*, 532, 1076.

[41] NRSV.

[42] Tatar, *The Hard Facts*, 124–25.

[43] Ibid.

[44] Rockwell, *Giving Voice to the Bear*, 116–21, 137–40.

[45] Tatar, *The Hard Facts*, 124.

[46] Zipes, *Breaking the Magic Spell*, 6–7.

[47] Jablow and Withers, *The Man in the Moon*, 14.

[48] Opie, *The Classic Fairy Tales*, 253–55.

[49] Jack Zipes, *Fairy Tale as Myth/Myth as Fairy Tale* (Lexington: University Press of Kentucky, 1994), 53–54.

[50] *Standard Dictionary of Folklore*, s.v. "box dropping from sky."

[51] Barber, *Women's Work*, 207–8.

[52] Klein, *Etymological Dictionary*, 1489, 1495.

[53] Bram, "Moon," 89.

[54] "The Name of the Helper: Folktales of the type 500, and related tales, in which a mysterious and threatening helper is defeated when the hero or heroine discovers his name," trans. and/or ed. D. L. Ashliman [copyright 1998]; available at http://www.pitt.edu/~dash/type0500.html.

Chapter 6: Goosey, Goosey Gander

[1] Notes in William S. Baring-Gould and Ceil Baring-Gould, *The Annotated Mother Goose* (New York: Bramhall House, 1962), 87.

[2] Gimbutas, *The Language of the Goddess*, 317.

[3] Ibid., 3–4.

[4] Walker, *Woman's Encyclopedia of Myths*, 349.

[5] Stutley and Stutley, *Harper's Dictionary of Hinduism*, 108.

[6] Chevalier and Gheerbrant, *A Dictionary of Symbols*, 446.

[7] Ibid.

[8] Walker, *Woman's Dictionary of Symbols*, 402.

[9] *Standard Dictionary of Folklore*, s.v. "goose."

[10] Ibid.

[11] Krupp, "Celestial Analogy and Cyclical Renewal," 4.

[12] Chevalier and Gheerbrant, *A Dictionary of Symbols*, 446.

[13] Standard Dictionary of Folklore, s.v. "goose."

[14] Walker, *Woman's Encyclopedia of Myths*, 349.

[15] Iona Opie and Peter Opie, eds., *The Oxford Dictionary of Nursery Rhymes* (Oxford: Oxford University Press, 1952), 33.

[16] Opie and Opie, *The Classic Fairy Tales*, 18–25.

[17] Baring-Gould and Baring-Gould, *The Annotated Mother Goose*, 17.

[18] Ibid., 16–17.

[19] Ean Begg, *The Cult of the Black Virgin* (New York: Arkana, Penguin Books, 1985), 32–33.

[20] *Standard Dictionary of Folklore*, s.v. "Berchta."

[21] Gimbutas, *The Language of the Goddess*, 209.

[22] Ibid., s.v. "Holde."

[23] Ibid., s.v. "goose god."

[24] Frazer, *The Golden Bough*, 486–87.

[25] Eliade, *Patterns in Comparative Religion*, 180.

[26] Walker, *Woman's Dictionary of Symbols*, 402.

[27] *Standard Dictionary of Folklore*, s.v. "Holde."

[28] Baring-Gould and Baring-Gould, *Annotated Mother Goose*, 17.

[29] *Standard Dictionary of Folklore*, s.v. "goose."

[30] Ibid.; and Stutley and Stutley, *Harper's Dictionary of Hinduism*, 108.

[31] Opie and Opie, *Oxford Dictionary of Nursery Rhymes*, 191–93.

[32] Baring-Gould and Baring-Gould, *Annotated Mother Goose*, 70.

[33] Sabine Baring-Gould, *Curious Myths of the Middle Ages*, ed. Edward Hardy (New York: Oxford University Press, 1978), 75.

[34] Diana Brueton, *Many Moons: The Myth and Magic, Fact and Fantasy of Our Nearest Heavenly Body* (Englewood Cliffs, N.J.: Prentice Hall, 1991), 30.

[35] Chevalier and Gheerbrant, *Dictionary of Symbols*, 587.

[36] *Gidja the Moon.*

[37] As quoted in Belting, *The Moon Is a Crystal Ball*, 13.

[38] Jablow and Withers, *The Man in the Moon*, 6.

[39] Belting, *The Moon Is a Crystal Ball*, 12.

[40] Harley, *Moon Lore*, 24–25.

[41] J.E. Cirlot, *A Dictionary of Symbols*, trans. Jack Sage (New York: Philosophical Library, 1962), 106.

[42] Hentze, *Mythes et symboles lunaires*, 153.

[43] Ibid., 153–54.

[44] Mary Miller and Karl Taube, *The Gods and Symbols of Ancient Mexico and the Maya: An Illustrated Dictionary of Mesoamerican Religion* (New York: Thames and Hudson, 1993), 164–65.

[45] Hentze, *Mythes et Symboles Lunaires*, 153–54.

[46] Chevalier and Gheerbrant, *Dictionary of Symbols*, 722.

[47] Graves, *The White Goddess*, 445.

[48] Harley, *Moon Lore*, 23.

Chapter 7: Diddle, Diddle, Dumpling

[1] Opie and Opie, *Oxford Dictionary of Nursery Rhymes*, 246.

[2] Brueton, *Many Moons*, 190–91.

[3] Klein, *Etymological Dictionary*, 831.

[4] Cirlot, *Dictionary of Symbols*, 129.

[5] NRSV

[6] Margaret Hodges, *Buried Moon* (New York: Little, Brown, 1990).

[7] Hamilton, *Mythology*, 119.

[8] Campbell, *The Mythic Image*, 470–71.

[9] G. A. Gaskell, *Dictionary of All Scriptures and Myth* (New York: Gramercy Books, 1960), 338.

[10] Chevalier and Gheerbrant, *Dictionary of Symbols*, 587.

[11] Ibid., 722.

[12] Walker, *Woman's Encyclopedia of Myth*, 944–45.

[13] Gaskell, *Dictionary of All Scriptures*, 349–50.

[14] Chevalier and Gheerbrant, *Dictionary of Symbols*, 721.

[15] Gimbutas, *The Language of the Goddess*, 305.

[16] Scarre, *Smithsonian Timelines*, 61.

[17] Gimbutas, *The Language of the Goddess*, 305–7.

[18] Rockwell, *Giving Voice to Bear*, 137–38.

[19] Shepard and Sanders, *The Sacred Paw*, 77–79.

[20] Ibid., 124.

[21] *Standard Dictionary of Folklore*, s.v. "Bear's Son."

[22] Ibid.

[23] Rhys Carpenter, *Folktale, Fiction and Saga in the Homeric Epics* (Berkeley and Los Angeles: University of California Press, 1946), 136–56

[24] Hamilton, *Mythology*, 117–30.

[25] Gimbutas, *The Language of the Goddess*, 305

Chapter 8: Jack Be Nimble

[1] Opie and Opie, *Oxford Dictionary of Nursery Rhymes*, 226–27.

[2] Ibid.

[3] Stutley and Stutley, *Harper's Dictionary of Hinduism*, 114.

[4] Frazer, *The Golden Bough*, 705–32.

[5] Ibid.

[6] Ibid., 743–53.

[7] Ibid., 731.

[8] Hamilton, *Mythology*, 65–66.

[9] Harley, *Moon Lore*, 149.

[10] A1142.5.1.1, in Thompson, *Motif-index of Folk-literature*.

[11] Frazer, *The Golden Bough*, 524–25.

[12] Gimbutas, *Language of the Goddess*, 317.

[13] Chevalier and Gheerbrant, *Dictionary of Symbols*, 472–75.

[14] Harley, *Moon Lore*, 64.

[15] Slote, *Moon in Fact and Fantasy*, 76–82.

[16] *To the Moon!* 17.

[17] Ibid., 21–24.

[18] Harley, *Moon Lore*, 125.

[19] *Standard Dictionary of Folklore*, s.v. "Ostara."

[20] Harley, *Moon Lore*, 66.

[21] Bram, "Moon," 89.

[22] Cirlot, *Dictionary of Symbols*, 133.

[23] Gail and Houlding, *Day of the Moon Shadow*, 225.

[24] Erdoes and Ortiz, *American Indian Myths*, 139–40.

[25] *Standard Dictionary of Folklore*, s.v. "rabbit."

[26] *To the Moon!* 14–16.

[27] Cole, *Best-Loved Folktales of the World*, 712–18.

[28] Klein, *Etymological Dictionary*, 128.

[29] *Standard Dictionary of Folklore*, s.v. "Ma" and "Mama."

[30] Erdoes and Ortiz, *American Indian Myths*, 169–71.

[31] Gwydion O'Hara, *Moonlore: Myths and Folklore from Around the World* (St. Paul: Llewellyn Publications, 1996), 30–32.

[32] Stewart, *Astrology*, 28.

[33] Bram, "Moon," 89.

[34] Harley, *Moon Lore*, 173–74.

[35] *Standard Dictionary of Folklore*, s.v. "eclipses."

[36] Guirma, *Princess of the Full Moon*.

[37] Harley, *Moon Lore*, 160.

[38] Frazer, *The Golden Bough*, 705–32.

Chapter 9: There Was a Man and He Had Nought

[1] Baring-Gould and Baring-Gould, *The Annotated Mother Goose*, 95.

[2] Opie and Opie, *Oxford Dictionary of Nursery Rhymes*, 285.

[3] Ibid.

[4] Jablow and Withers, *Man in the Moon*, 97–98.

[5] Ibid., 21.

[6] Rama P. Coomaraswamy, *The Door in the Sky: Coomaraswamy on Myth and Meaning* (Princeton, N.J.: Princeton University Press, 1997), 24.

[7] Ibid., 28.

[8] Ibid., 218–19.

[9] Erdoes and Ortiz, *American Indian Myths*, 143–45.

[10] Ibid., 168–71.

[11] Tony van Renterghem, *When Santa Was a Shaman: The Ancient Origins of Santa Claus and the Christmas Tree* (St. Paul, Minn.: Llewellyn Publications, 1995), 103.

[12] Chevalier and Gheerbrant, *Dictionary of Symbols*, 191.

[13] Alan Blackwood, *Festivals: New Year* (East Sussex, England: Wayland, 1985), 35.

[14] van Renterghem, *When Santa Was a Shaman*, 125.

[15] Rockwell, *Giving Voice to the Bear*, 170.

[16] van Renterghem, *When Santa Was a Shaman*, 101, 113.

[17] *Standard Dictionary of Folklore*, s.v. "Knecht Rupert," "Saint Nicholas."

[18] Ibid., s.v. "rods of life," "stick dances."

[19] R. Chambers, ed., *The Book of Days: A Miscellany of Popular Antiquities in Connection with the Calendar including Anecdote, Biography, & History, Curiosities of Literature and Oddities of Human Life and Character* (London: W. & R. Chambers, Ltd., c. 1887; Detroit: Gale Research, 1967), 1:573.

[20] Ibid.

[21] Ibid.

[22] Vickery, *Dictionary of Plant-Lore*, 320–21.

[23] *Standard Dictionary of Folklore*, s.v. "Jack in the Green."

[24] van Renterghem, *When Santa Was a Shaman*, 44, 142.

[25] Marguerite Ickes, *The Book of Festival Holidays* (New York: Dodd, Mead, 1964), 30.

[26] *Standard Dictionary of Folklore*, s.v. "sun dance."

[27] NRSV.

[28] *Standard Dictionary of Folklore*, s.v. "fire."

[29] Ibid., s.v. "knocks."

[30] Baring-Gould and Baring-Gould, *Annotated Mother Goose*, 28.

Chapter 10: Little Polly Flinders

[1] Baring-Gould and Baring-Gould, *Annotated Mother Goose*, 125.

[2] Eliade, *Shamanism*, 64.

[3] Robert Bly, *Iron John: A Book about Men* (New York: Addison-Wesley, 1990), 179–80.

[4] Stutley and Stutley, *Harper's Dictionary of Hinduism*, 139.

[5] Frazer, *The Golden Bough*, 705–43.

[6] Margaret Read MacDonald, ed., *The Folklore of World Holidays* (Detroit: Gale Research, 1992), 599–600.

[7] Chevalier and Gheerbrant, *Dictionary of Symbols*, 49.

[8] Frazer, *The Golden Bough*, 716–17.

[9] Walker, *Woman's Encyclopedia of Myths*, 66–67.

[10] Erdoes and Ortiz, *American Indian Myths*, 136–39.

[11] Ibid., 161–62.

[12] Harley, *Moon Lore*, 33–35.

[13] Ibid.

[14] Ibid., 57.

[15] Edsman, "Bears," 88.

[16] Shepard and Sanders, *The Sacred Paw*, 137–38.

[17] Clement Moore, *A Visit from Saint Nicholas*; available at "Christmas Stories and Poems," http://www.night.net/christmas/Twas-night01.html.

[18] Chevalier and Gheerbrant, *Dictionary of Symbols*, 752–53.

[19] Robert Bauval and Adrian Gilbert, *The Orion Mystery: Unlocking the Secrets of the Pyramids* (New York: Crown Trade Paperbacks, 1994), 198–99.

[20] Thich Nhat Hanh, *Living Buddha, Living Christ* (New York: Riverhead Books, 1995).

[21] Chevalier and Gheerbrant, *Dictionary of Symbols*, 752–53.

[22] NRSV.

Chapter 11: Jack and the Beanstalk

[1] The version of "Jack and the Beanstalk" reprinted in full in this chapter is from Joseph Jacobs, *English Folk and Fairy Tales: Folk and Fairy Tales from Many Lands*, 3rd ed., rev. (New York: G. P. Putnam's Sons, [1900]), 59–68.

[2] Bram, "Moon," 87.

[3] Harley, *Moon Lore*, 92–93.

[4] Bram, "Moon," 87.
[5] Chevalier and Gheerbrant, *Dictionary of Symbols,* 237–38.
[6] Ibid.
[7] Stutley and Stutley, *Harper's Dictionary of Hinduism*, 101.
[8] Harley, *Moon Lore,* 133.
[9] Chevalier and Gheerbrant, *Dictionary of Symbols,* 237–38.
[10] Walker, *Woman's Dictionary of Symbols*, 481.
[11] *Standard Dictionary of Folklore,* s.v. "beans."
[12] Ibid.
[13] Chevalier and Gheerbrant, *Dictionary of Symbols,* 74.
[14] *Standard Dictionary of Folklore,* s.v. "overlooking."
[15] Andrew Lang, ed., *The Red Fairy Book* (New York: McGraw-Hillbrook, 1967), 133.
[16] Walker, *Woman's Encyclopedia of Myths,* 598.
[17] Chevalier and Gheerbrant, *Dictionary of Symbols,* 237–38.
[18] "Jack and the Beanstalk," in E. Nesbit, *The Old Nursery Stories* (London: Henry Frowde and Hodder & Stoughton, 1908). From "The Jack and the Beanstalk and Jack the Giant-Killer Project," ed. Michael N. Salda, located at the de Grummond Children's Literature Research Collection, University of Southern Mississippi. Available at http://www-dept.usm.edu/~engdept/jack/jackhome.html.
[19] *The Old Farmer's Almanac* (Dublin, N.H.: Yankee Publishing, 1997), 68, 80.
[20] Heinberg, *Celebrate the Solstice,* 11.
[21] *Old Farmer's Almanac,* 1988–98.
[22] Chevalier and Gheerbrant, *Dictionary of Symbols,* 370.
[23] Ibid., 387–88.
[24] Schimmel, *Mystery of Numbers,* 108–9.
[25] Joseph Gaer, *Holidays Around the World* (Boston: Little, Brown, 1953), 71–72.
[26] Derek Walters, *Chinese Mythology: An Encyclopedia of Myth and Legend* (London: Aquarian/Thorsons, HarperCollins, 1992), 65–66.
[27] Li-Ch'en, *Annual Customs in Peking,* 3.
[28] *Standard Dictionary of Folklore,* s.v. "New Year."
[29] Rockwell, *Giving Voice to Bear,* 172.
[30] Graves, *The White Goddess,* 69.
[31] *Standard Dictionary of Folklore,* s.v. "Jacob's ladder."
[32] Eric Partridge, *Dictionary of Slang and Unconventional English*, 8th ed., ed. Paul Beale (New York: Macmillan, 1984), 606–10.
[33] In Salda, "The Jack and the Beanstalk and Jack the Giant-Killer Project,".
[34] *Standard Dictionary of Folklore,* s.v. "beans."
[35] Jablow and Withers, *The Man in the Moon,* 120.
[36] Harley, *Moon Lore,* 171.
[37] Chevalier and Gheerbrant, *Dictionary of Symbols,* 1105.
[38] *Standard Dictionary of Folklore,* s.v. "whipping."
[39] Eliade, *Shamanism,* 490.
[40] Frances Carpenter, "Heng O, the Moon Lady," in *To the Moon!* 4.
[41] Jablow and Withers, *The Man in the Moon,* 11–13.

[42] Ibid., 19.

[43] *Standard Dictionary of Folklore*, s.v. "ascent to upper world."

[44] Belting, *The Moon Is a Crystal Ball*, 136–43.

[45] Slote, *Moon in Fact and Fantasy*, 101–06.

[46] Opie, *Classic Fairy Tales*, 211–26.

[47] Carpenter, *Folktale, Fiction, and Saga in the Homeric Epics*, 129–35.

[48] Klein, *Etymological Dictionary*, 1078.

[49] Shepard and Sanders, *The Sacred Paw*, 136.

[50] *Standard Dictionary of Folklore*, s.v. "coin of the dead."

[51] In Salda, "The Jack and the Beanstalk and Jack the Giant-Killer Project."

[52] Bram, "Moon," 90.

[53] Barmbrack bread and other traditional holiday breads are available from the Breadman Bakery in Foster, Virginia.

[54] Marina Warner, *From the Beast to the Blond: On Fairy Tales and Their Tellers* (New York: The Noon Press, Farrar, Strauss and Giroux, 1994), 128.

[55] Walker, *The Woman's Dictionary of Symbols*, 5.

[56] Bram, "Moon," 88.

[57] Eric Hadley and Tessa Hadley, *Legends of the Sun and Moon*, illus. Jan Nesbitt (New York: Cambridge University Press, 1983).

[58] Desmond Varley, *Seven: The Number of Creation* (London: G. Bells & Son, 1976), 24.

[59] Shepard and Sanders, *The Sacred Paw*, 131.

[60] *Standard Dictionary of Folklore*, s.v. "looking tabu."

[61] Slote, *Moon in Fact and Fantasy*, 18.

[62] Lois Ehlert, *Moon Rope: A Peruvian Folktale* (San Diego: Harcourt Brace Jovanovich, 1992).

[63] Joseph Bruchac and Gayle Ross, *The Girl Who Married the Moon: Tales from Native North America* (New York: Troll Medallion, 1994), 116–24.

[64] Harley, *Moon Lore*, 176–77.

[65] Erdoes and Ortiz, *American Indian Myths*, 168–69.

[66] Walker, *Woman's Encyclopedia of Myths*, 672.

[67] Krupp, *Beyond the Blue Horizon*, 96–98.

[68] Walker, *Woman's Encyclopedia of Myths*, 905.

[69] *Standard Dictionary of Folklore*, s.v. "dragon" and "Marduk."

[70] Ibid., s.v. "ascent to upper world."

[71] Opie and Opie, *Classic Fairy Tales*, 211–26.

Chapter 12: Three Blind Mice

[1] Baring-Gould and Baring-Gould, *Annotated Mother Goose*, 156.

[2] Opie and Opie, *Oxford Dictionary of Nursery Rhymes*, 306.

[3] Ibid.

[4] Chevalier and Gheerbrant, *Dictionary of Symbols*, 100.

[5] *Standard Dictionary of Folklore*, s.v. "Tiresias."

[6] Chevalier and Gheerbrant, *Dictionary of Symbols*, 100.

[7] Ibid., 721.

[8] Lummis, *Man Who Married the Moon*, 71–73.

[9] Eliade, *Patterns in Comparative Religion*, 128, 180.

[10] Jablow and Withers, *Man in the Moon*, 79–80, 21–22.

[11] Edwards, *Sun Stories*, 31–35.

[12] Edsman, "Bears," 88.

[13] *Standard Dictionary of Folklore*, s.v. "mouse."

[14] Harley, *Moon Lore*, 71.

[15] Anthony Aveni, *Conversing with the Planets: How Science and Myth Invented the Cosmos* (New York: Kodasha International, 1992, 1994), 106.

[16] *Standard Dictionary of Folklore*, s.v. "mouse."

[17] Chevalier and Gheerbrant, *Dictionary of Symbols*, 967.

[18] Partridge, *A Dictionary of Slang*, 1194.

[19] Walker, *Woman's Encyclopedia of Myths*, 856–57.

[20] Chevalier and Gheerbrant, *Dictionary of Symbols*, 573.

[21] *Standard Dictionary of Folklore*, s.v. "moon."

[22] Ibid., s.v. "iron."

[23] A700.5 in Thompson, *Motif-index of Folk-literature*.

[24] Chevalier and Gheerbrant, *Dictionary of Symbols*, 365.

[25] *Standard Dictionary of Folklore*, s.v. "overlooking."

[26] Schimmel, *The Mystery of Numbers*, 115–16.

[27] Robert M. Lombardo, "The Genesis of Organized Crime in Chicago," in *IASOC Criminal Organizations*, 10:2; Available at http://www.acsp.uic.edu/iasoc/crim_org/vol10_2/art_4k.htm.

[28] Stutley and Stutley, *Dictionary of Hinduism*, 110–11.

[29] G303.4.4.1 in Thompson, *Motif-index of Folk-literature*.

[30] Campbell, *The Mythic Image*, 337, 290.

Chapter 13: There Was a Man Lived in the Moon

[1] Baring-Gould and Baring-Gould, *Annotated Mother Goose*, 157–58.

[2] Harley, *Moon Lore*, 204–8.

[3] Bram, "Moon," 88.

[4] Hamilton, *Mythology*, 227.

[5] Stutley and Stutley, *Harper's Dictionary of Hinduism*, 282–84.

[6] Campbell, *The Mythic Image*, 89.

[7] Harley, *Moon Lore*, 11.

[8] Alfredo Lopez-Austin, *The Rabbit on the Face of the Moon: Mythology in the Mesoamerican Tradition*, trans. Bernard R. Ortiz de Montellano and Thelma Ortiz de Montellano (Salt Lake City: University of Utah Press, 1996), 5.

[9] Philip, *Illustrated Book of Myth*, 38–39.

[10] Krupp, *Beyond the Blue Horizon*, 72–74.

[11] *Standard Dictionary of Folklore*, s.v. "eclipses."

[12] Ibid., s.v. "food tabu in the land of the dead."

[13] Belting, *The Moon Is a Crystal Ball*, 72–74.

[14] Krupp, *Beyond the Blue Horizon*, 167–68.
[15] Ibid., 193–97.
[16] Aveni, *Conversing with the Planets*, 58.
[17] Walker, *Woman's Dictionary of Symbols*, 74–75.
[18] Schimmel, *The Mystery of Numbers*, 107–8.
[19] Aveni, *Conversing with the Planets*, 30.
[20] Gimbutas, *Goddesses and Gods of Old Europe*, 152.
[21] Baring-Gould and Baring-Gould, *Annotated Mother Goose*, 158.
[22] Opie and Opie, *Oxford Dictionary of Nursery Rhymes*, 54.

Chapter 14: Little Red Riding Hood

[1] Household Stories from the Brothers Grimm, 132–35.
[2] Klein, *Etymological Dictionary*, 1062.
[3] Warner, *From the Beast to the Blonde*, 86–87.
[4] Walker, *Woman's Encyclopedia of Myths*, 38–40.
[5] *Standard Dictionary of Folklore*, s.v. "Janus."
[6] Walker, *Woman's Encyclopedia of Myths*, 717.
[7] Begg, *Cult of the Black Virgin*, 46.
[8] *Standard Dictionary of Folklore*, s.v. "Anahita," "Anath," "Cybele," "Inanna," and "Nanna."
[9] Alan Dundes, "Interpreting Little Red Riding Hood Psychoanalytically" in *The Brothers Grimm and Folktale*, ed. James M. McClatchery (Chicago: University of Illinois Press, 1988), 26.
[10] Walker, *Woman's Dictionary of Symbols*, 376.
[11] Chevalier and Gheerbrant, *Dictionary of Symbols*, 435–37.
[12] *Standard Dictionary of Folklore*, s.v. "Wolf."
[13] Chevalier and Gheerbrant, *Dictionary of Symbols*, 1121.
[14] Ibid.
[15] Begg, *Cult of the Black Virgin*, 117.
[16] Chevalier and Gheerbrant, *Dictionary of Symbols*, 709–10.
[17] *Standard Dictionary of Folklore*, s.v. "oak."
[18] Ibid., s.v. "hazel."
[19] Vickery, *A Dictionary of Plant-Lore*, 172–74.
[20] Chevalier and Gheerbrant, *Dictionary of Symbols*, 476.
[21] *Standard Dictionary of Folklore*, s.v. "hazel."
[22] Yvonne Verdier, "Le Petit Chaperon Rouge dans la tradition orale," quoted in Dundes, "Interpreting Little Red Riding Hood Psychoanalytically," 28.
[23] Rockwell, *Giving Voice to the Bear*, 15–18.
[24] *Standard Dictionary of Folklore*, s.v. "menstruation."
[25] Rockwell, *Giving Voice to the Bear*, 185.
[26] Bram, "Moon," 90.
[27] *Standard Dictionary of Folklore*, s.v. "menstruation."

[28] See charts in Toni Weschler, *Taking Charge of Your Fertility: The Definitive Guide to Natural Birth Control and Pregnancy Achievement* (New York: HarperCollins, 1995).

[29] *Standard Dictionary of Folklore*, s.v. "childbirth," and "menstruation."

[30] Walker, *Woman's Encyclopedia of Myths*, 644.

[31] Rockwell, *Giving Voice to the Bear*, 125.

[32] "Fairy Lore: Fairyland," on *Fairy Tale–A True Story* Homepage, [Paramount Pictures, 1997]; available at http://www.fairytalemovie.com/lore/fairyland.html.

[33] *Standard Dictionary of Folklore*, s.v. "Oats Goat."

[34] P. Saintyves [E. Nourry], "Little Red Riding Hood; or, The Little May Queen," trans. Catherine Rouslin, in *Little Red Riding Hood: A Casebook*, ed. Alan Dundes (Madison: University of Wisconsin Press, 1989), 79.

[35] Dundes, "Interpreting Little Red Riding Hood Psychoanalytically," 20.

[36] Walker, *Woman's Encyclopedia of Myth*, 1070.

[37] Harley, *Moon Lore*, 170–75.

[38] O'Hara, *Moonlore*, 7–8.

[39] Harley, *Moon Lore*, 156.

[40] Walters, *Chinese Mythology*, 74.

[41] Slote, *Moon in Fact and Fantasy*, 36–40.

[42] Ehlert, *Moon Rope*.

[43] Bram, "Moon," 88.

[44] *Standard Dictionary of Folklore*, s.v. "light."

[45] Harley, *Moon Lore*, 35

[46] O'Hara, *Moonlore*, 9–10.

[47] Calvin, *How the Shaman Stole the Moon*, 80.

[48] Joan Borysenko, *The Ways of the Mystic: Seven Paths to God* (Carlsbad, Calif.: Hay House, 1997), 2.

[49] Walker, *Woman's Encyclopedia of Myth*, 582–83.

[50] Durdin-Robertson, *Year of the Goddess*, 30.

[51] *Standard Dictionary of Folklore*, s.v. "cross."

[52] Harley, *Moon Lore*, 107.

[53] *Standard Dictionary of Folklore*, s.v. "cross."

[54] Julien Ries, "Cross," in *The Encyclopedia of Religion*, ed. Mircea Eliade, 4:157.

[55] George R. Elder, "Crossroads," in *The Encyclopedia of Religion*, ed. Mircea Eliade, 4:166.

[56] Hamilton, *Mythology*, 65–66.

[57] Opie and Opie, *The Classic Fairy Tales*, 122–5.

[58] Eliade, *Patterns in Comparative Religion*, 160.

[59] *Standard Dictionary of Folklore*, s.v. "dog."

[60] Paul Delarue, "The Story of Grandmother," in *Little Red Riding Hood: A Casebook*, 17–20.

[61] Hamilton, *Mythology*, 227.

[62] Dundes, "Interpreting Little Red Riding Hood Psychoanalytically," 22–23.

[63] Wolfram Eberhard, "The Story of Grandaunt Tiger," in *Little Red Riding Hood: A Casebook*, 56–57.

[64] Yangsook Choi, *The Sun Girl and the Moon Boy: A Korean Folktale* (New York: Alfred A. Knopf, 1997).

[65] Eberhard, "The Story of Grandaunt Tiger," 60–63.

[66] *Standard Dictionary of Folklore*, s.v. "Little Red Riding Hood."

[67] Campbell, *The Mythic Image*, 471–78.

[68] Ed Young, *Lon Po Po: A Red Riding Hood Story from China* (New York: PaperStar, the Putnam Berkley Group, 1989).

[69] Walker, *Woman's Encyclopedia of Myth*, 1070.

[70] *Wolves at Our Door*, prod. Dutcher Film Productions, 50 min., Discovery Channel Video, 1997, videocassette.

[71] Warner, *From the Beast to the Blonde*, 181–83.

Chapter 15: The Grimms' Cinderella

[1] Jablow and Withers, *Man in the Moon*, 10.

[2] Aveni, *Conversing with the Planets*, 106.

[3] *Standard Dictionary of Folklore*, s.v. "moon."

[4] Harley, *Moon Lore*, 56.

[5] James Holding, "The Boy Who Fished for the Moon: A Tale of the South Seas," in *To the Moon!* 9–12.

[6] Nai-Tung Ting, *The Cinderella Cycle in China and Indo-China*, FF Communications no. 213 (Helsinki, Finland: Academia Scientarum Fennica, 1974), 17.

[7] *New Saint Joseph Sunday Missal*, 1359.

[8] Padraic Colum, "Hina, the Woman in the Moon: A Hawaiian Legend," in *To the Moon!* 12–13.

[9] Philip, *The Cinderella Story*, 78.

[10] Chevalier and Gheerbrant, *Dictionary of Symbols*, 753–54.

[11] *Cassell's New Latin Dictionary: Latin-English, English-Latin*, s.v. focus.

[12] *Standard Dictionary of Folklore*, s.v. "lares," "fairy."

[13] Walker, *Woman's Encyclopedia of Myths*, 1046.

[14] Chevalier and Gheerbrant, *Dictionary of Symbols*, 742.

[15] Vickery, *Dictionary of Plant-Lore*, 278.

[16] Walker, *Woman's Dictionary of Symbols*, 405.

[17] Shirley Climo, *The Korean Cinderella*, illus. Ruth Heller (New York: HarperCollins, 1993).

[18] Paul Delarue, "From Perrault to Walt Disney: The Slipper of Cinderella," in *The Brothers Grimm and Folktale*, 110–14.

[19] Aarland Ussher, "The Slipper on the Stair," in *Cinderella: A Casebook*, ed. Alan Dundes (Madison: University of Wisconsin Press, 1982), 193–99.

[20] "Fairy Lore: Fairyland," on *Fairy Tale–A True Story* Homepage, [Paramount Pictures, 1997]; available at http://www.fairytalemovie.com/lore/fairyland.html.

[21] Walker, *Woman's Encyclopedia of Myths*, 532.

[22] Carl Withers, *Painting the Moon: A Folktale from Estonia*, illus. Adrienne Adams (New York: E. P. Dutton, 1970).

[23] *Standard Dictionary of Folklore*, s.v. "Brer Rabbit."

[24] Ibid., s.v. "horseshoe."

[25] Ibid., s.v. "horse."

[26] Walker, *Woman's Dictionary of Symbols*, 379.

[27] *Standard Dictionary of Folklore*, s.v. "horse."

[28] Ibid., s.v. "Bear's Son."

[29] Anna Birgitta Rooth, *The Cinderella Cycle* (Lund, Sweden: C. W. K. Gleerup, 1951), 69–71.

[30] Shirley Climo, *The Egyptian Cinderella*, illus. Ruth Heller (New York: Thomas Y. Crowell, 1989).

[31] Eliade, *Patterns in Comparative Religion*, 130.

Chapter 16: Other Cinderellas

[1] *Standard Dictionary of Folklore*, s.v. "Cinderella."

[2] "Cinderella: Aarne-Thompson folktale type 510A and related stories of persecuted heroines," trans. and/or ed. D. L. Ashliman [copyright 1998]; available at http://www.pitt.edu/~dash/type0510a.html#grimm.

[3] Alan Dundes, "To Love My Father All," in *Cinderella: A Casebook*, 229–41.

[4] Roger Lacelyn Green, *Once Long Ago: Folk and Fairy Tales of the World*, illus. Vojtech Kubasta (London: Golden Pleasure Books, 1962), 82–85.

[5] "The Father Who Wanted to Marry His Daughter: Folktales of Aarne-Thompson Type 510B," trans. and/or ed. D. L. Ashliman [copyright 1998]; available at http://www.pitt.edu/~dash/type0510b.html.

[6] *Standard Dictionary of Folklore*, s.v. "moon," "Salt Woman."

[7] Chevalier and Gheerbrant, *Dictionary of Symbols*, 823.

[8] "Fairy Lore: People and Fairies," on *Fairy Tale–A True Story* Homepage.

[9] Articles in the *Altoona (Pennsylvania) Mirror* newspaper provided by John Orr, Altoona Area High School English teacher.

[10] Rockwell, *Giving Voice to the Bear*, 172.

[11] *The New Webster Encyclopedic Dictionary of the English Language*, s.v. "Mary."

[12] Stutley and Stutley, *Harper's Dictionary of Hinduism*, 300–301.

[13] Walker, *Woman's Encyclopedia of Myth*, 66, 69–70, 267, 450–56.

[14] Stutley and Stutley, *Harper's Dictionary of Hinduism*, 137.

[15] Begg, *Cult of the Black Virgin*.

[16] See notes in *New Oxford Annotated Bible*, 441OT.

[17] Above material on the Queen of Sheba is from Warner, *From the Beast to the Blonde*, 97–128.

[18] Theodor Vernaleken, *Kinder- und Hausmarchen, dem Volke treu nacherzahlt*, no. 33 (Vienna and Leipzig: Wilhelm Braumuller, 1896), 144–48, trans. and ed. D. L. Ashliman [copyright 1998]; available at http://www.pitt.edu/~dash/type0510b.html.

[19] Chevalier and Gheerbrant, *Dictionary of Symbols*, 256–57.

[20] "Fairy Lore: Fairyland," on *Fairy Tale–A True Story* Homepage

[21] Gerina Dunwich, *The Wicca Book of Days: Legend and Lore for Every Day of the Year* (New York: A Citadel Press Book, Carol Publishing Group, 1995), 5.

[22] Chevalier and Gheerbrant, *Dictionary of Symbols*, 256–57.

[23] *Standard Dictionary of Folklore*, s.v. "Wu Yo."

[24] Julien Ries, "Cross," in *The Encyclopedia of Religion*, ed. Mircea Eliade, 4:158.

[25] Schimmel, *Mystery of Numbers*, 113, 120.

[26] Eliade, *Patterns in Comparative Religion*, 166.

[27] See charts in Toni Weschler, *Taking Charge of Your Fertility*.

[28] Ries, "Cross," in *The Encyclopedia of Religion*, 156.

[29] Gaskell, *Dictionary of All Scriptures and Myths*, 323.

[30] Joseph Jacobs, *The Buried Moon*, illus. Susan Jeffers (Englewood Cliffs, N.J.: Bradbury Press, 1969).

[31] Gimbutas, *The Language of the Goddess*, 305–09.

[32] Walker, *Woman's Encyclopedia of Myth*, 117.

[33] MacDonald, *The Folklore of World Holidays*, 89.

[34] *Standard Dictionary of Folklore*, s.v. "Brigit," "Saint Brigit."

[35] "O S. Brigits Countrey, Parents, Birth, and many vertues and especially of her charithy to the poore: Abridged out of what Cogitosus her owne nepheu, and Ioannes Capgravivs have written," [1625]; available at "Tales of Brigit–The Mary of the Gael," http://www.ncf.carleton.ca/~dc920/saintale.html.

[36] Shirley Toulson, *The Celtic Year* (Rockport, Mass.: Element, 1993), 80.

[37] Frazer, *The Golden Bough*, 155.

[38] "Saint Brigid: The Mary of the Gael," Part 2, "The Shepherdess," [Catholic Information Network, copyright 1997]; http://www.cin.org/saints/bridget.html.

[39] *Standard Dictionary of Folklore*, s.v. "Saint Brigit."

[40] *The Catholic Encyclopedia* (1907), s.v. "Brigid."

[41] *Lives of the Saints for Every Day of the Year: In Accord with the Norms and Principles of the New Roman Calendar*, rev. and ed. Hugo Hoever (New York: Catholic Book Publishing, 1989), 56–57.

[42] Diana Ferguson, *The Magickal Year* (New York: Quality Paperback Book Club, 1996), 81.

[43] *Standard Dictionary of Folklore*, s.v. "goose that laid the golden egg."

[44] "Saint Brigid: The Mary of the Gael."

[45] "Saint Brigid a.k.a. The Mary of the Gael," in "Irish/Celtic Seasonal Celebrations," available at http://www.ncf.carleton.ca/~bj333/HomePage. season.html#briget.

[46] Wendy M. Reynolds, "The Goddess Brighid," available at http://www.oz. net/~dmagnat/wendybrig.html.

[47] *Standard Dictionary of Folklore*, s.v. "Berchta," "Holde."

[48] "St. Brigid (St. Bride's Day)," in Peter N. Williams, "The Traditions of the Northern Celts," available at http://britannia.com/celtic/celtictraditions.html.

[49] *Standard Dictionary of Folklore*, s.v. "Berchta," "Perchten."

[50] Gimbutas, *The Language of the Goddess*, 298.

[51] Durdin-Robertson, *The Year of the Goddess*, 31.

[52] Dunwich, *Wicca Book of Days*, 6.

[53] Walker, *Woman's Encyclopedia of Myth*, 117.

[54] Reynolds, "The Goddess Brighid."

[55] MacDonald, *The Folklore of World Holidays*, 89.

[56] Jon Bonsing, "Brighid: Flame of Springtime," [1996]; available at http://people. enternet.com.au/~havok/brighid.htm.

[57] Serena Roney-Dougal, "Glastonbury–Bride's Mound," [1996]; available at http:// www.glastonbury.co.uk/articles/bridesm-serana01.html.

[58] Durdin-Robertson, *The Year of the Goddess*, 39.

[59] MacDonald, *The Folklore of World Holidays*, 89.

[60] *Standard Dictionary of Folklore*, s.v. "Saint Brigit."

[61] Frazer, *The Golden Bough*, 155.

[62] "Celtic Goddess, Christian Saint," available at http://atlanticonline.ns.ca/celtic/ stbrigid.html.

[63] *Standard Dictionary of Folklore*, s.v. "swan maiden."

[64] "Under Brigid's Mantle," available at http://www.azstarnet.com/~gallae/brigit. htm.

[65] MacDonald, *The Folklore of World Holidays*, 89.

[66] Durdin-Robertson, *The Year of the Goddess*, 37–40.

[67] Ferguson, *The Magickal Year*, 74.

[68] *Standard Dictionary of Folklore*, s.v. "Saint Brigit."

[69] "O S. Brigits Countrey, Parents, Birth, and many vertues."

[70] MacDonald, *The Folklore of World Holidays*, 89.

[71] "From Lady Gregory," available at "Tales of Brigit–The Mary of the Gael," http://www.ncf.carleton.ca/~dc920/saintale.html.

[72] Philip, *The Cinderella Story*, 17–20.

[73] Ibid., 5–7.

[74] Ibid., 36–38.

[75] *Standard Dictionary of Folklore*, s.v. "goose," "swan maiden."

[76] Rooth, *The Cinderella Cycle*, 17–18.

[77] Philip, *The Cinderella Story*, 46–50.

[78] Edsman, "Bears," 87–88.

[79] Guirma, *Princess of the Full Moon*.

[80] Brueton, *Many Moons*, 26.

[81] Ting, *Cinderella Cycle in China*, 19.

[82] Miranda J. Green, *The World of the Druids* (New York: Thames and Hudson, 1997), 10–13.

[83] Philip, *The Cinderella Story*, 7.

[84] Robert D. San Souci, *Sootface: An Ojibwa Cinderella Story*, illus. Daniel San Souci (New York: Bantam Doubleday Dell Books for Young Readers, 1994).

[85] Ting, *Cinderella Cycle in China*, 11.

[86] Penny Pollock, *The Turkey Girl: A Zuni Cinderella Story*, illus. Ed Young (New York: Little, Brown, 1996).

[87] Philip, *The Cinderella Story*, 79.

[88] Simms, *Moon and Otter and Frog*.

Chapter 17: Conclusion

[1] Fideler, *Jesus Christ, Sun of God*, 233.

[2] As quoted by Jan de Vries, "Theories Concerning 'Nature Myths,'" 35–36.

[3] *Standard Dictionary of Folklore*, s.v. "Erinyes," "Fates," "fairy," "Keres," "Moirae," "Norns."

[4] Campbell, *The Inner Reaches of Outer Space*, 70.

[5] *Standard Dictionary of Folklore*, s.v. "cross."

[6] Chevalier and Gheerbrant, *Dictionary of Symbols*, 257.

References

Ashe, Geoffrey. *Dawn Behind the Dawn: A Search for the Earthly Paradise.* New York: Henry Holt and Company, 1992.

Ashliman, D. L., ed. "Folklore and Mythology Electronic Texts." [University of Pittsburgh, copyright 1998]. Available at http://www.pit.edu/~dash/folktexts.html.

Aveni, Anthony. *Conversing with the Planets: How Science and Myth Invented the Cosmos.* New York: Kodasha International, 1992, 1994.

Barber, Elizabeth Wayland. *Women's Work: The First Twenty-Thousand Years: Women, Cloth, and Society in Early Times.* New York: W. W. Norton, 1994.

Baring-Gould, Sabine. *Curious Myths of the Middle Ages.* Ed. Edward Hardy. New York: Oxford University Press, 1978.

Baring-Gould, William S., and Ceil Baring-Gould. *The Annotated Mother Goose.* New York: Bramhall House, 1962.

Bauval, Robert, and Adrian Gilbert. *The Orion Mystery: Unlocking the Secrets of the Pyramids.* New York: Crown Trade Paperbacks, 1994.

Beach, Edward A. "The Ecole Initiative: The Eleusinian Mysteries." [Copyright 1995]. Available at http://www3.erols.com/nbeach/eleusis.html.

Begg, Ean. *The Cult of the Black Virgin.* New York: Arkana, Penguin Books, 1985.

Belting, Natalia. *The Moon Is a Crystal Ball: Unfamiliar Legends of the Stars.* New York: Bobbs-Merrill, 1952.

Blackwood, Alan. *Festivals: New Year.* East Sussex, England: Wayland, 1985.

Bly, Robert. *Iron John: A Book About Men.* New York: Addison-Wesley, 1990.

Borysenko, Joan. *The Ways of the Mystic: Seven Paths to God.* Carlsbad, Calif.: Hay House, 1997.

Bram, Jean Rhys. "Moon." In *The Encyclopedia of Religion,* ed. Mircea Eliade, 10:83–91.

Bruchac, Joseph, and Gayle Ross. *The Girl Who Married the Moon: Tales from Native North America.* New York: Troll Medallion, 1994.

Brueton, Diana. *Many Moons: The Myth and Magic, Fact and Fantasy of Our Nearest Heavenly Body.* Englewood Cliffs, N.J.: Prentice Hall, 1991.

Calvin, William H. *How the Shaman Stole the Moon: In Search of Ancient Prophet-Scientists from Stonehenge to the Grand Canyon.* New York: Bantam Books, 1991.

Campbell, Joseph. *The Hero with a Thousand Faces.* Bollingen Series 17. Princeton, N.J.: Princeton University Press, 1949, 1968.

———. *The Inner Reaches of Outer Space: Metaphor as Myth and as Religion.* New York: Harper & Row, 1986.

———, assisted by M. J. Abadie. *The Mythic Image.* Princeton, N.J.: Princeton University Press, 1974.

———. *The Power of Myth with Bill Moyers.* Ed. Betty Sue Flowers. New York: Doubleday, 1988.

Carpenter, Rhys. *Folktale, Fiction and Saga in the Homeric Epics.* Berkeley and Los Angeles: University of California Press, 1946.

Chambers, R., ed. *The Book of Days: A Miscellany of Popular Antiquities in Connection with the Calendar including Anecdote, Biography, and History, Curiosities of Literature and Oddities of Human Life and Character.* London: W. & R. Chambers, Ltd., c. 1887; Detroit: Gale Research, 1967.

Chevalier, Jean, and Alain Gheerbrant. *A Dictionary of Symbols.* Trans. John Buchanan-Brown. New York: Penguin Books, 1994.

Choi, Yangsook. *The Sun Girl and the Moon Boy: A Korean Folktale.* New York: Alfred A. Knopf, 1997.

Cirlot, J. E. *A Dictionary of Symbols.* Trans. Jack Sage. New York: Philosophical Library, 1962.

Climo, Shirley. *The Egyptian Cinderella.* Illus. Ruth Heller. New York: Thomas Y. Crowell, 1989.

———. *The Korean Cinderella.* Illus. Ruth Heller. New York: HarperCollins, 1993.

Cole, Joanna, comp. *Best-Loved Folktales of the World.* New York: Anchor Books, Doubleday, 1982.

Coomaraswamy, Rama P. *The Door in the Sky: Coomaraswamy on Myth and Meaning.* Princeton, N.J.: Princeton University Press, 1997.

de Santillana, Giorgio, and Hertha von Dechend. *Hamlet's Mill: An Essay on Myth and the Frame of Time.* Boston: Gambit, 1969.

de Vries, Jan. "Theories Concerning 'Nature Myths.'" In *Sacred Narrative: Readings in the Theory of Myth,* ed. Alan Dundes, 30–40. Berkeley and Los Angeles: University of California Press, 1984.

Dorson, Richard M. "The Eclipse of Solar Mythology." *Journal of American Folklore* 68 (1955): 393–416.

Dundes, Alan, ed. *Cinderella: A Casebook.* Madison: University of Wisconsin Press, 1982.

————, ed. *Little Red Riding Hood: A Casebook.* Madison: University of Wisconsin Press, 1989.

Dunwich, Gerina. *The Wicca Book of Days: Legend and Lore for Every Day of the Year.* New York: A Citadel Press Book, Carol Publishing Group, 1995.

Durdin-Robertson, Lawrence. *The Year of the Goddess: A Perpetual Calendar of Festivals.* Wellingborough, Northamptonshire: The Aquarian Press, 1990.

Edsman, Carl-Martin. "Bears." Trans. Verne Moberg. In *Encyclopedia of Religion,* ed. Mircea Eliade, 2:86–89.

Edwards, Carolyn McVickar. *Sun Stories: Tales from Around the World to Illuminate the Days and Nights of Our Lives.* New York: HarperSanFrancisco, 1995.

Ehlert, Lois. *Moon Rope: A Peruvian Folktale.* San Diego: Harcourt Brace Jovanovich, 1992.

Elder, George R. "Crossroads." In *The Encyclopedia of Religion,* ed. Mircea Eliade, 4:166.

Eliade, Mircea, ed. *Encyclopedia of Religion.* 15 vols. New York: Macmillan, 1987.

————. *Patterns in Comparative Religion.* Trans. Rosemary Sheed. New York: Meridian Books, 1958.

————. *Shamanism: Archaic Techniques of Ecstasy.* Trans. Willard R. Trask. Bollingen Series 76. Princeton, N.J.: Princeton University Press, 1964.

Erdoes, Richard, and Alfonso Ortiz, eds. *American Indian Myths and Legends.* New York: Pantheon, 1984.

Ferguson, Diana. *The Magickal Year.* New York: Quality Paperback Book Club, 1996.

Fideler, David. *Jesus Christ, Sun of God: Ancient Cosmology and Early Christian Symbolism.* Wheaton, Ill.: Quest Books, The Theosophical Publishing House, 1993.

Frazer, James George. *The Golden Bough: A Study in Magic and Religion.* 1-vol. abridged ed. New York: Macmillan, 1922; Macmillan Paperbacks Edition, 1963.

Gaer, Joseph. *Holidays Around the World.* Boston: Little, Brown, 1953.

Gail, Judy, and Linda A. Houlding. *Day of the Moon Shadow: Tales with Ancient Answers to Scientific Questions.* Illus. Kimberly Louise Shaw. Englewood, Colo.: Libraries Unlimited, 1995.

Gaskell, G. A. *Dictionary of All Scriptures and Myths.* New York: Gramercy Books, 1981.

Gimbutas, Marija. *The Goddesses and Gods of Old Europe: 6500–3500 B.C. Myths and Cult Images.* Berkeley and Los Angeles: University of California Press, 1974; new and updated edition in paperback, 1982.

———. *The Language of the Goddess*. New York: HarperCollins, 1991.

Graves, Robert. *The White Goddess: A Historical Grammar of Poetic Myth*. New York: Farrar, Straus and Giroux, 1948.

Green, Miranda J. *The World of the Druids*. New York: Thames and Hudson, 1997.

Green, Roger Lacelyn. *Once Long Ago: Folk and Fairy Tales of the World*. Illus. Vojtech Kubasta. London: Golden Pleasure Books, 1962.

Grimm, Jacob, and Wilhelm Grimm. *The Complete Fairy Tales of the Brothers Grimm*. Trans. Jack Zipes. New York: Bantam Books, 1992.

Guirma, Frederic. *Princess of the Full Moon*. Trans. John Garrett. New York: Macmillan, 1970.

Gutsch, William A., Jr., *1001 Things Everyone Should Know About the Universe*. New York: Doubleday, 1998.

Hadley, Eric, and Tessa Hadley. *Legends of the Sun and Moon*. Illus. Jan Nesbitt. New York: Cambridge University Press, 1983.

Hamilton, Edith. *Mythology*. New York: A Mentor Book, Penguin Books, 1942.

Hanh, Thich Nhat. *Living Buddha, Living Christ*. New York: Riverhead Books, 1995.

Harley, Timothy. *Moon Lore*. London: Swann Sonnenschein, Le Bas and Lowrey, 1885.

Harrington, Philip S. *Eclipse! The What, Where, When, Why, and How Guide to Watching Solar and Lunar Eclipses*. New York: John Wiley & Sons, 1997.

Heinberg, Richard. *Celebrate the Solstice: Honoring the Earth's Seasonal Rhythms Through Festival and Ceremony*. Wheaton, Ill.: Quest Books, The Theosophical Publishing House, 1993.

Hentze, Carl. *Mythes et symboles lunaires: Chine ancienne, civilisations anciennes de l'Asie, peuple limitrophes du Pacifique*. Anvers: Editions "de Sikkel," 1932.

Hodges, Margaret. *Buried Moon*. New York: Little, Brown, 1990.

Hoever, Hugo, ed., *Lives of the Saints for Every Day of the Year: In Accord with the Norms and Principles of the New Roman Calendar*. Rev. ed. New York: Catholic Book Publishing, 1989.

Household Stories from the Collection of the Brothers Grimm. Trans. Lucy Crane. Illus. Walter Crane. New York: McGraw Hill, 1966. This is a reprint of the work first published by Macmillan & Co. in 1866.

Ickes, Marguerite. *The Book of Festival Holidays*. New York: Dodd, Mead, 1964.

Jablow, Alta, and Carl Withers. *The Man in the Moon: Sky Tales from Many Lands*. New York: Holt, Rinehart and Winston, 1969.

Jacobs, Joseph. *The Buried Moon*. Illus. Susan Jeffers. Englewood Cliffs, N.J.: Bradbury Press, 1969.

―――. *English Folk and Fairy Tales: Folk and Fairy Tales from Many Lands*. 3rd ed., rev. New York: G. P. Putnam's Sons, [1900].

James, E. O. *Seasonal Feasts and Festivals*. New York: Barnes & Noble University Paperback, 1963.

Jones, Steven Swann. "The Construction of the Folktale: 'Snow White.' " Ph.D. diss., University of California, Davis, 1979.

Klein, Ernest. *A Comprehensive Etymological Dictionary of the English Language: Dealing with the Origin of Words and Their Sense Development Thus Illustrating the History of Civilization and Culture*. New York: Elsevier, 1966.

Krupp, E. C. *Beyond the Blue Horizon: Myths and Legends of the Sun, Moon, Stars, and Planets*. New York: Oxford University Press, 1991.

―――. "Celestial Analogy and Cyclical Renewal: Configurational Approaches to Culture Through Analogy." Paper presented to the American Anthropological Association, Washington, D.C., November 19, 1993. Paper kindly provided to me by the author, who is director of the Griffith Observatory, Los Angeles, Calif.

―――. "Moon Maids," *Griffith Observer* 52 (December 1988): 2–15.

Lang, Andrew, ed. *The Red Fairy Book*. New York: McGraw-Hillbrook, 1967.

Leach, Maria, and Jerome Fried, eds. *Funk and Wagnalls Standard Dictionary of Folklore, Mythology, and Legend*. New York: HarperSanFrancisco, 1972.

Li-ch'en, Tun. *Annual Customs and Festivals in Peking as Recorded in the Yen-ching Sui-shih-chi*. Trans. Derk Bodde. 2nd ed. Hong Kong: Hong Kong University Press, 1965.

Lopez-Austin, Alfredo. *The Rabbit on the Face of the Moon: Mythology in the Mesoamerican Tradition*. Trans. Bernard R. Ortiz de Montellano and Thelma Ortiz de Montellano. Salt Lake City: University of Utah Press, 1996.

Lummis, Charles F. *The Man Who Married the Moon and Other Pueblo Indian Folk-stories*. New York: The Century Co., 1894; reprinted by AMS Press, New York, 1976.

MacDonald, Margaret Read, ed. *The Folklore of World Holidays*. Detroit: Gale Research, 1992.

McGlathery, James M., ed. *The Brothers Grimm and Folktale*. Urbana: University of Illinois Press, 1988.

Miller, Mary, and Karl Taube. *The Gods and Symbols of Ancient Mexico and the Maya: An Illustrated Dictionary of Mesoamerican Religion*. New York: Thames and Hudson, 1993.

Mitchell, Stephen. *Genesis: A New Translation of the Classic Biblical Stories*. New York: HarperCollins, 1996.

Moore, Thomas. *The Planets Within: The Astrological Psychology of Marsilio Ficino*. Hudson, N.Y.: Lindisfarne Press, 1982.

Myss, Carolyn. *Why People Don't Heal and How They Can*. New York: Harmony Books, 1997.

The New Oxford Annotated Bible with Apocryphal/Deuterocanonical Books: New Revised Standard Version. Ed. Bruce M. Metzger and Roland E. Murphy. New York: Oxford University Press, 1994.

New Saint Joseph Sunday Missal Complete Edition: The Complete Masses for Sundays, Holy Days and the Easter Triduum. New York: Catholic Book Publishing, 1986.

O'Hara, Gwydion. *Moonlore: Myths and Folklore from Around the World*. St. Paul: Llewellyn Publications, 1996.

Opie, Iona, and Peter Opie, eds. *The Oxford Dictionary of Nursery Rhymes*. Oxford: Oxford University Press, 1952.

————. *The Classic Fairy Tales*. New York: Oxford University Press, 1980.

Partridge, Eric. *Dictionary of Slang and Unconventional English*. 8th ed. Ed. Paul Beale. New York: Macmillan, 1984.

Philip, Neil. *The Cinderella Story*. New York: Penguin Books, 1989.

Pollock, Penny. *The Turkey Girl: A Zuni Cinderella Story*. Illus. Ed Young. New York: Little, Brown, 1996.

Ries, Julien. "Cross." In *The Encyclopedia of Religion,* ed. Mircea Eliade, 4:155–66.

Rockwell, David. *Giving Voice to the Bear: North American Indian Rituals, Myths, and Images of the Bear*. Niwot, Colo.: Roberts Rinehart, 1991.

Roebuck, Valerie J. *The Circle of Stars: An Introduction to Indian Astrology*. Rockport, Mass.: Element Books Limited, 1992.

Rooth, Anna Birgitta. *The Cinderella Cycle*. Lund, Sweden: C. W. K. Gleerup, 1951.

Salda, Michael N., ed. "The Jack and the Beanstalk and Jack the Giant-Killer Project." At the de Grummond Children's Literature Research Collection, University of Southern Mississippi. Available at http://www-dept.usm.edu/~engdept/jack/jackhome.html.

San Souci, Robert D. *Sootface: An Ojibwa Cinderella Story*. Illus. Daniel San Souci. New York: Bantam Doubleday Dell Books for Young Readers, 1994.

Scarre, Chris. *Smithsonian Timelines of the Ancient World*. New York: Dorling Kindersly, 1993.

Schimmel, Annemarie. *The Mystery of Numbers*. New York: Oxford University Press, 1993.

Shepard, Paul, and Barry Sanders. *The Sacred Paw: The Bear in Nature, Myth, and Literature*. New York: Arkana, Viking Penguin, 1985.

Simms, Laura. *Moon and Otter and Frog*. Illus. Clifford Brucelea. New York: Hyperion Books for Children, 1995.

Sleator, William. *The Angry Moon*. Illus. Blair Lent. Boston: Atlantic Monthly Press, Little, Brown, 1970.

Slote, Alfred. *The Moon in Fact and Fantasy*. Illus. John Kaufmann. New York: World Publishing, 1967.

Spenser: Poetical Works. Ed. J. C. Smith and E. de Selincourt. New York: Oxford University Press, 1912.

Stewart, J. V. *Astrology: What's Really in the Stars?* Amherst, N.Y.: Prometheus Books, 1996.

Stewig, John Warren. *The Moon's Choice*. Illus. Jan Palmer. New York: Simon and Schuster, 1993.

Stutley, Margaret, and James Stutley. *Harper's Dictionary of Hinduism: Its Mythology, Folklore, Philosophy, Literature, and History*. San Francisco: Harper & Row, 1977.

Tatar, Maria. *The Hard Facts of the Grimm's Fairy Tales*. Princeton, N.J.: Princeton University Press, 1987.

Tester, S. J. *A History of Western Astrology*. Wolfeboro, N.H.: Boydell Press, 1987.

Tezise, Percy, and Dick Roughsey. *Gidja the Moon*. Milwaukee, Wisc.: Gareth Stevens, 1984.

Thompson, Stith. *Motif-index of Folk-literature: A Classification of Narrative Elements in Folktales, Ballads, Myths, Fables, Mediaeval Romances, Exempla, Fabliaux, Jest-books, and Local Legends*. Bloomington: Indiana University Press, 1966.

Ting, Nai-Tung. *The Cinderella Cycle in China and Indo-China*. FF Communications no. 213. Helsinki, Finland: Academia Scientarum Fennica, 1974.

Toulson, Shirley. *The Celtic Year*. Rockport, Mass.: Element, 1993.

Tripp, Edward. *Crowell's Handbook of Classical Mythology*. New York: Thomas Y. Crowell, 1970.

Vandergrift, Kay E. "Snow White Text: Snow White Alternative Texts." Created January 6, 1997. Available at http://www.scils.rutgers.edu/special/kay/snowwhite.html.

van Renterghem, Tony. *When Santa Was a Shaman: The Ancient Origins of Santa Claus and the Christmas Tree*. St. Paul, Minn.: Llewellyn Publications, 1995.

Varley, Desmond. *Seven: The Number of Creation*. London: G. Bells & Son, 1976.

Vernaleken, Theodor. *Kinder- und Hausmarchen, dem Volke treu nacherzahlt.* No. 33. Vienna and Leipzig: Wilhelm Braumuller, 1896. Trans. and ed. D. L. Ashliman. [Copyright 1998]. Available at http://www.pitt.edu/~dash/type0510b.html.

Vickery, Roy, comp. *A Dictionary of Plant-Lore.* New York: Oxford University Press, 1995.

Walker, Barbara G. *The Woman's Dictionary of Symbols and Sacred Objects.* New York: HarperSanFrancisco, 1988.

———. *The Woman's Encyclopedia of Myths and Secrets.* New York: Harper & Row, 1983.

Walters, Derek. *Chinese Mythology: An Encyclopedia of Myth and Legend.* London: Aquarian/Thorsons, HarperCollins, 1992.

Warner, Marina. *From the Beast to the Blond: On Fairy Tales and Their Tellers.* New York: The Noon Press, Farrar, Strauss and Giroux, 1994.

Weschler, Toni. *Taking Charge of Your Fertility: The Definitive Guide to Natural Birth Control and Pregnancy Achievement.* New York: HarperCollins, 1995.

Withers, Carl. *Painting the Moon: A Folktale from Estonia.* Illus. Adrienne Adams. New York: E. P. Dutton, 1970.

Wolves at Our Door. Prod. Dutcher Film Productions. 50 min. Discovery Channel Video, 1997, videocassette.

Wright, Hamilton, Helen Wright, and Samuel Rapport, eds. *To the Moon!* New York: Meredith Press, 1968.

Young, Ed. *Lon Po Po: A Red Riding Hood Story from China.* New York: PaperStar, the Putnam Berkley Group, 1989.

———. *Moon Mother: A Native American Creation Tale.* New York: HarperCollins, Willa Perlman Books, 1993.

Zerubavel, Eviatar. *The Seven Day Circle: The History and Meaning of the Week.* New York: The Free Press, Macmillan, 1985.

Zipes, Jack. *Breaking the Magic Spell: Radical Theories of Folk and Fairy Tales.* Austin: University of Texas Press, 1979.

———. *Fairy Tale as Myth/Myth as Fairy Tale.* Lexington: University Press of Kentucky, 1994.

Index